# Playing Heaven

# Playing Heaven

## REDISCOVERING OUR PURPOSE AS PARTICIPANTS IN THE MISSION OF GOD

R. PAUL STEVENS

REGENT COLLEGE PUBLISHING
Vancouver, British Columbia

*Playing Heaven:*
*Rediscovering Our Purpose as Participants in the Mission of God*
Copyright © 2006 R. Paul Stevens
All rights reserved.

Published 2006 by Regent College Publishing
5800 University Boulevard, Vancouver, BC V6T 2E4 Canada
Web: www.regentpublishing.com
E-mail: info@regentpublishing.com

Views expressed in works published by Regent College Publishing
are those of the author and do not necessarily represent the
official position of Regent College <www.regent-college.edu>.

On the cover: "Allegory of the Good Government: Effects of the
Good Government in the City," by Ambrogio Lorenzetti (c.1311-
1348). Fresco. Fourteenth-century Siena becomes the image of the
ideal city. The dance of the women alludes to the theme of living in
peace. Education, building and trade all speak to the way the town
works. Reproduced by permission of Art Resource, New York.

Library and Archives Canada Cataloguing in Publication

Stevens, R. Paul (Robert Paul), 1937–
    Playing Heaven: Rediscovering Our Purpose as Participants
in the Mission of God / R. Paul Stevens.

    Includes bibliographical references.
    ISBN 1-57383-352-5

1. Work–Religious aspects–Christianity. 2. Christian life. I. Title.
BV4501.3.S74 2006        248.4            C2005-904613-9

# CONTENTS

# ACKNOWLEDGEMENTS

This book was created as a way of honouring the long and distinguished service of R. Paul Stevens to Regent College and the invaluable advice and encouragement that he has offered to generations of Regent College students. While Paul officially retired in 2005 as the David C. Brown Family Professor of Marketplace Theology he continues to teach for the College and to travel throughout the world meeting the hundreds of Regent alumni with whom he retains connections.

Thanks are to be expressed to those who had major roles in putting this work together: to Dal Schindell, our ever-creative director of publications at Regent College; to Rosi Petkova, the layout artist responsible for the look of the book; to Rob Clements who helped to bring the book through the press; and to Karen Wuest, our excellent editor and literary advisor who worked to bring these chapters together into a coherent whole.

~ Donald M. Lewis
*Academic Dean, Regent College*

# FOREWORD

It's now fifteen years since I first met Paul Stevens. I knew him only from his writings and had been disappointed to find he was on one of his periodic trips overseas when I visited Regent College from Australia a few years earlier. Given our overlapping interests and commitments, when we did meet it was no surprise that we soon developed a strong personal as well as professional friendship.

Several things impressed me about Paul from the start. His warmth and approachability. His quick mind and well-crafted way with words, including his soft Canadian accent. His passion for equipping the laity, both in the church and the world. His commitment to networking, not only in North America but increasingly throughout the world, and encouragement of indigenous Christians. His dedication to writing for the average person as well as those in professional ministry. His love of the creation, embodied in his self-built house on Ruxton Island, one of the Gulf Islands, and his adventures in white-water rafting. Finally, in and through all of these, his boundless energy and capacity.

I also soon came to admire features of Paul's approach to teaching and ministering. Instead of taking this up early on as a full-time career, he partly supported himself in ordinary employment, as a carpenter. When he gained a full-time position at a theological college, he began the practice of regularly spending a week alongside one of his mature age students in their workplace, seeking to understand the responsibilities, pressures, challenges and opportunities they faced. More recently, his organizing groups of business people travel for a period of time in developing countries to learn theologically and practically how to integrate their faith and their work.

While Paul's writings have mostly been in Practical Theology, they have covered a range of genres within this area. Some have concentrated on theological, others on ethical, issues. Some on vocational, others on spiritual, concerns. Some on pastoral, others on educational, matters. The form his writings has taken has also been varied and creative. Alongside his many books and articles, Paul has developed a number of in-depth and stimulating Bible Study Guides. He has collaborated on the production of Manuals on the family, the workplace and everyday life. He has produced several works in a more reflective devotional mode.

Since Paul has written many pieces that have only been available in less well-known publications, it is wonderful to have the most significant of those collected here in one volume. A glance at the headings under which these are grouped in the List of Contents reveals most of his major preoccupations, for instance, calling and vocation, work and rest, theology of the everyday, and living in but not of the world. Within these areas many of his central themes also appear, namely, the role of values, mission, risk-taking and spirituality in the marketplace, the connection between the Trinity, sacrament, people of God, sabbath, powers and principalities and ordinary life.

We also see his awareness of the different generational contexts in the West and cross-cultural contexts in the Two-Thirds World. He uses different formats, for example, lecture, dialogue, reflection, sermon and review to communicate his ideas and convictions. Some of these contributions provide background to what he has written elsewhere. Some encapsulate that more concisely and trenchantly. Some provide expansions of his thinking and practice that are available in other forms. In all we find the same simplicity of language, surprising turn of phrase, and gracefulness of attitude, familiar to us from his better known writings.

Paul, all this will be appreciated by those who have benefited from your wisdom and experience. It would be wonderful if this collection also attracts a new audience for whom it will be a gateway to your more extensive contributions. This collection comes to you with the heartfelt appreciation of your colleagues and all those who have had a hand in bringing it together. We thank you, we congratulate you and we honour you, for all you have done and, will continue to do in your new phase of life.

~ Robert Banks
*Sydney, Australia*

# CALLING & VOCATION

# REAL CALL

*From* Vocatio, *vol. 2, no. 1 (January 1999)*

The English word "vocation" comes from the Latin *vocatio*, which means "calling"; they are the same thing, though this is not obvious to the people who use these words. Most of the world today has strayed from the authentic meaning of calling and defines it as a self-chosen career.

The fact that many people still speak of their jobs as their "vocation," while pastors and missionaries speak of "being called," shows how inadequately we have grasped the universal call of God to every Christian. As Os Guinness says, calling means that our lives are so lived as a summons of Christ that the expression of our personalities and the exercise of our spiritual gifts and natural talents are given direction and power precisely because they are done not for our families, our businesses or even mankind, but for the Lord. And he will hold us accountable for them.

Negatively, calling in Scripture is neither limited to nor equated with work. Positively, calling is to Someone, not to something or somewhere. This last statement is sublimely significant but missed in this post-vocation world.

## Misunderstanding Calling

There are many indications that we are living in a post-vocation world.

First, there is *secular misunderstanding.* In the secular mindset, calling has been reduced to the occupation we choose. But "choosing one's vocation" is a misnomer! To speak of calling invites the question, "By whom?" Certainly not oneself! In line with this, vocational guidance has been reduced to career selection. As a secular perversion of calling, careerism invites people to seek financial success, security, access to power and privilege, and the guarantee of leisure, satisfaction and prestige.[1]

Second, there is *ecclesiastical misunderstanding*. In most churches the average Christian has a job or profession that they chose. The minister, however, has a calling. The professional ministry has been elevated as the vocation of vocations and the primary work to which a person should give evidence of a "call." Luther was eloquent on the tragic results of this two-level view of vocation, stemming as it did from medieval monasticism, though it now extends into modern Christianity.

Monastic vows rest on the false assumption that there is a special calling, a vocation to which superior Christians are invited to observe the counsels of perfection while ordinary Christians fulfill only the commands. But there simply is no special religious vocation since the call of God comes to each at the common tasks.[2]

As we will see, this profound misunderstanding is partly responsible for the widespread difficulty of relating Sunday to Monday and translating Christian faith into everyday activities. Unfortunately, the Reformation itself introduced another distortion.

## Reformational Misunderstanding

Following the Protestant Reformation, calling became equated exclusively with the personal experience of the providence of God, placing us in a "station" or "calling" where we were to serve God as ministers. Called people live in harmony with their gifts and talents, discerning circumstances and accepting their personalities and life situations as God's "call." The Reformers did not universally teach this. On the basis of 1 Corinthians 7:17 ("Each one should retain the place in life that the Lord assigned to him and to which God has called him"), Luther opposed the prevailing idea that in order to serve God fully one should leave one's previous way of life and become a member of the priesthood or of a religious order.[3]

In fact this is the one place where Paul, or any other New Testament writer, seems to use call language for the "place in life" or "station" we occupy (slave, free, married, single, etc.). It is complicated by the fact that in verse 17, Paul speaks of the situation as that "to which God has called him" and in verse 20 as the situation "which he was in when God called him." Though such life situations get taken up in God's call and are transformed by it, the call of God comes to us in these situations (1 Cor 7:20) and it is much more than occupation, marital status or social position. Although Paul comes very close to seeing the setting in which one is called as "calling" itself, he never quite makes that jump. At most "calling" refers to the circumstances in which the calling took place. This does not mean that a person is locked forever in a particular situation. "Rather, Paul means that by calling a person within a given situation, that situation itself is taken up in the call and thus sanctified to him or her."[4]

This Reformational overemphasis on staying where God has placed us has led to reducing mission, suspecting charismatic gifts and, ironically, to downplaying non-clerical ministry. But there is a half-truth in this distortion. The purpose of God is revealed in our personality and life-path. Elizabeth O'Connor says, "We ask to know the will of God without guessing that his will is written into our very beings."[5]

## Call Language in the Bible

"Call" (Qara) language in the Old Testament is used primarily for the people of God who are summoned to participate in God's grand purpose for the world. It is a call to salvation, a call to holiness and a call to service. In the New Testament it is the same. "Call" (kaleo and klesis) is used for the invitation to salvation through discipleship to Christ, the summons to holy corporate and personal living, as well as the call to serve. All are called. All are called together. All are called for the totality of everyday life.

### *The One and the Three*

In the Bible there is only one call of God that comes to God's people, but there are three dimensions in that call: to belong, to be and to do.

First, there is the call to belong to God, to become persons who have their identity as children of God and members of the family of God.

Second, there is the call to be God's people who exist for the praise of his glory as we live out our true identity in all aspects of life in the church and world.

Third, there is the call to do God's work, to enter into God's service in both the church and the world. This involves gifts, talents, ministries, occupations, roles, work and mission.

In this way Christian vocation fulfills the human vocation mandated in Genesis 1:27–28, a vocation also with three parallel parts:

1. the call to enjoy communion with God (belonging), a communion lost through sin;
2. the call to community building (being) and the mandate to build a family; and
3. the call to co-creativity (doing), through which humankind expresses stewardship of the earth and makes God's world work.

Unfortunately, most discussions of the human vocation centre on the third dimension exclusively. In reaction to this, Christians normally focus on the "Great Commission" (Mt 28:18–20) without understanding that Christ's work of salvation enables people to recover their full humanity and embrace the three-fold creation mandate. A truncated understanding of vocation as merely relating to the Great Commission has resulted in the tragic loss of dignity to persons working in various so-called "secular" occupations. The gospel involves us in serving God's purposes in the world through civic, social, political, domestic and ecclesiastical roles.

Further, there is no authority in the Bible for a special, secondary call from God as a prerequisite to enter the professional ministry. The call to leadership in the church comes from the church! While a special existential "call" may be given by God in some cases, the primary biblical bases upon which a person may enter pastoral leadership is character—a good reputation, ethical behaviour—and God-given gifts of leadership (1 Tm 3; 1 Pt 5:1–10). There is no status difference between leaders and people, so-called clergy and so-called laity, and there is only a functional distinction in some areas.

In the same way, there is no need to be "called" through an existential experience to an occupation or other responsibilities in society. God gives motivation and gift; God arranges circumstances and guides. Through God's leading, work, family, civil vocation and neighbouring are encompassed in our total response to God's saving and transforming call in Jesus. Misunderstanding on this point has been promoted by the overemphasis on 1 Corinthians 7:17 mentioned previously. Focusing on this one text has had several side effects: (1) it minimizes the corporate (people of God) aspect of vocation; (2) it makes too much of the specific place one occupies in society as though the place itself were the calling; (3) it focuses on task/doing to the exclusion of being. Nevertheless, one should regard the various contexts of life—marriage and singleness, workplace, neighbourhood, society—as taken up into the call of God and therefore expressed in terms of holiness and service rather than arenas chosen for personal self-fulfillment.

So vocational guidance is not discerning our "call" but, in the context of our call to discipleship, discerning the guidance of God in our lives and learning how to live in every dimension of our lives in response to God's call.

## Living as Called People

Understanding and experiencing calling can bring a deep joy to everyday life. Paraphrasing Os Guinness, I note several fruits of living vocationally rather than simply yielding to careerism, occupationalism or professionalism.

First, calling enables us to put work in its proper perspective—neither a curse nor an idol, but taken up into God's grand purpose. Second, calling contributes to a deep sense of identity that is formed by whose we are rather than what we do. Third, calling balances personal with public discipleship by keeping our Christian life from becoming privatized, on the one hand, or politicized on the other hand. Fourth, it deals constructively with ambition by creating boundaries for human initiative so that we can offer sacrificial service without becoming fanatical or addicted. Fifth, it equips people to live with single-mindedness in the face of multiple needs, competing claims and diversions—the need is not the call. Sixth, it gives people a deep sense of integrity under pressure by inviting them to live in a counterculture and a counter-community—the people of God—so we can never become "company people." Seventh, it makes sense of the brevity of our lives, realizing that just as David "had served God's purpose in his own generation, [and] fell asleep" (Acts 13:36), we can live a meaningful life even if our vision cannot be fully realized in one short lifetime. Eighth, the biblical approach to calling assures us that every believer is called into full-time ministry—there are no higher and lower forms of Christian discipleship.

*Reprinted with permission from* The Complete Book of Everyday Christianity, *ed. Robert Banks and R. Paul Stevens (Downer's Grove, IL: InterVarsity Press, 1997).*

## Endnotes

[1] James A. Donahue, "Careerism and the Ethics of Autonomy: A Theological Response," *Horizons* 15, no. 2 (Fall 1988): 318.

[2] Roland Bainton, *Here I Stand: A Life of Martin Luther* (Nashville: Abingdon, 1978).

[3] Marc Kolden, "Luther on Vocation," *Word and World* 3, no. 4 (): 382–390.

[4] Gordon D. Fee, *First Corinthians,* NICNT (Grand Rapids: Eerdmans, 1987), 309–210.

[5] Elizabeth O'Connor, *The Eighth Day of Creation: Gifts and Creativity* (Waco, Texas: Word, 1971), 14–15.

## Works Cited

Louis T. Almen, "Vocation in a Post-Vocational World," *Word and World* IV, no. 2 (Spring, 1984): 131–140.

Roland Bainton, *Here I Stand: A Life of Martin Luther* (Nashville: Abingdon, 1978).

Klaus Bockmuehl, "Recovering Vocation Today," *Crux* XXIV, no. 3 (September 1988): 25–35.

L. Coenen, "Call," *NIDNTT,* vol. 1 (Exeter: Paternoster Press, 1975), 271–276.

James A. Donahue, "Careerism and the Ethics of Autonomy: A Theological Response," *Horizons* 15, no. 2 (Fall 1988): 316–33.

William Dumbrell, "Creation, Covenant and Work," *Crux* XXIV, no. 3 (September 1988): 14–24.

David Falk, "A New Testament Theology of Calling with Reference to the 'Call to the Ministry'" (unpublished MCS Thesis, Regent College, May 1990).

Gordon D. Fee, *First Corinthians,* NICNT (Grand Rapids: Eerdmans, 1987).

Os Guinness, "The Recovery of Vocation for Our Time" (unpublished audiotape).

Marc Kolden, "Luther on Vocation," *Word and World* 3, no. 4: 382–390.

Paul Marshall, "Calling, Work and Rest," *Christian Faith and Practice in the Modern World* (Grand Rapids: Eerdmans, 1988).

Elizabeth O'Connor, *The Eighth Day of Creation: Gifts and Creativity* (Waco, Texas: Word, 1971).

Greg Ogden, *The New Reformation: Returning the Ministry to the People of God* (Grand Rapids: Zondervan, 1990), 188–215.

William Perkins, *The Works of That Famous Minister of Christ in the University of Cambridge* (London: John Legatt, 1626).

Karl Ludwig Schmidt, *kaleo,* in *Theological Dictionary of the New Testament,* vol. 3, ed. Gerhard Kittel, trans. Geoffrey W. Bromile (Grand Rapids: Eerdmans, 1965) , 487–491.

# THE MARKETPLACE:

## MISSION FIELD OR MISSION?

*From* Crux, *vol. 37, no. 3 (September 2001)*

Among Christians throughout the world, there is an unquestionable hierarchy of sacredness in human occupations: the missionary (or martyr) is at the top and the businessperson is near the bottom. So in one sense the answer to the question posed by the title of this article seems obvious: the marketplace is simply one more arena where Christians who must work in business may be able to "do the Lord's work" by witnessing.[1] It is a mission field, though a hard one. There is greed, rapacious competition, sinful inequalities between the rich and the poor, exploitation and idolatrous demands made on some workers. It is thought that the following poem is right:

> Only one life,
> T'will soon be past
> Only what's done for Christ
> Will last.

In this light, the only lasting work is to save souls until we are evacuated from the earth and enjoy the bliss of immortality in heaven. This poem, insofar as it represents the ethos and informal learning that takes place in seminaries and churches, has been part of driving a whole generation of people into so-called "full-time ministry" as the vocation of vocations (per Calvin). "Full-time ministry," I argue, is a misleading phrase, perhaps even a dangerous one, and should never be used exclusively for a Christian service career or a church leader. In fact there is no part-time option available for disciples of Christ. But in what sense may the marketplace be a context for "full-time ministry"?

**Innate Vice or Innate Virtue?**

The marketplace is a place where goods, services and values are exchanged, whether that place is a stock exchange, store, mall, village marketplace, Internet, trade show or convention. Since it is based on profit and greed, the marketplace seems intrinsically opposed to the kingdom of God, which is about sharing and love. Not surprisingly there is a long history of this antipathy of the church toward business—except for the value attributed to businesspeople who give their tithes and sit on church boards—and also to the idea that business only has extrinsic value through what it produces: pay, a platform for missions and tithes to the "Lord's work." Origen criticized those who did not sell their possessions and give to the poor; the church councils and Luther condemned usury (this being one of the major theological issues of the Middle Ages); Pope Paul VI condemned the "international imperialism of money"; and Bonino, an Argentinean, rejected capitalism for "raising man's grasping impulse." As Michael Novak concludes, "this places the businessman [sic] in an intolerable position of being either corrupt or naïve."[2] Not surprisingly many businesspeople live bifurcated lives—so the saying goes, "Mr. Business went to heaven for what he did on Sunday. Mr. Business went to hell for what he did on Monday."

The church is influenced not only by the contemporary prioritization of the professional ministry, aided and abetted by Calvin's doctrine of a "secret call"[3] and by Medieval dualism, but also by the Greek world, which can be traced as far back as the birthing culture. In the ancient world, work was a curse and the life of contemplation was essentially antithetical to the life of trade. "There is the higher mind and lower body. Spirituality and materialism are great opposites within a single monistic system and...the increase of one brings the decrease of the other..."[4] Thus there came the separation of the *vita contempliva* (contemplation) from the *vita activa* (action).[5]

**Tentmaking Mission**

One practical implication of this in the modern and postmodern worlds is that tentmaking mission, often deemed to be the future of the global mission of the church, normally depreciates the actual work that people perform to gain entry to a restricted-access country. The work itself, whether it is business or teaching English, is not considered to have any intrinsic value. Its value is only extrinsic—access. Not surprisingly, converts aspire to what is modelled—professional Christian service.[6]

In a 1984 essay on "the Lay Task of Co-Creation," Michael Novak explores the "innate virtue of enterprise." Enlarging on the idea of human beings as co-creators with God, as mandated God-imaging creatures, Novak says:

> The task of laypersons in the economic order, whether investors, workers, managers, or entrepreneurs, is to build cooperative associations respectful of each other's full humanity. Such enterprises should be so far as is feasible participative and creative, in order to bring out from creation the productive possibilities and the human resources that the Creator, in his bounty, has hidden within it. Economic activity is a direct participation in the work of the Creator himself.[7]

## Marketplace as Mission Field

Before I tackle this much harder part of the question—whether business and marketplace activity in some sense engages the mission of God—I want to affirm that the marketplace is a mission field, indeed one of the greatest and most promising in the world.

### *William Carey and International Trade*

William Carey envisioned the gospel going into all the world through the means of international trade. He drew on the text in Isaiah 60:9:

> Surely the islands look to me; in the lead are the ships of Tarshish, bringing your sons from afar, with their silver and gold, to the honour of the Lord your God, the Holy One of Israel, for he has endowed you [Zion] with splendour.[8]

In Carey's view it was inexcusable not to go into all the world to preach the gospel once we had the mariner's compass and could safely cross any sea—and indeed already did so for trade.[9] International trade, whether on a small scale of entrepreneurial import-export businesses or the grand scale of multinational corporations, represents an unprecedented opportunity for believers to be present in the world God loves, to make contacts with people, to earn the right to speak and to share the wonderful good news of Jesus.[10] It is being done today by thousands of believers in places where the formal missionary is excluded. Even in so-called "open countries," such as post-Christian Europe and post-Christian Canada—truly "hard-to-reach" though not "closed countries"—trade brings us into contact with people who would never darken the door of a church. Commenting on the global picture, Dr. Ralph McCall, a venture capitalist residing in Switzerland, proposed in an address to students at Regent College that "the unreached world" today is Europe, and the lost tribe is the multinational corporation.

### The Ordinary Christian at Work

Reflect for a moment on the millions of believers who will never be able to cross an international frontier, but who will spend most of their active waking hours in the workplace. It is estimated that the average North American Christian spends 88,000 hours of her lifetime in the workplace—more if one is a farmer or a professional. Indeed it is becoming more for everyone, with the whittling down of leisure time by more than 50% over the last three decades to a mere thirteen hours a month. At the same time, these same believers spend less than 4,000 hours in the church building engaged in church-related activities that focus almost entirely on the 4,000 hours rather than the 88,000. Perhaps we are reverting to the situation of the first two centuries, when much of the work of evangelism was done by slaves working eighteen hours a day.

A gracious transformation in local church culture could be accomplished by refusing for fifty-two weeks to give "air time" in the Sunday service to returning missionaries, visiting clergy and professors from theological colleges and, in its place, interviewing for five minutes an ordinary member of the congregation along these lines: "What do you do for a living? What are the issues you face in your daily work? What difference does your faith make in the way you deal with these issues? How can we pray for you in your ministry in the marketplace?"

### The Reasons for Marketplace Witness

The reasons for thinking that the marketplace is a key mission field are so obvious that one could only think that an enemy has blinded our eyes to the possibilities.

- First, *access*: The marketplace gives access to people who work there while it denies access to outsiders, especially religious professionals, except in a few cases where industrial or corporate chaplaincy is accepted.

- Second, the *relational context*: The corporation is a community—literally a company is *com-pani* (shared bread)—of shared life and enterprise, providing a relational context for ministry that is often deeper than the local church or the neighbourhood.

- Third, sheer *time*: Most working adults spend most of their waking hours in this community.

- Fourth, *intrinsic issues and values*: The marketplace itself raises issues that are openings for the gospel and pastoral care: identity, relationality, priorities, credibility, life-purpose, success and failure.

- Fifth, *life-centredness*: The opportunities abound for relational evangelism, in which a person may hear the gospel not only in word, but also in the lived-out behaviour of the witness, far surpassing the openings created by parachuting into a new neighbourhood, door-to-door visitation or short-term missions. In this context note Paul's emphasis on "my way of life" (1 Cor 4:17; 2 Tm 3:10). As R.F. Hock has indicated in his study of Paul's tentmaking, far from being at the periphery of his life, "Paul's tentmaking was actually central to [his life]…and his trade was taken up into his apostolic self-understanding, so much so that, when criticized for plying his trade, he came to understand himself as the apostle who offered the message free of charge."[11]

- Sixth, *proximity to people in need and crisis*: When trouble and hardship hit, a worker is more inclined to share this with a colleague at work than a religious professional in the church. The opportunities for pastoral care in the marketplace—that is, caring for the whole person (body, soul and spirit) in the light of the love and pastoral care of God—are enormous, so much so that several theologically trained people known to me have gone into pastoral ministry in business rather than the church. Instead of a few hours of direct pastoral care one can have in church leadership, one has forty hours a week.

What would happen if every theological student preparing for pastoral ministry were to spend a semester in the workplace listening and learning how to empower people for full-time service in the marketplace? What change of perspective would be brought about if every professor of theology in a seminary spent two weeks each year in a professional office or a factory? What gain could be made in modeling if every theological faculty included people who modeled full-time ministry in the world, since education is essentially an imitation process and students become "like" their teachers (Lk 6:40)? Consider the transformation that would come if every local church recognized that not only ordinary members working in businesses, but also traveling businesspeople going to other countries are missionaries with significant opportunities with governments and industries. Are they not as deserving of prayer support and commissioning as a team of people going to Mexico to help build a church building?[12] What message and meta-message would be communicated if we opened our pulpits, at least occasionally, for thoughtful businesspeople to speak God's Word from the integrative perspective of being a businessperson, a schoolteacher or a lawyer?

## Marketplace as Mission

A mission field, yes. But mission?

### *Relating Business and Mission*

Sunki Bang, who leads the Business Ministry Institute in Seoul, Korea, has helpfully suggested several ways of relating business and mission.

- *Business and mission*: two isolated activities.

- *Business for mission*: using the proceeds of business as a way of financing mission.

- *Business as a platform for mission*: work and professional life as a means of channeling mission throughout the world (in Korea they are called "Businaries").

- *Mission in business*: hiring non-believers with a view of leading them to Christ; offering chaplaincy services.

- *Business as mission*: business as part of the mission of God in the world.[13]

It is this last option that we must now consider. To do so, first we will address the question, what is the mission of God? Then we will ask whether enterprise in the marketplace participates in the mission of God in whole, part or not at all.

Three factors in contemporary mission *theoria* (thinking) and *praxis* (action) make gaining a biblical theology of mission problematic and may explain, in part, why we seldom think of business itself as mission.

## Misunderstanding Mission

First, there is the notion that mission is essentially a human activity undertaken in response to God's love or as a duty to fulfill the Great Commission. In fact mission starts not with human action but with God's action in sending himself. Augustine once said (and Moltmann elaborated on this) that in the Triune God, there is a lover, a beloved and love itself.[14] In the same way, there is sender, sent and sending (Jn 17:18; 20:21). The term "mission" comes from the Latin, "to send." It was used exclusively for the mission of God until recently.[15] In creation God was already the God in mission, with his Word and Spirit as "missionaries."[16] The church does not create mission. God's mission creates the church. It is not an activity of the church that certain people, especially those interested, undertake on behalf of the church. Mission is the sending of God in which the people of God are called to participate.

Second, there is the false notion that "mission is what missionaries do."[17] Thus, it is thought that our participation in the mission of God is done representatively or vicariously by certain designated people called "missionaries." As John Davis has shown in his research of the interpretation of the Great Commission, it is not merely the apostles (and missionaries) that are called to preach, teach and disciple, but the whole people of God.[18] Indeed, to say that the church does not *have* a mission but *is* one does not go far enough, though it underscores that all the people of God are missionaries and not just the missionaries working on behalf of the church. The church itself is created through the mission of God and participates in the mission of God; and it does this not only in its gathered (ecclesial) life, but also in its dispersed (diaspora) life as members fan out into the world as agents of the kingdom of God. So the source of the church's mission is not human obedience, not even human duty, but the Incarnation, the outpoured Spirit, the sending of apostles by the Son and of the Son and the sending of the church by the Triune God.[19]

Third, there is the tragic separation of the Great Commission (Mt 28:18–20) from the creation mandate to subdue and care for creation (Gn 1:26–28). Whole denominations of Christians line up after one or the other as the mandate for the church's life. There are three full-time jobs for Adam and Eve (and their progeny) in Genesis 1 and 2: communion with God, community building and co-creativity with God (something Karl Barth would call sub-creativity).[20] This tragic separation has led to varying lists of priorities as to which work is more sacred and the unfortunate debate in the Western world of the conflicting values of evangelism and social justice.[21]

Far more helpful would be to speak of the *Greatest Commission*, found in John 17:18 and 20:21, where Jesus says, "As the Father has sent me, I am sending you" (20:21). God sends us in a fully incarnational mission with all the resources of the Triune God whose mission we are entering.

### The Mission of God

My colleague Charles Ringma helpfully defines mission as *joining God in God's caring, sustaining and transforming activity on earth.* This involves both building the faith community and also building the human community. Mission is good news to the world both because it brings people into relation with Jesus, and also because it promises to bring *shalom* into the world. The ultimate goal of mission is the Sabbath *shalom:* the threefold harmony of God, creation and humankind, which will finally be obtained when Christ comes again and the kingdom of God is consummated.[22] In the meantime we work towards that end, finding meaning in our imperfect and fragmented efforts on earth in view of the certain end, the full realization of the kingdom of God in a new heaven and earth. Significantly, Jürgen Moltmann claims that eschatology is the most pastoral of all theological disciplines, because it shows us that we are not at high noon but at the breaking of a new day.[23] Some of the great biblical theological doctrines illuminate this beautifully.

### Mission and Christian Truth

#### The Doctrine of Creation: Relationality and Regency

The doctrine of creation, for example, shows that work is intrinsic to human nature. It is part of what it means to be made in the image of God. The Bible opens with God working. The image, as we are to understand it strictly from the text of Genesis 1:26–31, involves *relationality* ("male and female he created them") and *regency* ("fill the earth and subdue it"). God is a worker, and we are God-like in our work[24] just as we are God-like in love and community building. Work of all kinds has intrinsic value (it is good in itself, not merely for what it produces) in that it sustains and develops God's creation and is part of the dignity of being God-imaging creatures. Business and commerce are implicit in the creation mandate to subdue and care for creation.[25] This seems apparent from the list of occupations for Cain's descendents:

- Jabal—the father of those who dwell in tents and have livestock, which implies commerce.

- Jubal—the father of those who play the harp and flute, which implies culture.
- Tubal-Cain—who forged all kinds of tools of bronze and iron, which implies crafts.

### The Doctrine of Redemption: Personal and Creational Transformation

In the same way, the doctrine of redemption points towards a this-worldly and whole-person mission. Reflecting on Colossians 1:15–20 and Romans 8:19–23, Paul Marshall says, "the scope of redemption in Christ is the same as the scope of creation."[26] It started with God's work during the Old Testament. God's redemptive purpose through Israel, which includes the stewardship of the land, economic laws and the development of creation, sought "to restore a measure of conformity to the original economic purposes of God in creation."[27] The failure to see the unity of the Testaments (Old Testament/New Testament) has contributed to the erroneous view that "the New Testament is more 'spiritual' than the Old, and is, because of this, superior to it."[28]

Turning to the New Testament, we discover that Jesus, in announcing his ministry in terms of the Jubilee (Lk 4:18; Lv 25), declared the full extent of his kingdom ministry—to make people fully human and to humanize the earth. We know from Leviticus 25 that this involves even economic *shalom*. As agents of the kingdom, the people of God[29] are to proclaim the Word of God, show love and compassion, exercise responsible stewardship of creation and engage in spiritual warfare against Satan's dark kingdom. All human work that embodies kingdom values and serves kingdom goals—to extend God's kingdom on earth—can be rightly termed as kingdom ministry and should be regarded as kingdom work. Gospel work and so-called "secular work" are actually independent. Biblically we should speak of a single mission rather than prioritizing evangelism and social action/stewardship of creation.[30]

### The Doctrine of Last Things: Continuity and Consummation

Moltmann refers to eschatology as the "doctrine of the return to the pristine beginning" through which God will achieve his purpose for creation in "'the new creation of all things' and [in] the universal indwelling of God in that creation."[31] The doctrine of the last judgment means that we are accountable for our use of talents and the stewardship of our lives (Mt 25:14–30). Judgment and accountability mean that our work and lives are meaningful, resultful and significant. The resurrection of the body as the Christian's future means that "our labour in the Lord is not in vain" (1 Cor 15:58).[32] As Miroslav Volf notes, "the continuity or discontinuity between the present and future orders is the key issue in developing a theology of work."[33]

### Work that Lasts

There are nine biblical reasons why we can expect that some of our work in non-gospel activity may last and contribute to the new heaven and the new earth:

1. There is continuity between this life and the next.

2. The new Jerusalem is related to this world—a city, the land (Rv 21–22).

3. The kings of the earth bring their glories into the new heaven and new earth (Rv 21:24); the glory and honour of the nations is found in the Holy City (Rv 21:26).

4. The Old Testament prophesies that during the reign of the Messiah we will not cease to work: "my chosen ones will long enjoy the works of their hands" (Is 65:21–22).

5. The resurrected body of Jesus bore scars from this life—but these scars were transfigured (Jn 20:27).

6. In the final judgment Jesus declares that he personally received even humble acts of service in our everyday life (Mt 25:31–46).

7. The fire of judgment (2 Pt 3:7) does not mean annihilation but transformation, for "in keeping with his promise we are looking forward to a new heaven and a new earth" (2 Pt 3:13).

8. Romans 8:19–22 proclaims that the earth groans and waits for liberation from bondage, this being associated with the revelation of the children of God.

9. Revelation 14:13d indicates that the deeds of the Christians will follow them, "the indelible imprint" of their work on their lives.[34]

Miroslav Volf wisely cautions that while God will somehow include our efforts in the new creation, we must not imagine that the "results of human work should or could create and replace 'heaven.'"[35] Along the same lines and with consummate wisdom, Lesslie Newbigin says:

> We can commit ourselves without reserve to all the secular work our
> shared humanity requires of us, knowing that nothing we do in itself
> is good enough to form part of that city's building, knowing that
> everything—from our most secret prayers to our most public political
> acts—is part of that sin-stained human nature that must go down
> into the valley of death and judgement, and yet knowing that as we
> offer it up to the Father in the name of Christ and in the power of the
> Spirit, it is safe with him and—purged in fire—it will find its place
> in the holy city at the end.[36]

Work, including work in the marketplace, has intrinsic value because it
has eternal implications and eternal significance. We are held accountable
for our work. Our deeds follow after us. We are in some way "playing
heaven," as children do when they anticipate their grown-up life by
"playing house." In the same way we anticipate and work toward our
grown-up life in the perfectly consummated creation and community.

In summary the full scope of God's mission involves personal salvation
for individuals. But it also includes the whole of society—thought-forms
and cultures that shape the way people think and act as well as the
principalities and powers: personal, social, human, creational, temporal
and eternal. Obviously marketplace activity cannot express the full scope
of God's mission, but it undertakes part of that mission. As Newbigin
says, "Christ is not just the Lord of Christians; he is Lord of all, absolutely
and without qualification. [Therefore] the entire membership of the
Church in their secular occupations are called to be signs of his lordship
in every area of life."[37]

### Rethinking Business as Mission

There are several reasons for affirming that business can be, and often is,
part of what God is doing in mission:

First, business is a *morally serious enterprise*. It calls for creditability
and deals with values. Significantly, the Chinese word for "business" is
composed of two pictograms, which together say, "create meaning."

Second, it involves the use of *talents* for the common good. It enlists
creativity, inventiveness and cooperation in harnessing and developing the
potential of the earth and the enhancement of human life. As such it is a
direct participation in the work of the creator.

Third, it is a valid form of *community building*.

Fourth, it is one of the best hopes for *the poor* of the world, for it creates new wealth rather than merely distributing existing resources.

Fifth, by developing creation, albeit so imperfectly, and creating new wealth, it *points to the final consummation* of history in the new heaven and the new earth.

## Mission Practice in the Marketplace

Summarizing the mission of the people of God in the marketplace includes the following dimensions:

- The *kerygmatic* (proclamation) role: We are called to bear God's word and the good news of the kingdom in the marketplace as well as everywhere else.

- The *diakonic* (service) role: We are serving God and God's purposes (the real meaning of "ministry") in the marketplace as we release talents, create community and serve our neighbour by providing goods and services. We also serve God by being pastors, shepherding and caring for the people with whom we are brought into proximity through the marketplace.

- The *koinonic* (fellowship and partnership) role: We build community by caring for our neighbour in the workplace and creating corporate and professional cultures that reflect in some measure the presence of the kingdom—people-affirming, interdependent communities that give people significance, release talents and help people learn to love.

- The *prophetic* (discernment) role: We serve God by calling the marketplace to accountability for injustice, rapacious competition, idolatrous demands made on workers, unjust and unfair remuneration patterns and participation in global inequities. In this way we engage not only individual sin but also systemic evil, what Paul called "the principalities and powers."[38] We also work prophetically by pointing to the final consummation of history and the new heaven and new earth, giving meaning to this worldly activity.

So it is not *either* mission field *or* mission, but *both* mission field *and* mission.[39] Regarding the marketplace as "mission field" serves to build the *faith community* (one of the two dimensions of God's mission); viewing the marketplace as "mission" serves to build the *human community*. Sin pollutes this activity just as much as it twists the direct evangelistic efforts Christians undertake in the church and the world, but taken together, as both mission field and mission, business activity is one way of serving God and God's purposes in the world. We cannot pray, "thy kingdom come, thy will be done on earth," without including the possibility that we are both cooperating with God now in accomplishing his will on earth while also working toward the second coming of Christ, when the "not yet" and "coming" of the kingdom will become "now" and "here."

Steve Brinn, a self-proclaimed "sinful capitalist" asks:

> Why shouldn't Christians be up to their ears in tough stuff—and aren't most of our reasons for shying away from it shallow or false? From the time I entered business more than 22 years ago, Christ to me has been a model of engagement. Dangerous engagement in life, where there was high exposure with questionable people and complicated issues, entailing prospects for great conflict and trouble. Christ's invitation to be like him led me, in the business context, from safe harbours to open water.[40]

## Endnotes

[1] I acknowledge my indebtedness to an article by John Jefferson Davis, who traced the history of the interpretation of Matthew 28:18–20 from the early church to the present, showing how the full meaning of the text was obscured by ecclesiastical controversies with the full missiological implication emerging with William Carey. Davis notes, "the marketplace implications of this crucial text are just beginning to receive attention at the present time" (1). From "'Teaching Them to Observe All that I Have Commanded You,' The History of the Interpretation of the 'Great Commission' and Implications for Marketplace Ministries" (unpublished article from Gordon-Conwell Theological Seminary, South Hamilton, MA, 1998).

[2] Brian Griffiths, *The Creation of Wealth* (London: Hodder and Stoughton, 1984), 9–11.

[3] "I pass over that secret call, of which each minister is conscious before God, and which does not have the church as witness. But there is the witness of our heart that we receive the proffered office not with ambition or avarice, not with any other selfish desire, but with sincerity, fear of God and desire to build up the church. That is indeed necessary for each of us (as I have said) if we would have our ministry approved by God" (*Institutes*, II.1063). Calvin's concern was to prevent "noisy and troublesome men from rashly tak[ing] upon themselves to teach or to rule" (*Institutes*. II.1062).

[4] Max L. Stackhouse, et al, *On Moral Business: Classical and Contemporary Resources for Ethics in Economic Life* (Grand Rapids: Eerdmans, 1995), 137. Plotinus said: "The pleasure demanded for the Sage's life cannot be in the enjoyments of the licentious or in any gratifications of the body—there is no place for these, and they stifle happiness—not in any violent emotion—what could so move the Sage?—it can be only such pleasure as here must be where Good is, pleasure that does not rise from movement and is not a thing of process, for all that is good is immediately present to the Sage and the Sage is present to himself: his pleasure, his contentment, stands immovable" (139).

[5] Eusebius of Caesaria said: "Two ways of life are given by the law of Christ to his Church. The one is above nature, and beyond human living…Wholly and permanently separate from the common customary life of mankind, it devotes itself to the service of God alone…Such then is the perfect form of human life. And the other, more humble, more human, permits men to have minds for farming, for trade, and the other more worldly interests, as well as for religion…And a kind of secondary grade of piety is attributed to them." Quoted in Leland Ryken, *Redeeming the Time: A Christian Approach to Work and Leisure* (Grand Rapids: Baker, 1995), 74.

[6] See Siew Li Wong, "A Defence of the Intrinsic Value of 'Secular Work' in Tentmaking Ministry in the Light of the Theology Doctrines of Creation, Redemption and Eschatology" (unpublished MCS Thesis, Regent College, Vancouver, April 2000), 6–11. In the course of researching for the thesis, Ms. Wong interviewed executives in most of the tentmaking missions based in North America and found only one who indicated that the work that tentmaking missionaries do had any intrinsic value. It was merely instrumental.

[7] "The Lay Task of Co-Creation," in *Toward the Future: Catholic Social Thought and the U.S. Economy, A Lay Letter, Lay Commission on Catholic Social Teaching and the U.S. Economy* (North Tarrytown, NY: 1984), 25–45, quoted in Max L. Stackhouse, et al, op. cit., 905–6.

[8] William Carey, *An Enquiry into the Obligations of Christians to Use Means for the Conversion of the Heathens* (Leicester, 1792), 68. Carey says, "This seems to imply that in the time of the glorious increase of the church, in the latter days, commerce shall subserve the spread of the gospel."

[9] "As to their distance from us, whatever objections might have been made on that account before the invention of the mariner's compass, nothing can be alleged for it, with any colour of plausibility in the present age. Men can now sail with as much certainty through the Great South Sea, as they can through the Mediterranean, or any lesser Sea. Yea, and providence seems in a manner to invite us to the trial, as there are to our knowledge trading companies, whose commerce lies in many of the places where these barbarians dwell" (ibid., 67).

[10] See Michael C.R. McLoughlin, "Back to the Future of Missions," *Vocatio* 4, no. 2 (December 2000): 1–6.

[11] R.F. Hock, *The Social Context of Paul's Ministry: Tentmaking and Apostleship* (Philadelphia: Fortress Press, 1980), 166.

[12] A village church in Yorkshire recently honoured one of its members with a $90,000 stained glass window. The parishioner was Thomas Crapper, a plumber born in the nearby village of Thorne in 1836. As reported in *The Globe and Mail*, "the window incorporates a tastefully rendered silhouette of a toilet as part of a celebration of local achievements." Mr. Crapper was the inventor of the flush toilet. *The Marketplace: MEDA's Magazine for Christians in Business* (January–February 2001), 2.

[13] Bang notes that one of the dangers of taking the last position is the potential of minimizing evangelism, the matter I have explored in the first section. See Sunki Bang, "Tensions in Witness," *Vocatio* 1, no. 2 (July 1998): 17–18.

[14] Jürgen Moltmann, *The Trinity and the Kingdom*, trans. Margaret Kohl (San Francisco: Harper and Row, 1991), 32.

[15] This truth has been developed most completely by George F. Vicedom: "Catholic dogmatics since Augustine speak of sendings or the *missio* within the Triune God...Every sending of one Person results in the presence of the Other." From George F. Vicedom, *The Mission of God: An Introduction to a Theology of Mission*, trans. Gilbert A. Thiele and Dennis Hilgendorf (St. Louis: Concordia, 1965), 7.

[16] David Bosch, *Believing in the Future: Toward a Missiology of Western Culture* (Gracewing, 1995).

[17] In the same way, almost every theology of ministry published in the English language starts with the definition of ministry as what "the minister does"—proclamation of the Word and administering the sacraments. See R. Paul Stevens, *The Other Six Days: Vocation, Work and Ministry in Biblical Perspective* (Grand Rapids: Eerdmans/Regent Publishing, 1999), 132ff.

[18] See Davis, op. cit.

[19] See ibid., 191ff. and David J. Bosch, *Transforming Mission: Paradigm Shifts in Theology of Mission* (Maryknoll, NY: Orbis Books, 1996).

[20] Stevens, *The Other Six Days,* 91–104.

[21] Rene Padilla comments: "Every human need...may be used by the Spirit of God as a beach-head for the manifestation of his kingly power. That is why in actual practice the question of which comes first, evangelism or social action, is irrelevant. In every concrete situation the needs themselves provide the guidelines for the definition of priorities. As long as both evangelism and social responsibility are regarded as essential for mission, we need no rule of thumb to tell us which comes first and

when." From C. Rene Padilla, "The Mission of the Church in the Light of the Kingdom of God," *Transformation* 1, no. 2 (April–June 1984): 19.

[22] Adapted from Stevens, *The Other Six Days,* 204.

[23] I have often reflected on the fact that the whole culture of ancient Egypt was directed to the sunset of life and the world. All the pyramids and tombs are on the west side of the Nile. In contrast biblical faith looks towards the dawning of a new day. A similar contrast has been made between the perspective of African traditional religion and the Christian faith. The comparison is made between a person standing on a bridge over a river and looking one way or another, downstream or upstream. In African traditional religion the person is looking back, at the influence of the spirits or the ancestors coming towards him or her, while the biblical perspective is looking forward, to where we are being led by God.

[24] "The mind of the maker and the Mind of the Maker are formed on the same pattern," with the common characteristic of having both "the desire and the ability to make things." From Dorothy Sayers, *Christian Letters in a Post-Christian World: A Selection of Essays* (Grand Rapids: Eerdmans, 1969), 127, 101.

[25] See Michael Novak, *Business as a Calling: Work and the Examined Life* (New York: The Free Press, 1996), 37.

[26] Paul Marshall and Lela Gilbert, *Heaven is Not my Home: Learning to Live in God's Creation* (Nashville: Word Publishing, 1998), 46.

[27] Christopher J. H. Wright, *Living as the People of God: The Relevance of Old Testament Ethics* (Leicester: Inter-Varsity Press, 1998), 89.

[28] Bosch, op. cit., 405.

[29] The simplest definition of the kingdom is the rule of the sovereign plus the response of the people. Jesus, as Irenaeus said, embodied the kingdom and was the *autobasileia.* In contrast, Queen Elizabeth in England reigns but does not rule, which is the way many relate to God.

[30] See Rene Padilla, op. cit., 19.

[31] Jürgen Moltmann, *The Coming of God: Christian Eschatology,* trans. Margaret Kohl (Minneapolis: Fortress Press, 1996), 57.

[32] "The resurrection of Christ redeems from meaninglessness the whole of our life and work. It is in the resurrection of Christ that we find the final vindication of all the work we do in this life, our assurance that all our toil and struggle and sufferings possess abiding worth." From Alan Richardson, *The Biblical Doctrine of Work* (London: SCM Press, 1952), 58.

[33] Miroslav Volf, "Human Work, Divine Spirit, and the New Creation: Toward a Pneumatological Understanding of Work," *Pneuma: The Journal of the Society for Pentecostal Studies* (Fall 1987): 175. Volf contrasts the view of work as

cooperation with God in *creatio continua*, which has dominated Reformational theology, with work as cooperation with God in *transformatio mundi*.

[34] Ibid., 175–179.

[35] Miroslav Volf, *Work in the Spirit: Toward a Theology of Work* (New York: Oxford University Press, 1991), 92.

[36] Lesslie Newbigin, *Foolishness to the Greeks: The Gospel and Western Culture* (Grand Rapids: Eerdmans, 1986), 136.

[37] Lesslie Newbigin, *Unfinished Agenda: An Updated Autobiography* (St. Andrews, 1993), 203.

[38] See Stevens, "Resistance—Grappling with the Powers," in *The Other Six Days,* 215–242. Also see Stevens, "Principalities and Powers," *Vocatio* 3, no. 1 (December 1999).

[39] The Mennonite Economic Development Associates have as their mission statement: "As Christians in business our mission is to honour God in the world of business and economics by extending his reign to all our activities. With Jesus as Lord of the marketplace our task is to love, serve, preach and heal. We use our faith, skills and resources to correct inequities, work toward economic justice, seek righteousness, bring hope where is no hope, and make all things new." Quoted in Sunki Bang, "Tensions in Witness," 18.

[40] Steve Brinn, "Tough Business: In Deep, Swift Waters," *Vocatio* 2, no. 2 (July 1999): 3–6.

# VOCATIONAL CONVERSION:

# AN IMAGINARY PURITAN-BABY BOOMER

# DIALOGUE

*From* Crux, *vol. 37, no. 4 (December 2001)*

It has been said that the sixteenth-century Puritans[1] were people who had swallowed gyroscopes.[2] They were inwardly directed to the Lord's Kingdom and were not easily swayed by the attractions of the world. Crucial to this orientation was their understanding of the biblical doctrine of calling or vocation,[3] the idea that the whole of our life is a response to the summons of God and not merely a matter of self-directed development. William Perkins (1558–1602), while little known, deserves a modern hearing because he is the first Puritan[4] author to describe calling in a systematic way.[5] Thus sections of his *Treatise of the Vocations,*[6] written around the turn of the seventeenth century,[7] are paraphrased in an imaginary conversation between Perkins (P)[8] and a twentieth-century baby boomer (B), that demographic population bulge of people born between 1946 and 1964,[9] in order to contrast one modern view of vocation with a biblical view. The endnotes offer a few clarifying comments and corrections of the imbalance of the Puritan view of calling.

## Calling and Career

B: I am looking for a new set of satisfactions in my job.[10] It must be interesting, suitable to my talents and give me ample remuneration. Can Jesus give me this?

P: You would not be asking that question if you understood your life as a response to the call of God. There is no satisfaction apart from living

37

and acting within the compass of God's call.[11]

B: You agree, surely, that it is important for a person to find a job that is a good expression of one's personality? Didn't Jesus come to bring a satisfying and abundant life?

P: It is more important to discover what satisfies God. A calling is not self-chosen but imposed on humankind by God.[12] Calling is not to some *thing*, but to some *One*. It is not a mere job or career.

B: In my world if you don't get on the right escalator at the right time, you won't make it to the top.

P: A calling is for the common good, not just for your personal advancement. You are chosen by a loving God for a way of life and a particular path of service in the world.[13] Theology is the science of living well. And you cannot live well while ignoring social obligations.[14]

B: Why is the doctrine of calling so important?

P: God's word guides us to integrate every aspect of our lives under the rule of God. Whatever is not done within the compass of your calling is not done in faith, and this leaves you open to the punishments and displeasure of God.[15] Samson found that out the hard way.

B: Samson made the mistake of allowing his wife to give him a haircut!

P: No, it was much deeper than that. Samson lost his supernatural strength because he broke his Nazarite vow and so operated outside his calling (Jgs 13:1–5).[16] You will bring similar hardship on yourself if you do the same.

B: Samson was a special case.

P: Everyone is a special case[17] but always within a general calling that comes to all. The general calling comes when people allow Christ to win them from living for the world in order to live for God. All Christians are called to invoke the name of God in Christ, to further the good estate of the church, to serve one another in love and to walk worthily in their vocation of being a disciple of Jesus.[18]

B: But I thought you said that each of us is called individually?

P: First, I was speaking of the general calling that comes to each and every believer. This is the most important calling. Within the general call each person has a special way of serving God through the personal or particular calling. This involves the execution of some particular office or function that each of us plays in society and the church: the magistrate in governing, the minister in teaching the people, the physician in bringing health, the master in governing his family and the merchant in business.[19] Adam and Eve were the first to receive such a personal calling (in their case, to dress and keep the garden), and all who descend from Adam must have some calling to walk in, whether in public or private service, whether in the church, society or in the family.[20]

B: My generation is the first with less purchasing power than their parents at each stage of adulthood, the first generation that cannot afford what we have always had.[21] I wish I could be free from having to work except for the fun of it.

P: Damnable is the state of those enriched with great living and revenues, who spend their days in eating and drinking, in sports and pastimes, and do not employ themselves in service for the church or society.[22] Even servants, who have jobs that only occupy them for a short time each day and have positions that allow them to sleep around or spend their time playing games, have an insufficient calling. They need something more. Indeed, it is good for every man to have two strings to his bow.[23]

B: Please do not misunderstand me. I bring to work expectations other than gaining material success. I want a challenging involvement that is ecologically innocent, comfortable to my dignity, a call to growth and excitement, a meaningful contribution to society and all with a large paycheck.[24] I tend to measure my self-worth by how my work is valued and by my salary scale even more than the material goods money will buy.[25]

P: You seem to have missed the point. One cannot separate the practice of his or her particular calling from the general calling of being a Christian, the more important calling. Then and then only can you live an integrated life. The magistrate must be a Christian magistrate, not merely a magistrate. A husband must be a Christian not only when abroad in the town or in the church meeting, but in his deportment towards wife and children.[26]

## The Call to the Ministry

B: Then it seems to me that going into the ministry would be the best way of joining the general calling with the particular calling. Then everything one does will be service to God. Religious people can spend their time in contemplative prayer and serve God more completely, not being burdened with ordinary work in the world.

P: All Christians are equally called. I repudiate the idea that monks and friars think they live in a state of perfection because they live apart from normal society and are spiritually superior. The only place one can live the Christian life is in the world. Those who live from the support of others and do no useful work are not pleasing God. Every person must realize his or her personal calling in order to be a good and profitable member of some part of society or some corporate body in the world, including the church.[27]

B: What, then, makes a job Christian?

P: I am not talking about a job, but a calling that affects all aspects of your life.[28] All lawful callings are good. The dignity of our calling has nothing to do with the seeming importance of it.[29] Whether someone is a pastor, a magistrate or chimney sweep makes no difference. God looks on the heart of the worker. The action of the shepherd in keeping sheep is as good a work before God as the action of a judge in giving a sentence or a minister in preaching.[30]

B: Can one choose more than one calling?

P: Many of God's saints have, such as Melchizedek and Aaron. That is why I am unhappy with your constant preoccupation with your job. As I see it a person can be a merchant and a father in the family—two callings. Or take the apostle Paul. He was by one calling an apostle and by another a tentmaker because of the poverty of the church of the Corinthians, but also to stop the mouths of the false apostles who would have accused him of taking advantage of the gospel. Similarly, I think that many ministers now should have other callings, always remembering that there should be no hindrance to their principal calling of being a disciple of Jesus.[31]

B: You seem to make vocational decision-making unnecessary, unimportant or perhaps even impossible since you advise, it seems to me, merely submitting to God's will. Having a lot of choices is crucial for my generation. Personally, I like to keep my options open.

**Puritan Vocational Guidance**

P: The worst vocational mistake is not to *want* to do God's will. Within God's will and calling there are many choices.[32] In considering what calling is best for a person, three things must be considered. First, it must be an honest calling, not like that of the thief (Eph 4:28). Second, it must be suited to the person: every calling must be fitted to the man and the man must be fitted to the calling. To discover this, as you suggested, we must explore our affections, desires and gifts. But because we are often biased, we should consult the advice and help of others, especially if we sense that God's calling is in pastoral ministry.[33] Third, when there is a choice to be made, we simply should choose the best calling.[34]

B: So it is appropriate to offer yourself for a calling?

P: If your motive is right, that is fine,[35] as it was for Isaiah, who was ready to go when God called him.[36] I think parents have a particular responsibility to help their children discern their callings. For example, a parent who sees a child who has a love of learning, a love of hard work, a love of praise and a wit neither too quick nor too dull should discern that child fit for the academic world. Parents can do no greater wrong to their children and to society in general than to force them into callings for which they are unfit.[37]

B: How can I know that I have found the right career?

P: First, your indecision about your career is a sign that you are trying to establish your identity in your particular calling rather than your general calling. One discovers who one is through discipleship to Jesus. If your identity is well established there, and if you want to know God and glorify him in everything, it doesn't matter very much what you do for your particular calling.[38]

B: But what happens if I get into the wrong calling?

P: It is not so much a matter of the wrong calling as the wrong motive. Take the person who got married, a lawful calling, but got married for the wrong motive. The solution for that person is not to forsake the calling (and the spouse) but to repent of the bad attitude with which he or she entered marriage and then to continue in the calling for God's glory.[39]

B: As I search for fulfillment, I have, as some say, a sense of entitlement.

## Walking Worthily of One's Calling

P: You will never find your personal vocation in a spirit of grasping covetousness.[40] Walking worthily of your calling (Eph 4:1) is more important than finding the perfect situation.

B: Sometimes I feel resentment against God for denying me the right of satisfying and fulfilling work.

P: The principal end of our living is to perform service to humankind and in this service to do homage to God.[41] We walk worthily when we glorify God where we are, not in some other situation we covet. Usually the duty at hand opens up a ministry for us. A father and mother, for instance, are called not only to care for the bodies of their family but also for the souls of their household. Most homemakers are at fault in choosing the lesser duties.[42] You can always find God where you are if you are thankful enough to be content.

B: So what makes a personal calling Christian?

P: Three things: it must be done in obedience; it must be done in faith; and it must be directed to the glory of God.[43]

B: So it has little to do with our church work or our religious activity?

P: Rather, it is *how* we work and live, or more accurately, *for whom*. Injustice practised in our calling nullifies our worship, prayer, hearing the Word and receiving the sacraments. They become an abomination to the Lord. For example, God is grieved when doctors prescribe remedies without proper diagnosis, when merchants and tradesmen use false weights or dress up their wares to deceive the customer or sell in darkened shops so people cannot see what they are buying, when landlords take unreasonable rent or when a patron makes a public gesture about his generosity but secretly keeps back much for himself.[44]

B: Many who do this are saved people and claim to live by faith.

P: Faith is not merely saving faith but faith to please God in our callings. Faith must be joined to love as the left hand of the stonemason holds the ladder while the right hand holds the burden to be passed on to his fellow-worker. Love says that our labour must be for the good of others.[45]

## Overcoming the Lust of the Spirit

B: That is especially hard when others seem to have a better calling that you have.

P: That is why I said that calling is a matter of the heart. You cannot do well if you have a spirit of grasping and covetousness like Absalom and the sons of Zebedee.[46]

B: Such as wishing you had someone else's job or someone else's family situation?

P: Yes, a common fault in believers is that they do not attend to their own matters but look covetously at what others are doing.[47] Peter asked Jesus what John must do (Jn 21:21), but Jesus corrected him by saying, "If I want him to remain alive until I return, what is that to you?" (Jn 21:23).

B: My society daily encourages me to be discontent with what I have and who I am.

P: There is another way of looking at the difficulties we face in living according to our callings in this world. Since the fall of Adam there is no calling on earth without crosses and calamities.[48] We must labour to see every day that our situation is not an accident but part of God's providence— no matter how difficult it may be. We must resolve in our conscience that God is our portion (Ps 16:6), and we must resolve not to seek more in this world than we actually need. We have no warrant to pray for abundance.[49]

42

B: But what can we do when we see others placed in better situations than ourselves? [50]

P: We must consider that the great callings that others enjoy are not for their personal benefit but for the common good. [51]

B: You are asking for a completely different way of thinking.

P: Much more than thinking. Rather, vocational conversion. [52] We need to turn our affections from the world to set our minds on heavenly realities (Eph 1:18). We need to reflect constantly on our need for Christ and our hopeless state apart from the blood of Christ. We must in ourselves be as the wounded man that lay in the way so that Christ Jesus, the true Samaritan, may come to us to salve our wounds and to pour his precious blood into our souls. [53]

B: Is ambition wrong?

P: It is right to be faithful. Ambition is a vice whereby a person thinks better of himself than he should and thus becomes discontent with his particular calling. In this way, Absalom, through the ambition that arose from his natural self-love, was moved to seek his father's kingdom. He did not consider himself accurately. [54]

B: But surely we should be free to maximize our own potential if possible now, even if we have to change jobs many times.

P: You are once more talking about jobs rather than callings. If you understand your life around the truth of calling, you will see how inappropriate it is to change your calling for superficial reasons. And if you do, you should have in mind not your personal fulfillment but the public good. [55] That requires patience. Impatience is one of the things most lacking in those who do not walk worthily of their calling. We must be like the surgeon who continues to cut his patient even though the poor patient screams a lot. Similarly we must deal ruthlessly with impatience by constantly remembering that our calling is approved by God.

B: That seems like all work and no play.

## Leisure and the Ultimate Retirement

P: Personally I advise people to practise two kinds of vacations: first, keeping a weekly Sabbath, in which we forsake our normal calling for one full day; second, to engage in lawful recreation on workdays to refresh body and mind better to perform our duties. [56] Then, of course, there is a third vacation, which is a vacation of necessity due to prolonged illness or old age. [57]

B: When significant numbers of my generation retire, a significantly smaller

43

group in the population will be paying for our long-term care.[58] When can I hope to retire? Must I work until I die?

P: We never retire from our general calling, thank God.[59] Even the time for retirement from our particular calling is not of our own choosing but God's. For example, the Levites in the Bible took up their calling at age thirty and retired at fifty. No person should lay down his or her calling until with good conscience that person can say it is the good will and pleasure of God for him or her to cease these duties.[60] God will make the right time known.

B: In the meantime I am directing myself to the goal of living life to its fullest. I do not want to come to the end and judge that my life has been boring, wasteful and of no consequence.

P: My goal is to receive the approval of God. We must all give an account of our calling on the last day of Judgment.[61]

B: How can you know you have walked worthily of the calling you have received?

P: We must calculate our blessings, weigh all that was defective and then cleave to the reality of Christ, his death being all the satisfaction God needs.[62]

B: My success or failure can be assessed in this life. Can yours?

P: In this life, while the day of grace remains, we are to make a reckoning beforehand,[63] never resting until we have assurance in our consciences that the books in heaven are cancelled and that God is content to account Christ his satisfaction in our life as a payment for our sins. This being done, we shall be able to make a good account before the Lord at the last day of Judgment.[64]

## Endnotes

[1] In his masterful treatment of work and calling, Paul Marshall follows Basil Hall's definition of Puritans as "restlessly critical…members of the Church of England who desired some modifications in church government and worship, but not…those who removed themselves from the church." From Paul Marshall, *A Kind of Life Imposed on Man: Vocation and Social Order from Tyndale to Locke* (Toronto: University of Toronto Press, 1996), 38.

[2] Os Guinness, "Vocation and Calling," an audiotape produced by The London Institute of Contemporary Christianity (London: June 5–9, 1989).

[3] These two words mean substantially the same thing, though in modern usage "vocation" has been identified with career and "calling" with religious service or the work of a professional minister.

[4] Ian Breward notes that "Perkins himself showed little sign that he thought of himself as anything other than a normal and loyal member of the Church of England. He repudiated the label of 'puritan' except for those who believed that it was possible to live without sin in this life, and felt that it was possible to live without sin in this life." From Ian Breward, ed., *The Work of William Perkins* (Appleford, England: The Sutton Courtenay Press, 1969), 15.

[5] Marshall, *A Kind of Life Imposed on Man,* 41. Earlier Protestant writers had used the concept of vocation to reflect critically on the medieval idea that vocation had little to do with ordinary life in this world. Perkins used the doctrine of vocation to expound the Calvinist distinction between general and particular calling and to provide a firm link between justification and sanctification. He had the further interest of providing in the gospel a firm foundation for social stability and societal responsibility (Breward, *The Work of William Perkins,* 443).

[6] William Perkins, "A treatise of the Vocations, or Callings of Men, with the sorts and kinds of them and the right use thereof," in *The Workes of that Famous and Worthy Minister of Christ in the University of Cambridge, Mr. William Perkins* (London: John Legatt, 1626). This has been reprinted, with some portions deleted, in modern English in Breward, *The Work of William Perkins.*

[7] No precise date can be assigned to the *Treatise.*

[8] I have five reasons for making Perkins's thoughts available. First, Perkins is thoroughly biblical as he defends his views by biblical principle and text. Second, Perkins provides vocational counselling, as he is concerned with *how* vocational decisions are made. Third, his *Treatise* is practical, concerned with real issues of living in the world. Fourth, Perkins is lay-oriented, as he makes no distinction in dignity in the calling of the non-clergy laity and the clergy. Finally, Perkins is oriented to the heart and is concerned with evoking a deep personal spirituality that will result in the transformation of character.

[9] Paul C. Light, *Baby Boomers* (New York: W.W. Norton Company, 1988).

[10] Daniel Yankelovich, "New Rules In American Life: Searching for Self-Fulfilment in a World Turned Upside Down," *Psychology Today* (April 1981): 76.

[11] Perkins, "A treatise of the Vocations, or Callings of Men," 751.

[12] Ibid., 751.

[13] Ibid., 751.

[14] Breward, *The Work of William Perkins,* 444–445.

[15] Perkins, "A treatise of the Vocations, or Callings of Men," 751.

[16] Ibid., 752.

[17] In Perkins's view, all persons serve one another interdependently, each contributing uniquely, in work assigned by God for the preservation of the world.

[18] Perkins, "A treatise of the Vocations, or Callings of Men," 754. Perkins regarded society as having three aspects: church, commonwealth and family. For Perkins the general and the particular calling involved living for God in each of these three. Paul Marshall traces how Perkins's high view of "the interdependent division of labour among people working in a Godly fashion in their several estates and duties" became, in the later Puritans, "the interrelation of independent people working out their own salvation and prosperity" Marshall, *A Kind of Life Imposed on Man*, 52.

[19] Perkins, "A treatise of the Vocations, or Callings of Men," 754. Breward comments that "Perkins' doctrine did not succeed in holding the line against a growing individualism, but he did ensure as far as was possible when all he could appeal to was conscience that Christians did not luxuriate in pious feeling while ignoring social obligation" (Breward, *The Work of William Perkins*, 444–445).

[20] Perkins, "A treatise of the Vocations, or Callings of Men," 755.

[21] Doug Murren, a baby boomer pastor, notes nine reasons for the uniqueness of the baby boomer generation. "(1) We're the first generation to be raised, by and large, by absentee fathers. (2) We're also the first generation whose grandparents had no significant input in terms of life preparation and wage-earning skills. (3) We're the most educated generation in history. (4) We were raised in extreme affluence, with opportunities unimaginable to our parents. (5) We came into childhood and adolescence at the time of the greatest economic expansion in world history. (6) We're the first generation with less purchasing power than our parents at each stage of adulthood. (7) We're the first generation who can't afford what we've always had. (8) We're the first generation raised under the near-constant threat of nuclear war. (9) We're the first generation to be reared with television as a significant parenting tool" (Doug Murren, *The Baby Boomerang* [Ventura, CA: Regal Books, 1990], 33).

[22] Perkins, "A treatise of the Vocations, or Callings of Men," 756. Marshall points out that among the Puritans, the able-bodied but jobless were regarded as rats and weasels in the earth while the old, sick and weak were the poor to be loved as if each was Jesus. Marshall, *A Kind of Life Imposed on Man*, 5.

[23] Perkins, "A treatise of the Vocations, or Callings of Men," 756.

[24] Martin E. P. Seligman, "Boomer Blues," *Psychology Today* (October 1988).

[25] Perry G. Downs, "Baby Boomers' Ministry Needs" in *Christian Education Journal* 11, no. 1:25–32 (Autumn 1990): 27.

[26] Perkins, "A treatise of the Vocations, or Callings of Men," 756.

[27] Ibid., 755–756. It is noteworthy that Perkins, along with other reformers, was absolutely opposed to the life of the monk or nun as a superior way. It was not even an acceptable path of Christian service. This must be seen as a reaction

against the two-level spirituality of medieval Christianity. Unfortunately, it led practically, in the West, to the loss of the contemplative life in Protestantism.

[28] Os Guinness explains that with the industrial revolution work was secularized (and therefore absolutized) while calling was secularized and therefore regarded as irrelevant (Guinness, "Vocation and Calling").

[29] Marshall regards Perkins as ambiguous on the subject of the equality of callings since he placed greater priority on the "weighty" calling in the family (the master), the church (the minister) and the commonwealth (the magistrate), though his distinctions were functional rather than essential (Marshall, *A Kind of Life Imposed on Man*, 43).

[30] Perkins, "A treatise of the Vocations, or Callings of Men," 758. Commenting on the complexity and ambiguities in Perkins's teaching on callings, Paul Marshall concludes that "Perkins fused two different ideas of calling. He saw calling as honest, faithful labour *in* a God-given state; but he also saw it *as* that state, or the work of that state itself, which work must hence be rendered honest. There appeared to be a fusion of the English Reformation idea of calling as estates with the Lutheran, and semi-Calvinian, idea of calling as godly duty" (Marshall, *A Kind of Life Imposed on Man*, 41). Around the turn of the seventeenth century English Puritans began to use the words trade, employment, occupation, calling and vocation almost interchangeably (Ibid., 45). This led to a further secularization of calling and became linked with lawful prosperity (Ibid., 47). Still later in the seventeenth century, secularization brought about a cleavage between the general and the particular callings. Instead of the particular being a facet of the general, the two callings were envisioned side by side. The result was that particular calling was seldom understood as one's Christian duty or manner of life but rather one's job or trade in which one must work hard (Ibid., 52). Spirituality and calling were separated and piety took over.

[31] Perkins, "A treatise of the Vocations, or Callings of Men," 763.

[32] While Perkins does not use these words, they reflect the limited way Perkins approved of freedom of choice within one's calling.

[33] Perkins, "A treatise of the Vocations, or Callings of Men," 759.

[34] The note of listening to the voice of the Spirit, as well as the leading of the Spirit, is significantly lacking in Perkins's *Treatise*. Discerning one's calling comes dangerously close to reading circumstances.

[35] Perkins took "affection" (heart inclination and spiritual thoughtfulness) into serious consideration as a factor in the choice of a calling, more than did his Reformation predecessors. His use of "pollicie" (planning, rather than following the already given path) balanced the almost universal tendency to regard 1 Corinthians 7:17 as the only word of Scripture on vocational choices (more

accurately, on the fact that there is no choice).

[36] Perkins, "A treatise of the Vocations, or Callings of Men," 762.

[37] Ibid., 759.

[38] These words by James Houston are not even a loose translation of Perkins, but they reflect accurately his emphasis. James Houston, lecture in "Ministry and Spirituality" course, Regent College, Vancouver, 1990.

[39] Perkins, "A treatise of the Vocations, or Callings of Men," 762.

[40] James Houston, "Ministry and Spirituality" lecture.

[41] William Perkins, *The Workes of that Famous and Worthy Minister of Christ in the University of Cambridge, Mr. William Perkins* (three volumes, London, 1616–1618), 11, 323.

[42] Perkins, "A treatise of the Vocations, or Callings of Men," 764.

[43] Ibid., 758.

[44] Ibid., 771.

[45] Ibid., 772.

[46] Ibid., 756.

[47] Ibid., 764.

[48] Ibid., 760. Marshall comments: "Anyone who followed all the Puritans' proffered guidance needed to be prepared for a life of constant and earnest toil, repressing desire for fashion, riches, comfort and, often, rest" (Marshall, *A Kind of Life Imposed on Man*, 45).

[49] Perkins, "A treatise of the Vocations, or Callings of Men," 771.

[50] Ibid., 773.

[51] Ibid., 764.

[52] While not Perkins's phrase, I think this well expresses the intent of his teaching.

[53] Perkins, "A treatise of the Vocations, or Callings of Men," 770.

[54] Ibid., 773.

[55] Ibid., 776.

[56] While it appears that Perkins approves of leisure, he permits it as a stimulus to renewed energy in one's calling. Idleness was sin and a way of entertaining the devil's deception (Marshall, *A Kind of Life Imposed on Man*, 39–40).

[57] Perkins, "A treatise of the Vocations, or Callings of Men," 774.

[58] James A. Mathisen, "Who Are the Baby Boomers?" *Christian Education Journal* 11, no. 1:13–23 (Autumn 1990): 21.

[59] Perkins, "A treatise of the Vocations, or Callings of Men," 776.

[60] Ibid., 776.

[61] Ibid., 779.

[62] Ibid., 779.

[63] Max Weber noted that only the Protestant ethic of vocation provides religious motivation primarily through immersion in one's earthly vocation. As Paul Marshall comments, neither Weber nor anyone else has satisfactorily explained how Protestantism brought about this disposition, though it is unquestionable that "this 'innerworldly asceticism' created a *psychological* disposition toward continual, rational, restless labour," thus providing an impetus for the spirit of capitalism. From Paul Marshall, "Calling, Work and Rest," *The Best in Theology, Christianity Today*, ed. J.I. Packer (1989): 196. Perkins should be critiqued at this point for *over*emphasizing working out our general calling in the particular calling. A stronger emphasis on Sabbath would have brought this into better balance.

[64] Perkins, "A treatise of the Vocations, or Callings of Men," 779.

# REVIEW OF *CHANGING WORK VALUES:*
# *A CHRISTIAN RESPONSE*

*by Gordon Preece (Melbourne: Acorn Press, 1995)*

*From* Crux, *vol. 37, no. 3 (September 1996)*

Thankfully books on work and the Christian's ministry in the workplace are beginning to abound. Gordon Preece, chaplain and lecturer in Ethics and Lay Ministry at Ridley College, Melbourne, has added yet another substantial piece to the growing body of literature on the theology and philosophy of work. Its comprehensiveness is both its strength and its weakness.

Preece evaluates almost every theme it is possible to explore in the world of work: the much-heralded shift from industrial manufacturing to information technology, the influence of computers, the predictions of futurists concerning what it will be like to work in the twenty-first century, the effect of the globalizing of work and economics, the demise of the career, the continued out-sourcing of household work and the proliferation of lower-paid service jobs. Is it really true that the computer revolution indirectly created jobs for dishwashers at McDonalds? Read Preece to find out.

So much for the future. Next Preece considers the past. After surveying two influential figures on the doctrine of work—Karl Barth and Jacques Ellul—Preece revisits the Protestant work ethic (à la Max Weber), showing that this doctrine was formulated largely by people leaving Protestantism. Preece argues that a return to what the magisterial reformers and the early Puritans actually taught is exactly what is needed today to put work back into its proper place—i.e., work is neither to be one's god (to provide ultimate meaning and personal identity), nor to be viewed as a mere curse done of necessity. Rather, work is an aspect of our larger calling and a genuine sub-creativity shared with and under our working God. Here Preece leans hard on Jürgen Moltmann. He also explores the surprising discussion of the work ethic by Pope John Paul II in *Laborem Exercens*, once again offering a shrewd and constructive critique. Preece's is a fine piece of theological reflection.

The great strength of this book is its rootedness in the life of a specific Christian community where work, prayer and ministry are integrated. Were chapter three not seeded into the book, one might be tempted to relegate the book to its obvious Australian context and readership. But the most personal is indeed the most universal. Preece explains how WorkVentures, based in Australia, has sought to "harness the energy of the Third Wave of technological change for the benefit of local communities so that they are not left in its wake." The book is worth reading for this chapter alone.

The book tends to lack a focus and often makes for tiresome reading. But anyone wanting to understand "how come?" questions about the ministry of the laity will find *Changing Work Values*, as Robert Banks has noted, "a relevant, balanced and profoundly Christian understanding of the issues at hand."

# THEOLOGY OF WORK & REST

# TOWARD A MARKETPLACE SPIRITUALITY

*From* Crux, *vol. 41 no. 3 (Spring 2005)*

"No man [*sic*] can afford to live in the marketplace who
does not also live in the desert." *Archbishop Hume* [1]
"Someone asked Abba Anthony [the founder of Eastern
monasticism], 'What must one do in order to please God?'
The old man replied, 'Pay attention to [these three things]:
whoever you may be, always have God before your eyes
whatever you do; do it according to the testimony of the
holy Scriptures; in whatever place you live, do not easily
leave it.'" *The Sayings of the Desert Fathers* [2]

Spirituality is "in" today, but often it is the search for the divine being
inside the person. So a spate of books and seminars encourage us not
only to take our hands, minds and hearts to work, but our spirits as well.
Personally I welcome the recognition that human beings at work are not
merely thinking machines or heartless computers, but persons with spirits.
We bring our whole person to work—body, soul and spirit. But there is a
more critical reason for us to explore the spirituality of business.

## Busy, But Not Deep

Business is stressful. The sources of stress are not hard to find: shifts in the
work world—sometimes a weekly paradigm shift—technology, relational
pressures at work and home, the feeling that we have one continuous
work week, cultural shifts that press us to be politically correct and wary of
possible litigation, and the pressure of the global economy. But the most
pernicious source of stress is the drive within ourselves, which makes us

constantly busy. Not surprisingly, the word "business" is close to the word "busyness."

The symptoms of "busy" people are all too visible: they live compulsive, habitual lives, have no time for friends, are too occupied to keep Sabbath, feel guilty when resting or doing nothing and fill up every cancellation in their date book or Palm Pilot. They are consistently "overbooked." The professor in Ecclesiastes describes it well: "And I saw that all labour and all achievement spring from man's envy of his neighbour" (4:4). Commenting on this compulsive money-maker, Derek Kidner says, "he has surrendered to a mere craving and to the endless process of feeding it...Such a man [or woman], even with a wife [or husband] and children, will have little time for them, convinced that he [or she] is toiling for their benefit although his [or her] heart is elsewhere, devoted and wedded to his projects."[3] Mary Baechler, cofounder and president of Racing Strollers, in an article entitled "Death of a Marriage," says, "There was a fundamental moment when I chose the business over the marriage." Baechler asks reflectively, "How does someone who is obsessed live peacefully with someone who isn't?"[4]

Oftentimes the source of such busyness is the desire to find approval for one's accomplishments. But busy people may be unaware of the deep well of this negative motivation within because they do not know themselves. Many leaders, whether in business, politics or church, are escaping from themselves. They have what Eric Fromm calls "market-oriented personalities," and they sell themselves to be or do whatever purchases them signs of acceptance.

Good questions for the perpetually busy person to ask are: Why am I so sensitive to criticism? Why do I fill up the gaps in my date book? Why do I find it hard to give up places, positions and ministries? Why am I so competitive? Why is it so important for me to succeed? Why am I unable to let go of others' pain? Why am I afraid to be alone? Why do I always seem to need people? Why am I so discontent? Why do I need to control others? Why am I so busy? Why do I burn out relationships? Why am I sometimes so unmotivated?

### Christian Spirituality

Christian spirituality is a way of life for disciples of Christ. It is the lived experience of God, rooted in the revealed word of God, grounded in community and illuminated by the rich tradition of the church. It is concerned with all of life, not merely piety and not exclusively prayer. It is individual and corporate, churchly and worldly, inward and outward, concerned with personal relationship with God and with justice in the world. Furthermore, Christian spirituality is biblical and Trinitarian.

Biblical spirituality is characterized by the irruption of God in the thick of life, where we see through life, issues, situations and places as though we were looking through a Kodachrome transparency. Open the Bible and we see God at work in the world. More than that, the Bible "reads" us—telling us who we are and revealing what we are doing. Eugene Peterson puts it this way: "'Biblical' means an orientation and immersion in the large, immense world of God's revelation in contrast to the small, cramped world of human 'figuring out.'"[5]

A fully Christian spirituality is also Trinitarian. That is, the lived experience relates to the Triune God—Father, Son and Spirit. There are several dimensions of a Trinitarian spirituality. First, it means that our fellowship and community is not just with other seekers and disciples; we are actually taken into the fellowship and love-life of Father, Son and Spirit (1 Jn 1:3). Speaking to this with great eloquence, Thomas Torrance says that the doctrine of the Holy Trinity is "the fundamental grammar of our knowledge of God...Through his self-revelation in the incarnation God has opened himself to us in such a way that we may know him in the inner relations of his divine Being and have communion with him in his divine life as Father, Son and Holy Spirit."[6]

Second, a Trinitarian spirituality means that the God whom we know is not distant in heaven but immanent and present, not only in sacred places and sacred time, but also in the warp and woof of everyday life. Through the incarnation of God in Jesus and the empowering presence of the Holy Spirit, God is with us in the grittiest business situation.

Third, our lived experience of God is like the interpenetration but not the merging of Father, Son and Spirit. The word we have used for this is *perichoresis*. We are becoming truly ourselves in the context of a love relationship. *Perichoresis* is communion with God, not being swallowed up in God, like a drop of water in the ocean. The apostle Paul spoke of this as "I in Christ" and "Christ in me."

Fourth, the concern and purpose of God into which we are immersed is not merely redemptive and curative (saving souls and mending people) but also unitive and creative (bringing things and people together and making beautiful things).

And finally, the Trinity helps us to pray. Prayer is not easy, but as my colleague Edwin Hui says, "Paul has anticipated our difficulties and has reminded us of the most fundamental experience or reality of the life of prayer (and there is no other life than the life of prayer...): first, even as 'we do not know what we ought to pray for, but the Spirit himself intercedes for us with groans that words cannot express' (Rom 8:26), and second, 'Christ Jesus…is at the right hand of God and is also interceding for us'" (Rom 8:34). So, continues Hui, "In this praying event, the person who prays has an unmistakably three-facets 'experience' of the Triune God as she is being incorporated by the 'Spirit' into the life of the 'Son' towards the 'Father.' It is an experience of…being invited into the conversation of God to God in and through the one who prays."[7]

"I have no time to pray," says a busy executive. But it is not just executives. Recently I went for two days of prayer to a Benedictine monastery near Vancouver. The guest master, whom I have known for thirty years, said to me, "How I would love to go to a monastery to have two days of quiet. The phone rings. There are endless e-mails and letters and the constant duties of my work!" Not a few businesspeople feel "burned out" after a few decades in the commercial world and think that they want to do something "significant" by getting out of business. But the solution is in another direction. It starts with recognizing that God is not absent from the marketplace. Ironically, this message is coming largely from people outside the church.

### Spirituality Without Religion

There is a spate of books and articles on "the new business spirituality." Representative of this flood of information is John Renesch, the editor of *New Traditions in Business: Spirit and Leadership in the Twenty-First Century.*[8] Bringing together twelve leading thinkers about business tomorrow, Renesch proposes a new way of doing business:

- The company is a community, not a corporation, a system for being, not merely a system for production and profit.
- The new image of the manager is that of a spiritual elder.
- Employees are members of the body working interdependently for the common good.
- While mission statements, vision, goals and values will continue to *push* a company, a "Higher Purpose" (parallel to the "Higher Power" made popular by AA) will *pull* a company forward.
- The corporation is an equipping (learning) organization that provides an environment for every-member service (ministry) so each person will become more human, more creative and more integrated with the higher purpose.

Renesch and his associates are not alone. In 1997 the British economist Charles Handy wrote eloquently in *The Hungry Soul* about the need for a recovery of spirit in business. An annual corporate leadership and ethics forum at Harvard involving key corporate leaders in North America, including the Canadian psychologist Martin Rutte, is currently exploring the recovery of spiritual values in the marketplace. *The Vancouver Sun* recently carried an article on Tanis Helliwell, a Canadian New Age therapist and business consultant, who offers a seminar titled, "Take Your Soul to Work." There is indeed a host of authors, conferences, seminars and travelling gurus promoting something that is neither simply traditional religion (though it draws heavily on it) nor simply New Age spirituality (though there are affinities).

My thesis student, Jeff Sellers, has helpfully summarized this mixture of New Age and traditional religious spiritualities under three aspects: 1) the corporate aspect, which values higher purpose over higher profit and ecological sensitivity; 2) the personal aspect, which values self-actualization, autonomy, creativity and spiritual motivation; 3) the cosmic aspect, which values cooperation, harmony, spiritual evolution and global synergy. [9]

The language being used today by many businesspeople taken up with the movement seems like a return to the revival tents of frontier Christianity: caring, love, spiritual, the human spirit, awakening, backsliding, new heresy, inner resources, inner authority, inner wisdom, soul, the search for a deeper sense of life purpose, co-creation, the pursuit of unconditional love, *metanoia* (repentance), the business leader as a spiritual elder, the need for transcendence, relationship with God, wonderment, evoking spirit, celebration, the corporate cathedral, the higher purpose, communion, spiritual values, disciplines and, remarkably, tradition. One of Renesch's authors analyses the reason: "The basic positivistic and reductionistic premises of scientific materialism are being replaced by a new set of beliefs that include increased faith in reason guided by deep intuition. In other words, a 'respiritualization' of society is taking place that is more experiential and less fundamentalistic than most of the historically familiar forms of structured religion."[10] The alleged paradigm shift of the century is not a return to religion, but to spirituality without religion.

The corporation again has a soul and a calling. Vision is replacing profit as the *raison d'être* of a company. A corporation exists to make a long-term contribution to society, indeed to the globe. As older social cultures, cities, neighbourhoods and churches have become atomised, business cultures will be the new tribes, the new neighbourhoods. Corporations *are* our new communities. One indication of this change of focus is reflected in the re-minted mission statements of large corporations so that their purposes are perceived as "not mainly for profit" but "for good." Samples include:

- Du Pont: "A new partnership with nature."
- Mary Kay Cosmetics: "To give unlimited opportunity to women."
- Merk: "To preserve and improve human life."
- Sony: "To experience the joy of advancing and applying technology for the benefit of the public."
- Wal-Mart: "To give ordinary folk the chance to buy the same things as rich people."
- Walt Disney: "To make people happy."[11]

Crucial to this "respiritualization" of business is the role of intuition and awakening of will, joy, strength and compassion through the liberating power of relating to a higher purpose that inspires creativity and a calling. Thus we are challenged with soul work, not merely remuneration or the challenge of a career. Most commonly this higher purpose is not thought of as a being or power outside the system because nothing is outside the system! The new business spirituality affirms "inner wisdom, authority, and resources, challenging the scientific materialism that was dominant in the earlier part of the century."[12] The private corporation, it is claimed, has the potential of providing spiritual eldership for the young and of extending creation across geographical, cultural and political boundaries—the most powerful institution on earth. So the church of Max Weber's study has been reinvented as the corporate cathedral.

Who would have thought that post-Protestant Calvinism, which fired one generation of entrepreneurs, would be replaced after several decades of spiritual wilderness with business spirituality without religion? Many of the concepts of the new business spirituality are entirely congruent with historic Christianity and Judaism: co-creativity, spirit, love, service (the same word as "ministry" in Greek), interdependence, community, relationality, global concern, ecological sensitivity, vocation or calling. The new business spirituality movement reflects, on the one hand, the insatiable hunger of the human being for someone beyond humankind, for authentic community and for significant service. On the other hand, there are presuppositional questions that need to be addressed.

For example, the new business spirituality assumes the intrinsic goodness of human beings without any consideration of people's brokenness and sinfulness, the latter being the only Christian doctrine that is empirically verified! "Human transcendence," one of the buzzwords of the movement, is an oxymoron. Human beings cannot transcend themselves, though the attempt to do so is the tree of the knowledge of good and evil extended into the twenty-first century (Gn 2:17; 3:5). Nor can we save ourselves. But in the new business spirituality, there is new life without new birth, repentance without turning to God, hope without a substantial worthy end for the whole human story, god without God and faith without a transcendent divine being.[13] It was only a few decades ago that the psychiatrist R.D. Laing, ahead of his time, said that Amos had prophesied that there would be a famine, "not a famine of food or a thirst for water, but a famine of hearing the words of the LORD" (Am 8:11). That time, Laing prophesied, has come.[14] The new business spirituality is addressing the God-sized vacuum in the souls of people in the workplace, a gap that has unfortunately been left unattended by the religiously occupied church and the secular humanism of Western culture. But there is another way, and it is one rooted in the long tradition of the Christian faith.

**The Mixed Life**

In *One Minute Wisdom,* Anthony de Mello relates the following conversation:

> Said the Master to the businessman, "As the fish perishes on dry land, so you perish when you get entangled in the world. The fish must return to the water, you must return to solitude. The businessman was aghast. "Must I give up my business and go into the monastery?" "No, no. Hold onto your business and go into your heart."[15]

In the history of Christian spirituality this has been called the "mixed life." It is a life of active engagement mixed with withdrawal to know God and ourselves—John Calvin's famous "double knowledge," which he said was the heart of true religion. The mixed life was expounded brilliantly by Walter Hilton, a fourteenth-century Augustinian canon, in *Letters to a Layman.* Responding to a businessperson who wanted to leave business to know God better, Hilton wrote:

> You ought to mingle the works of an active life with spiritual endea-vours of a contemplative life, and then you will do well. For you should at certain times be busy with Martha in the ordering and care of your household, children, employees, tenants, or neighbours. If they do well, you ought to comfort and help them in this; if they do

badly, then teach them to amend themselves and correct them. And you should regard and wisely know how your property and worldly goods are being administered, conserved, or intelligently invested by your employees, in order that you might, with the increase, the more bountifully fulfil the deeds of mercy to your fellow Christians. At other times you should, with Mary, leave off the busyness of the world and sit down meekly at the feet of our Lord, there to be in prayer, holy thought and contemplation of him, as he gives you grace. And so you should go from one activity to the other in maintaining your stewardship, fulfilling both aspects of the Christian life. In so doing, you will be keeping well the order of charitable love.[16]

This is precisely what Jesus did. As I read the gospels I am convinced that Jesus did not live a "balanced life," with everything scheduled and poised, as some have proposed. There were times he could not eat because of the press of activity. But Jesus did live a disciplined life. There were times of fasting, whole nights given to prayer and special times of intercession (Lk 22:32). But most evident is his rhythm of engagement and withdrawal—what we are here calling the mixed life. In John 6:15 we have a brief reference to this practice when people were about to take him by force and make him king. Luke tells us that "Jesus often withdrew to lonely places and prayed" (Lk 5:16). In Mark 6:45 we have the strange, even shocking words, "he dismissed the crowd." The crowds did not leave on their own accord. He sent them away, saying "no" to the sick, wounded, guilt-ridden and demon-possessed while he went to be alone with the Father. For Christians the need of the world is not the call of God. The call comes from God and we will need to withdraw frequently and regularly from compulsive need-meeting in order to hear the voice of God.

Critical to living the mixed life is knowing that we are beloved of God, that God takes delight in us and that we do not have to do anything to gain God's love and approval. My colleague Darrell Johnson puts it this way: "Jesus played to an audience of one (the Father)." This is in stark contrast with the Pharisees. "How can you believe," Jesus asked them, "if you accept praise from one another, yet make no effort to obtain the praise that comes from the only God?" (Jn 5:44). Many leaders in business, politics and religion are deeply insecure, and out of that insecurity they base their leadership on the search for one of three things: power, intimacy or status. The ultimate solution for this is living in the delight of God (Is 42:1). We will not know this deep within ourselves without reflection, prayer and hearing the Word of God.

Can this be done in the context of work? Today there are many problems with praying and reflecting in the workplace itself. Prior to the information age there were "down" and "in between" times. But now with cell phones attached to our belts or in our purses and hands-free phones in cars, there is hardly a moment left to be contemplative. We have to create those moments and turn off the phones. We need to go for short walks and sometimes be unavailable. Most of our work, though, demands our total attention, unlike the repetitive work that Brother Lawrence enjoyed in the monastery kitchen in his delightful book, *The Practice of the Presence of God*. Many of our prayers in the workplace will be "arrow prayers" like that of Nehemiah in the high pressure of court life: "Then I prayed to the God of heaven and I answered the king" (Neh 2:4). There will be charismatic moments when there will be an "aha," a celebration of something new and great. And we can relate to our fellow workers sacramentally: they are image bearers.

A difficult assignment is an opportunity for prayer. Brother Lawrence used to say to the Lord at the beginning of a task, "I cannot do this unless you help me." When he made a mistake, he would turn this into a prayer: "Lord I will never do otherwise unless you mend what is amiss in my life." But there is also the need for longer seasons of withdrawal to pray, celebrate and refresh oneself in priorities. Following are seven time-tested disciplines that require us to set aside a block of time, and sometimes a whole day, for withdrawal.[17]

First, we can practise invocation and commendation habits at the start or end of the day. Steve Brinn speaks about "simmering" in the morning rather than bounding out of bed.

Second, there is *lectio continua*, the continuous reading of Scripture to saturate mind and heart with the wide world of God's presence and activity. When we read the Bible from the perspective of life in the world, we make several discoveries. The Bible describes ordinary people working and being apprehended by God in the context of everyday life. God reveals himself not mainly in the tent, temple and church, but in the workplace and neighbourhood. The Bible shows us how to live in the marketplace with justice, faith and even shrewdness. Ministry can take place in the context of marketplace activity, as it did with Paul, Aquila and Priscilla, tentmakers. We discover that the marketplace is a metaphor for the Kingdom of God, inspiring many of the parables of Jesus. We get refreshed in vision and perspective. Personally I follow a plan of Bible reading that takes me through the Old Testament once a year and the New Testament and Psalms twice a year by reading four chapters a day, two from each testament.[18]

Third, there is *lectio divina*, the slow, meditative reading of Scripture accompanied by prayer. This can be accompanied by meditation on a specific text and memorization of certain texts.

Fourth, in journal keeping, we record in writing our feelings, emotions, longings and prayers in the presence of God, without self-criticism. Psalm 42:5 is a journal entry: "Why are you cast down, O my soul, and why are you disquieted within me? Put your hope in God, for I will yet praise him, my saviour and my God." David is talking to God about his own depression in the light of something greater than his experience. In his *Confessions*, Augustine said, "For it is better for them to find you and leave the question unanswered than to find the answer without finding you."[19]

Fifth, there is fasting from food to be quiet for God or from things to give control to God or from people to be alone with God.

Sixth, confession is expressing to God with complete candour and honesty a Spirit-born brokenness not only for inappropriate behaviour and thoughts, but also for the breach in our relationship with God (1 Jn 1:9). Augustine said, "I will confess therefore what I know of myself, and what I do not know: for what I know of myself, I know through the shining of your light; and what I do not know of myself, I continue not to know until my darkness shall be made as noonday in your countenance."[20] Confession to another believer is being honest with God in the presence of another (Jas 5:16). The benefits are a free conscience, inner healing and sometimes physical healing. Bonhoeffer, in his classic *Life Together*, comments on this: "He who is alone with his sin is utterly alone…The final breakthrough to fellowship does not occur, because, though they have fellowship with one another as believers and as devout people, they do not have fellowship as the undevout, as sinners. The pious fellowship permits no one to be a sinner. So everybody must conceal his sin from himself and from the fellowship." Bonhoeffer continues, "Many Christians are unthinkably horrified when a real sinner is suddenly discovered among the righteous. So we remain alone without sin, living in lies and hypocrisy. The fact is that we are sinners!"[21]

Finally, there is Sabbath. The word "Sabbath" means to cease, to desist from work and striving, preferably for a complete day each week. We do not "keep" Sabbath; Sabbath keeps us—it keeps us focused on God as the ultimate reality, keeps us rightly ordered in terms of priorities and keeps us mindful that we are not accepted by the most important person in the universe because of our performance. My friend, Justyn Rees, is right when he suggests that more people have died by not keeping this law in the Ten Commandments than by not keeping the "thou shalt not commit murder" law. Stress takes its toll and lots of people die because they do not have a mixed life. And if we are not keeping one day for play, prayer, worship and contemplation we are probably taking ourselves too seriously. Worse than that, we are hurting ourselves. We were made for this weekly celebration, and church worship may well be part of it, but not if Sunday becomes a day of meetings and, in effect, one more workday.[22]

**Living the Tension Well**

"Going deep" will not eliminate tension. Jacques Ellul puts it this way: "The Bible tells us that the Christian is in the world, and that there he or she must remain…"[23] Some try to disconnect the spiritual life from the material one. Ellul says, others moralize and "Christianize" life in the marketplace, "covering it up with an ethical glaze." Yet we cannot deny the tension: we live in a sinful world and we cannot change it, or at least not much; at the same time, we cannot accept it as it is.

> He has sent us into the world, and just as we are involved in the tension between sin and grace, so also we are involved in the tension between these two very contradictory demands. It is a very painful, and a very uncomfortable, situation, but it is the only position which can be fruitful for the action of the Christian in the world, and for his [sic] life in the world…We must accept—in a spirit of repentance—the fact that our life in the world is necessarily 'scandalous'…To be honest, we must not accept this tension of the Christian, or of the Christian life, as an abstract truth. It must be *lived*, it must be realized, in the most concrete and living way possible.[24]

*Adapted from chapter seven of* Doing God's Business: Meaning and Motivation for the Marketplace *(Grand Rapids: Eerdmans, forthcoming 2006).*

## Endnotes

[1] Quoted by Bruce Hindmarsh, "Via Activa or Via Contemplativa?" (paper presented at Regent College Vocatio Institute, Vancouver, May 2004).

[2] Benedicta Ward SLG, trans., *The Sayings of the Desert Fathers: The Alphabetical Collection* (1974; reprint, London: Cistercian Publications, 1985), 2.

[3] Derek Kidner, *The Message of Ecclesiastes: A Time to Mourn and a Time to Dance* (Downers Grove: InterVarsity Press, 1976), 47.

[4] Mary Baechler, "Death of a Marriage," *INC* (April 1994).

[5] Eugene Peterson (lecture, Regent College, Vancouver).

[6] Thomas F. Torrance, *Trinitarian Perspective: Toward Doctrinal Agreement* (Edinburgh: T&T Clark, 1994), 1.

[7] Edwin Hui (presentation on Spiritual Theology at the Regent College "Whirlwind Tour of the Faculty," Vancouver, 2000).

[8] Authors taking up this challenge include L. Bolman and T. Deal, *Leading with the Soul: An Uncommon Journey of Spirit* (San Francisco: Jossey-Bass, 1995); Denis Breton and Christopher Largent, *The Soul of Economics: Spiritual Evolution Goes to the Marketplace* (Wilmington, Delaware: Idea House Publishing Co., 1991)—they reinterpret the law, beatitudes and Lord's prayer as a mythical structure for rethinking economics; Jack Cranfield and Jacqueline, *Heart at Work: Stories and Strategies for Building Self-Esteem and Reawakening the Soul at Work* (New York: McGraw Hill, 1996); Gilbert Fairholm, *Capturing the Heart of Leadership: Spirituality and Community in the New American Workplace* (Westport, Conn.: Praeger, 1997); Charles Garfield, et al with Michael Toms, *The Soul of Business* (Carlsbad, Calif.: Hay House Inc., 1997); Emilie Griffin, *The Reflective Executive: A Spirituality of Business and Enterprise* (New York: Crossroad, 1993); Os Guinness, *Winning Back the Soul of American Business* (Washington, D.C.: Hourglass Publishers, 1990); Ian Percy, *Going Deep* (Toronto: MacMillan Publishing Co., 1998); John Renesch, ed. *New Traditions in Business: Spirit and Leadership in the 21st Century* (San Francisco: Berrett-Koehler Publishers, 1992).

[9] Jeff Sellers, "New Age or Kingdom Come? Description and Critique of the 'New Business Spirituality' in Light of a Biblical Spirituality of Work" (master's thesis, Regent College, April 2000).

[10] Willis Harmen, in *New Traditions in Business: Spirit and Leadership in the 21st Century,* ed. John Renesch (San Francisco: Berrett-Koehler Publishers, 1992), 16.

[11] Charles Handy, *The Hungry Spirit: Beyond Capitalism—A Quest for Purpose in the Modern World* (London: Hutchinson, 1997), 78.

[12] Harmen, in *New Traditions in Business,* 15.

[13] One issue is anthropology, the implicit view of the human person. Much of the new business spirituality deifies the person in speaking of the "the limitless potential of the individual," and the "Divinity that is at our deepest

core" (William Miller, in *New Traditions in Business*, ed. John Renesch, 71). Authors in the field of business spirituality use "transcendence" for the Buddhist experience of transcending all distinctions so that emptiness equals fulfillment (Maynard in *New Traditions in Business*, ed. John Renesch, 42). Second, there is the issue of soteriology or redemption. The new business spirituality appeals to the intrinsic goodness of humankind without dealing with human brokenness and disorder (sin). Theory X and Y wrestles with these double truths about humankind (see Lee Hardy, *The Fabric of This World*). While human beings cooperate with God in the process of redemption, ultimately humankind cannot save itself. Third, there is the issue of epistemology and ontology. The acceptance of the subjective principle of epistemology—we invent what we know; what we believe is what is—leads to a multiverse.

[14] R. D. Laing, *The Politics of Experience and the Bird of Paradise* (Harmondsworth, England: Penguin Books, 1967), 118.

[15] Elizabeth A. Dreyer, *Earth Crammed with Heaven: A Spirituality of Everyday Life* (New York: Paulist Press, 1994), 89.

[16] Walter Hilton, *Toward a Perfect Love*, trans. David Jeffrey (Portland: Multnomah Press, 1985), 8–9.

[17] I acknowledge my indebtedness for some of these suggestions to my colleague Bruce Hindmarsh for his presentation, "A Mixed Life or a Mixed-Up Life?" (paper presented at Regent College marketplace cohort meeting, Knoxville, TN, May 2004).

[18] *McCheyne's Calendar for Daily Readings*, Banner of Truth Trust (P.O. Box 621, Carlisle, Pennsylvania, 17013, USA).

[19] Saint Augustine, *Confessions*, trans. R.S. Pine-Coffin (Harmondsworth, UK: Penguin Books, 1961), I, 6.

[20] Saint Augustine, quoted in Kenneth Leech, *True Prayer: An Invitation to Christian Spirituality* (San Francisco: Harper & Row, 1980), 123.

[21] Dietrich Bonhoeffer, *Life Together* (San Francisco: Harper & Row, 1954), 110.

[22] In Scripture Sabbath is a law to be kept, a law not rescinded but fulfilled by Jesus (Ex 20:8–11; Mk 2:28). It is a blessing, a gift, as we celebrate creation (Ex 20:8–11) and redemption (Dt 5:12–15). It is a calling, a vocation; even God rests (Gn 2:2). It is a sacrament in time and a sign of our relationship with God (Ex 31:12–13, 17). It is a metaphor of salvation (Heb 4:9; Mt 1:18) and a prophecy and foretaste of the New Heaven and New Earth, when there will be a continuous Sabbath of the threefold harmony of God, creation and humankind.

[23] Jacques Ellul, *The Presence of the Kingdom*, trans. Olive Wyon (New York: Seabury Press, 1948), 7.

[24] Ibid., 17.

# SPIRITUAL & RELIGIOUS SOURCES OF ENTREPRENEURSHIP: FROM MAX WEBER TO THE NEW BUSINESS SPIRITUALITY

*From* Crux, *vol. XXXVI, no. 2 (June 2000)*

There can be no capitalist development without an entrepreneurial class; no entrepreneurial class without a moral charter; no moral charter without religious premises. *Gianfranco Poggi*[1]

In the classic film *Wall Street*, Gordon Gekko (Michael Douglas) typifies the entrepreneur for many. "The lesson in business," he tells Bud Fox (Charlie Sheen), is "don't get emotional about stock, it clouds the judgment." Gekko is constantly in a telephone conversation, using language such as "block anybody else's merger efforts," "Christmas is over, business is business," and "I want every orifice in his body flowing red." In a famous scene, Gekko redefines greed: "Greed is good, greed is right, greed works; greed clarifies, cuts through, and captures that essence of the evolutionary spirit." It is interesting that Gekko uses the word "spirit" in a film that exemplifies the secular humanism that has been the dominant cultural environment of business in the Western world for several decades. But there is a change in Western culture that makes the question of a moral charter for entrepreneurship and even the search for a religious/spiritual foundation apt if not urgent.

**The Elusive Entrepreneur**

Defining entrepreneurship is not an easy task. Entrepreneurship involves three facets: envisioning, inventing (creativity) and implementing—any one of which, by its absence, renders an activity as less than fully entrepreneurial.[2] "Entrepreneur" is a French term that in the Middle Ages was used to describe a cleric who was in charge of a great architectural work such as a cathedral or a castle. The word combined the functions of inventor, planner, architect, manager, employer and supervisor. An earlier form of the word was used as early as the fourteenth century. According to Bert Hoselitz, the term was used in the sixteenth and seventeenth centuries for government contractors. But in the eighteenth century, this French term became infused with "a precise economic content" in the writings of the eighteenth-century businessman, Richard Cantillon.[3] The trio of qualities noted above—envisioning, inventing and implementing— seem indispensably linked with the idea of entrepreneurship: not just envisioning, not just inventing, not just implementing, but all three. Admitting the complexity of defining an entrepreneur, Robert Hebert and Albert Link suggest a similarity with the Heffalump in *Winnie the Pooh*: "All who claim to have caught sight of him report he is enormous, but they disagree on his particularities."[4]

In this paper I wish to revisit Max Weber's thesis in *The Protestant Ethic and the Spirit of Capitalism*. As Michael Novak notes, there are at least two good reasons why Weber has earned an immortal place in intellectual history. First, "he identified something new in economic history and glimpsed...its moral and religious dimensions. Second, he suggested in advance why Marxism, both as an explanatory theory and a vision of paradise, was doomed to fail: Its resolute materialism excluded the human spirit."[5] I then wish to explore an extraordinary irruption of spirituality in business in the Western world, loosely called the "New Business Spirituality." Is this a confession of the bankruptcy of secular humanism—humankind left alone without a transcendent reference point? Dr. H.J. Blackham, one-time director of the British Humanist Society, said that the most drastic objection to humanism is that it is too bad to be true! While the phrase "paradigm shift" is undoubtedly overused, I think this is what we are experiencing. Finally, I wish to reflect on Weber and the New Business Spirituality on the basis of a classic Judeo-Christian theology of entrepreneurship, both to welcome congruencies and to indicate some ways that a lasting and life-giving centre for the entrepreneurial imperative can be found.[6]

Unquestionably, entrepreneurial activity requires faith, whether that faith is a "push" from within (drivenness that arises from unmet human needs) or a "pull" from without (a calling from a significant Other). Most of the contemporary theories of entrepreneurship do not consider this aspect. Factors usually identified include personality traits, such as risk-taking, independence, internal locus of control, self-confidence,[7] the environment or "the times"[8] and the possession of skills that can be learned.[9] The most plausible theory is the systemic one, namely that multiple interdependent factors work together to create the entrepreneurial imperative that has led to the flourishing of Western capitalism. With the exception of the much-debated 1904–1905 essay by Max Weber, there is a surprising lack of study and literature on the spiritual/religious sources of entrepreneurship.[10]

### Weber's "Partial, Complex and Momentous" Thesis

The Protestant work ethic is blamed (not without reason) for anti-leisure attitudes (the so-called "Calvinist feeling that work alone is good").[11] The popular version of the Protestant work ethic involves the following beliefs: idleness is sinful;[12] industriousness is a religious ideal; waste is a vice; frugality is a virtue; leisure is earned by work and a preparation for work; complacency and failure are outlawed; ambition and success are sure signs of God's favour; wealth is a special sign of God's favour.[13]

Some of these beliefs stem directly from the Protestant Reformation. The magisterial Reformers (Luther and Calvin) not only "reformed" the way in which people came to know their acceptance with God, but also their attitudes to the world and work in particular.[14] Lutheranism enjoins the entrepreneur to consider his economic activity as a calling (*Beruf*), though according to Max Weber, the Lutheran's commitment to his worldly calling or station does not involve strenuous effort to master, rationalize and innovate.[15] As Weber viewed the matter, something more would be needed to ratchet up the believer's intensity to a passion for entrepreneurship. Gianfranco Poggi puts it this way: "Only a religious vision that turns worldly reality into a field of experimentation, and the individual into a 'tensed-up being,' relentlessly working that field in the pursuit of a dynamic design, could plausibly be said to have offered such an inspiration."[16] According to Weber this is what Calvinism supplied— not the Calvinism taught by the Reformers, but the reception of that teaching by what he calls "the lay practitioners of religion."[17] Weber's thesis can be summarized in this way: For capitalism to flourish there must be both intensive activity and the imperative to save. The rise of both spirits can be traced to Calvinism. As to the first, with the closing of the monastery door as a way to prove one's merit before God, the fervent believer was enjoined to prove oneself by intensive work in the world in his or her calling. For the second, Calvinism taught self-denial and self-sacrifice, the very delayed gratification that is essential for accumulating capital. The theological underpinning for this, according to Weber, was supplied by the twin doctrines of Calvinism—the transcendence of God and predestination.[18] These allowed believers to operate in the world as God's instruments and in the process to gain some assurance of their own status as the elect.[19] The Calvinist Puritans recommended living the life one would live if one was sure of his or her salvation thus inciting "intense worldly activity." Weber cites Baxter to show that living with discipline, productivity and self-restraint shows you are saved. The first doctrine "cranks up the tension" and the second "opens the believer to the world."[20] "Thus all the Calvinist faithful's ethical eggs were placed in the basket of his calling."[21]

> The attainment of [wealth] as a fruit of labour in a calling was a sign of God's blessing. And even more important: the religious valuation of restless, continuous, systematic work in a worldly calling, as the highest medium of asceticism, and at the same time the surest and most evident proof of rebirth and genuine faith, must have been the most powerful conceivable lever for the expansion of that attitude toward life which we have here called the spirit of capitalism.[22]

Implicit in the Calvinism that Weber studied is a particular concept of the stewardship of money, only potentially useful, and of time, involving a methodological attitude to time that monitors the environment and makes adjustments, maximizing the time.[23] Catholicism proposed extensive interpenetration of the sacred and profane, discouraging "the faithful from treating the latter as a religiously neutral field, deprived of ritual significance, and open to his 'tinkering' and rearranging."[24] In contrast, Calvinism led believers to adopt an ethical posture, an inner-worldly asceticism in the context of intensive "tinkering" in the world.[25] When you combine the attainment of wealth (acquisitive activity) as the fruit of labour and a sign of God's blessing with the limitation of consumption (saving), the inevitable result is the accumulation of capital.[26] This is powerful incentive for envisioning, inventing and implementing. The spirit of this motivation is typified by the words of the evangelical John Wesley, founder of the Methodists, in his famous sermon on the use of money: "Gain all you can [a push for entrepreneurship], save all you can [a push for capitalism], give all you can."[27] Poggi's conclusion is apt: Weber's argument is partial (addressing a distinctive part of a large historical problem), complex ("it comprises a number of discrete points, connected by a correspondingly high number of steps or transitions") and *momentous* (emphasis mine).[28]

Weber's thesis is hard to verify empirically but, as the British economist Brian Griffiths notes, "the Protestant ethic thesis turns out to be a specific example of a far more general thesis: namely that the economic process is related in an important way to cultural and religious values."[29] Entrepreneurship is inspired, and religious/spiritual sources are a powerful motivation. What is remarkable in *The Arc of Ambition* is that the authors, James Champy and Nittin Nohria, do not consider where ambition comes from. They note: "The pattern of achievement in virtually every field is about seeing beyond the accepted beliefs and conventions of the day. Achievers ignore the boundaries of the old and have the courage to explore the new. They see something others don't."[30] Champy and Nohria do acknowledge, however, that some Asian religions—Buddhism, for instance—discourage inventiveness by advising people to accept their life circumstances.[31]

### Reformational Sources of Entrepreneurship

The "Protestant work ethic" could be more accurately described as the "post-Protestant work ethic."[32] Weber rarely quotes Calvin.[33] He relies heavily on his observations that capitalism seems to have flourished better in Protestant countries than Catholic,[34] a matter explained differently by David Landes.[35] Weber also relied heavily on the later Puritans such as Richard Baxter,[36] Pietists in England and Holland, Methodists,[37] and deists such as Benjamin Franklin.[38]

Among the nominally religious and early post-Protestants, people moved away from dependence on the sufficiency of Christ's work for salvation and, during the industrial revolution, invested work with more religious significance as a means of proving one's acceptance with God. The vocation of rest, which was given proper emphasis by Calvin and the early Puritans, was lost.[39] Weber correctly observes that what got worked out in the Reformed churches and sects was a "reversion to the doctrine of salvation by works" rather than justification by grace through faith: God helps those who help themselves.[40] But Weber is incorrect in concluding that Lutheranism, "on account of its doctrine of grace, lacked a psychological sanction of systematic conduct to compel the methodical rationalisation of life."[41]

Both Luther and Calvin recalled people to the foundational document of the Christian faith (the Bible) and to the essential gospel experience. Thus they argued that the primary spiritual posture—and therefore the psychological force for life in this world—is neither existential anxiety (fear that one might not be approved by God) nor self-justification. Rather true spirituality is a combination of *gratitude* to God and *love* of neighbour. This is what should make people "tick." It is also a source of entrepreneurship, inspiring people to creative action, to dream dreams and to serve the common good. While these truly spiritual motives do not create "tensed-up" people, they do provide an empowering motivation for passionate and creative work, a motivation that can be sustained indefinitely as I will attempt to show later. Luther expressed this beautifully using the analogy of marriage (an analogy Calvin himself used):[42]

> When a husband and wife really love each other, have pleasure in each other, and thoroughly believe in their love, who teaches them how they are to behave one to another, what they are to do or not to do, say or not to say, what they are to think? Confidence alone teaches them all this, and even more than is necessary. For such a man there is no distinction in works. He does the great and the important as gladly as the small and the unimportant, and vice versa. Moreover, he does them all in a glad, peaceful, and confident heart, and is an absolute willing companion to the woman. But where there is any doubt, he searches within himself for the best thing to do; then a distinction of works arises by which he imagines he may win favour. And yet he goes about it with a heavy heart and great disinclination. He is like a prisoner, more than half in despair and often makes a fool of himself. Thus a Christian man who lives in this confidence toward God knows all things, can do all things, ventures everything that needs to be done, and does everything gladly and willingly, not that he may gain merits and good works, but because it is a pleasure for him to please God in doing these things. He simply serves God with no thought of reward, content that his service pleases God. On the other hand, he who is not at one with God, or is in a state of doubt, worries and starts looking for ways and means to do enough and to influence God with his many good works [Weber's "tensed-up" person!].[43]

As I will show later, the Judeo-Christian revelation of the God of grace positively inspires creativity, risk-taking and inventiveness not because a person is *unsure* of his or her status before God, but precisely because they have this gospel confidence. It is the one-talent person with a conception of a mean, demanding God that fails to invest (Mt 25:24–25).

Since the times of the magisterial Reformers (Luther and Calvin) and the post-Reformation Protestantism that Weber studied, the Western world has experienced decades of secular humanism. Speaking to this Keynes observed fairly that "modern capitalism is absolutely irreligious, without internal union, without much public spirit, often, though not always, mere congeries of possessors and pursuers."[44] The spirit has been quenched. Business is business. Greed is good. Self-interest is the primary motivation for entrepreneurship. The unhappy divorce of church/religion and business has left business on its own, and has left Christians (and other people of faith) living schizophrenic lives: God on Sunday, Mammon on Monday. The corporation is simply a profit-making machine. Two hundred years ago, Baron Thurlow, chancellor for King George III, said: "How can you expect a corporation to have a conscience, when it has no soul to be damned and no body to be kicked?"[45] There is, however, a cultural paradigm shift under way, in part due to postmodernity (however we define it). Speaking to the philosophical underpinnings of postmodernity, Thomas Oden says, "Postmodernity whether East or West will be searching for a way back to the eternal verities that grounded society before the devastations of late modernity."[46]

## The New Business Spirituality

One evidence of this recovery of soul and spirit is the spate of books of which John Renesch's *New Traditions in Business: Spirit and Leadership in the Twenty-First Century* is representative.[47] Coordinating twelve leading thinkers about the future of business, Renesch and others propose a new business model:

- The company is a community, not a corporation, a system for being, not merely a system for production and profit.
- The new image of the manager is that of a spiritual elder.
- Employees are members of the body working interdependently for the common good.
- While mission statements, vision, goals and values will continue to *push* a company, a "higher purpose" (parallel to the "Higher Power" made popular by Alcoholics Anonymous) will *pull* a company forward.
- The corporation is an equipping (learning) organization that provides an environment for every-member service (ministry) so that each person will become more human, more creative and more integrated with the higher purpose.

Renesch and his associates are not alone. In 1997 the British economist Charles Handy wrote eloquently on the need for a recovery of spirit in business world.[48] An annual corporate leadership and ethics forum at

Harvard involving key corporate leaders in North America, including the Canadian psychologist Martin Rutte, is currently exploring the recovery of spiritual values in the marketplace. *The Vancouver Sun* recently carried an article on Tanis Helliwell, a Canadian New Age therapist and business consultant, who offers a seminar entitled, "Take Your Soul to Work." There is indeed a host of authors, conferences, seminars and traveling gurus promoting something that is neither simply traditional religion (though it draws heavily on it) nor simply New Age spirituality (though there are affinities).

The language being used today by many entrepreneurs and CEOs seems like a return to the revival tents of frontier Christianity, employing words such as: caring, love, spiritual, the human spirit, awakening, backsliding, new heresy, inner resources, inner authority, inner wisdom, soul, the search for a deeper sense of life purpose, co-creation, the pursuit of unconditional love, *metanoia* (repentance), the business leader as a spiritual elder, the need for transcendence, relationship with God, wonderment, evoking spirit, celebration, the corporate cathedral, the higher purpose, communion, spiritual values, disciplines and tradition. The "basic positivistic and reductionistic premises (of scientific materialism) are being replaced by a new set of beliefs that include increased faith in reason guided by deep intuition. In other words, a 'respiritualization' of society is taking place that is more experiential and less fundamentalistic than most of the historically familiar forms of structured religion."[49] The alleged paradigm shift of the century is not a return to religion, but to spirituality without religion.[50]

Here the corporation again has a soul and a calling. Vision is replacing profit as the *raison d'etre* of a corporation. A corporation exists to make a long-term contribution to society, indeed to the globe. As older social cultures (cities, neighbourhoods, churches) have become atomized, business cultures will be the new tribes, the new neighbourhoods. "Corporations *are* our new communities."[51] One indication of this change of focus is reflected in the following list of reminted mission statements that are used by large corporations to reflect "not mainly for profit" but "for good":

- Du Pont: "A new partnership with nature."

- Mary Kay Cosmetics: "To give unlimited opportunity to women."

- Merk: "To preserve and improve human life."

- Sony: "To experience the joy of advancing and applying technology for the benefit of the public."
- Wal-Mart: "To give ordinary folk the chance to buy the same things as rich people."
- Walt Disney: "To make people happy."[52]

Crucial to this respiritualization of business is the role of intuition and the awakening of will, joy, strength and compassion through the liberating power of relating to a higher purpose that inspires creativity and a calling from deep sources within.[53] Thus we are challenged with soul work, not merely remuneration or the challenge of a career. Most commonly this higher purpose is not thought of as a being or power outside of the system, because nothing is outside of the system. The New Business Spirituality affirms "inner wisdom, authority, and resources, challenging the scientific materialism that was dominant in the earlier part of the century."[54] The private corporation, it is claimed, has the potential of providing spiritual eldership for the young and extending creation across geographical, cultural and political boundaries—to become the most powerful institution on earth.[55] The church of Weber's study has been reinvented in the corporate cathedral.

Who would have thought that post-Reformation Calvinism, which fired one generation of entrepreneurs, would be replaced after several decades of spiritual wilderness with a business spirituality without religion? As I will show in the following section, many of the concepts of the New Business Spirituality are entirely congruent with historic Christianity and Judaism: co-creativity, spirit, love, service (the same word as "ministry" in Greek), interdependence, community, relationality, global concern, ecological sensitivity and vocation or calling. The New Business Spirituality movement reflects, on one hand, the insatiable hunger of the human being for Someone beyond humankind, for authentic community and for significant service. On the other hand, there are presuppositional questions that need to be addressed from the point of view of the Judeo-Christian tradition.[56] In my opinion, the New Business Spirituality is addressing the God-sized vacuum in the souls of people in the workplace, a gap that has unfortunately been left unattended by the religiously occupied church and the secular humanism of Western culture.

We turn now to consider broadly what could be called a biblical theology of entrepreneurship, bearing in mind the seminal influence of Max Weber's thesis and the emerging New Business Spirituality.

## Towards a Judaeo-Christian Theology of Entrepreneurship

### The Human Vocation

Inventiveness, creativity and initiative derive from human beings created in the image of God (Gn 1:27) as sub-creators or co-creators with God, charged with the care of and development of the whole of creation (Gn 1:28; 2:15). Contrary to what is often alleged, the Judeo-Christian view of the so-called "creation mandate" is not a license to manipulate and control but a charge to care for and develop creation as trustees rather than owners. God intended for both human creatures and the rest of creation not simply to be left preserved but to flourish.[57]

This means enculturating the world by making tools, making places, making communities, making cities, making family, making communication, making beauty, making music, making meaning, making food, making wealth and making play. Humankind was commissioned to be entrepreneurial in just this—not merely to admire untouched creation but to develop it for the common good and for God's glory. In this way Adam and Eve were the first priests of creation. In the same way business entrepreneurs are priests of God and priests of creation, accountable to God for their stewardship since they are not owners but charged to be sub-creators through which they bless creation and others. As Novak says, we "bring the Creator's work to its intended fulfillment by being co-creators in a very grand project."[58] That we are invited and enlisted into a grand project is underscored in the New Testament, where the phrase "fellow-workers" with God is actually used (1 Cor 3:9). We are creating creatures.[59] The New Testament speaks of this as calling/vocation. Further, it announces that all are called, not just religious professionals.

### Community Building

God created humankind "male and female...in [God's] image" (Gn 1:27)—built for community, relationality and love. God's purpose is to build on earth both the faith community and the human community. Thus the Bible faithfully records the cooperative endeavour, often with humankind grievously failing, of building family, people, church, nation and ultimately a global community. The business corporation is part of this divine mission. The meaning of the word "company" is literally "shared bread" (Latin, com-panis), something practised by the first Christians in Jerusalem (Acts 2:42–47). It can be argued that the corporation used the model of the early church, which was a new pattern of mutual responsibility, accountability, structured authority and voluntary participation that was neither *oikos* (household) nor *polis* (state). Max Stackhouse claims that the church was the first "trans-ethnic and trans-national corporation."[60] The Benedictine monastic movement also became a precursor of the corporation since it gave the church a base that was neither *oikos* nor *polis*, but was a disciplined cooperative community outside the traditional structures. And it was also entrepreneurial.

### Initiative and Risk-Taking

There are risks—for God as well as humankind—in this great venture of unfolding the potential of creation and building community. All acknowledge that entrepreneurship involves risk, though usually it is a calculated one.[61] Here the parable of the talents, which Jesus taught, is especially insightful (Mt 25:14–30). The servant with five or two talents, entrusted with money by the master while he was away, invested and made more. Each was an entrepreneur. But the servant with one talent wrapped it up and hid it, only to be condemned by the master upon his return. Why did the first two servants risk failure and loss by investing their talents to make more? Why did the servant with one talent wrap it up in a handkerchief and keep it intact? Why was the judgment of this servant so harsh—experiencing the removal of the talent, being declared worthless and cast into outer darkness? (25:30). This seems all the more harsh because the servant with one talent did not throw the talent away, squander it or despise it. The reason for his lack of entrepreneurship was his conception of God: "I know you are a harsh man, harvesting where you have not sown and gathering where you have not scattered seed. So I was afraid and went out and hid your talent in the ground" (25:24–25). A God who is creative, loving, forgiving and good inspires risk-taking. With such a God, failure might even become a kind of success.

### A Proper Selfishness

The expectation of gain or profit is certainly the most complicated aspect of a theology of entrepreneurship. Both Adam Smith and many contemporary authors argue that while the entrepreneur's efforts may result unintentionally in the well-being of society, their primary aim is to make a profit. This, however, is not simply the case. Don Flow, a businessperson in the automotive industry, says that to accept no social responsibility other than making a profit is to fail ethically "to understand the systemic nature of the economy and human community." He uses the analogy of blood in the human body. We need blood to live, but we do not live for our blood. We need profit for a business to survive, but businesses do not exist for their own survival but to produce goods and services that sustain and enhance human experience.[62]

Significantly, Champy and Nohria distinguish good ambition from bad: "A good ambition is holistic. It's not simply adding more chips to a stack of successes. Ambitious people benefit themselves to the degree that in pursuing their dream, they also respect their own lives and loved ones. Ambitious people benefit society to the degree that their achievements enrich others as well as themselves."[63]

While Scripture condemns self-love (preoccupation with oneself as a form of idolatry) and selfish ambition (as a "work of the flesh" in Galatians 5, through which a person is defined by accomplishments and behaviour as in predatory competition), there is a place in Scripture for self-affirmation (appreciating one's value, dignity, talents and capacities). There is also a concern for profitability—seeing that one's life and one's investment leads to a worthwhile end (Mt 16:26). Charles Handy calls this a "proper selfishness" (I would substitute "entrepreneurship" for "proper selfishness").[64]

### The Promise and Will of God

Further, two great biblical doctrines are positively inspiring to self-assertion, passion, zeal and positive ambition. First, there is the promise of God given originally to Abraham, a promise that is God's settled promise to bless the people of God and through them to bless the earth and all peoples. This is at the heart of the faith of Israel and the faith of Christians (2 Cor 1:20). There are three parts to the promise: the blessing of the community (the family), the blessing of the land (the earth) and the blessing of the nations (global love). The promise is to be appropriated, lived out and embodied—a profound incentive to this-worldly entrepreneurial activity. Behind the promise is the gracious initiative of God, and in the centre is gratitude to God and love for neighbour.

Second, there is the doctrine of the will of God. God's will, profoundly revealed in God's interaction with Abraham, Isaac and Jacob, is not a divine fiat, an inexorable force to which one blindly and cravenly submits; nor is it chance or fate. God's will is an empowering vision, a dream of greatness (as with the dreams given to Joseph). God does not have a wonderful plan for our lives but a wonderful purpose. So the God of Abraham, Isaac and Jacob positively inspires envisioning, inventing and implementing.

### The Vision of the New Heaven and New Earth

As cited earlier, Novak claims Marxism had a vision of paradise that excluded the human spirit. The Judeo-Christian faith has an empowering vision of the future that positively inspires creativity and inventiveness.

The vision of the new heaven and the new earth at the end of the Christian Bible points powerfully to this ideal. It is the end to which God's and humankind's joint work is striving—not a "spiritual" heaven, but a new heaven and a new earth, a transfigured creation. Eschatology, the study of "end times," is central to the Judeo-Christian worldview since it shows us, as the theologian Jürgen Moltmann said so well, that we are placed not at sunset but at the dawning of a new day. God originally had in mind the marriage supper of the Lamb, that powerful metaphor of people, place and renewed creation that occupies Revelation 19–22, so he thought up the world, thought up a God-imaging creature and even sent his Son to redeem people and creation to that end. Without such a worthy end humankind has no final meaning for tasks in this world. But the end is a garden city, a community of all peoples experiencing the three-fold Sabbath harmony of God, creation and humankind. The end is a beginning; but the beginning of it all has this end in view.

### Jesus, Entrepreneur

On to the stage of human history strides Jesus, whom Bruce Barton in 1924 called *The Man Nobody Knows*, a book often scorned but containing some truth. The gospel, Barton argues, pictures Jesus running a small entrepreneurial business, engaging the powers, enjoying a feast, befriending the marginalized and changing the course of history. As Barton says,

> Jesus had no funds and no machinery. His organization was a tiny group of uneducated men, one of whom had already abandoned the cause as hopeless, deserting to the enemy. He had come proclaiming a Kingdom and was to end upon a cross; yet he dared to talk of conquering all creation.[65]

What was the secret of his "entrepreneurial success?" From the gospels Barton extracts several principles by which he argues that Jesus was the founder of modern business: whoever will be great must render great service; whoever will find himself at the top must be willing to lose himself at the bottom; the big rewards come to those who travel the second, undemanded mile.[66] A contemporary development of the same theme,

*Jesus CEO,* invites yet another book with the title, *Jesus Entrepreneur!*

Considering Jesus as a model entrepreneur is warranted not only on the basis of his three-year public ministry, but also because his occupation as a *tekton* (Greek), usually translated "carpenter," is more likely one who makes a project happen, as with designing and building a boat or a house.

## Conclusions

Undoubtedly the world has changed since the days of the Puritanism that Weber analyzed, though much of the "Calvinist" dread of God still lingers in many churches. We have moved from a culture informed by belief in a supreme being in which people lived out their lives in a calling, answerable in the end to God, to an anti-rational, humanistic and often nihilistic culture. Perhaps secular humanism has run its course. In recent years there has, in the West, been a recovery of spirit or soul. It is a mixed and ambiguous movement. One could cynically suggest that the New Business Spirituality is just one more manipulative device to be used by managers to crank up motivation in flagging workers—of instrumental rather than intrinsic value. The nature of true spirituality is that it is essentially gratuitous. But the New Business Spirituality invites a recovery of the great theological truths that fired the entrepreneurship of Jews, early Christians, Catholics and Protestants and all peoples of faith. What is certain is that, except in the Third World where traditional Christian faith is flourishing, we are witnessing a recovery of entrepreneurship through spirituality *without religion,* and therefore without a transcendent and universal basis of entrepreneurial initiative. Will the religious/spiritual form of the new humanism prove enough without a transcendent centre? Is something more needed? What ultimately is needed for sustained and healthy entrepreneurial activity is provided by the Judeo-Christian worldview, and by personal relationship with God—creativity, risk-taking, a "proper selfishness" and the dream of a new heaven and a new earth.

## Endnotes

[1] Gianfranco Poggi, *Calvinism and the Capitalist Spirit: Max Weber's Protestant Ethic* (London: Macmillan, 1983), 83.

[2] Jeffery A. Timmons, *New Venture Creation: Entrepreneurship in the 1990s* (Homewood, Il: Irwin, 1990), 17; Peter F. Drucker, *Innovation and Entrepreneurship: Practice and Principles* (New York: Harper & Row, 1985), 243.

[3] Robert F. Hebert and Albert N. Link, *The Entrepreneur: Mainstream Views and Radical Critiques* (New York: Praeger Publishers, 1982), 12–13.

[4] Ibid., 114.

[5] Michael Novak, *The Catholic Ethic and the Spirit of Catholicism* (New York: The Free Press, 1993), 9.

[6] In *Believers in Business,* Laura Nash (Harvard Business School) investigated the subject narrowly (how and why *evangelical* Christians have been motivated to lead very successful corporations) and approached her study empirically/ descriptively (through qualitative research, observing and interviewing). I am not examining the capacity of all religious systems to inspire entrepreneurial activity, though there is need for such a study. Poggi points to Max Weber's studies of other civilizations based on Confucianism, Hinduism, Buddhism and ancient Judaism, studies that show, at least to Weber's satisfaction, that in spite of other conditions being favourable, these societies did not provide an ethical understanding of entrepreneurial activity (Poggi, *Calvinism and the Capitalist Spirit,* 50). Weber's sweeping generalizations on this must be critically examined, though, as I will show, Abrahamic and Christian faith predisposes people *in theory* to creative and inventive activity and many religious expressions do not. But there are significant studies to show how in each religious system there is incentive to entrepreneurial activity in this world, even when that religion contains a call to withdrawal and contemplation (as does Christianity). An excellent survey of reflections on capitalism within Islam, Hinduism, Buddhism and Chinese philosophy is found in Max Stackhouse, Dennis P. McCann and Shirley Roels, eds., *On Moral Business: Classical and Contemporary Resources for Ethics in Economic Life* (Grand Rapids: Eerdmans, 1995), 335–427. See also Ashis Gupta, *Indian Entrepreneurial Culture: Its Many Paradoxes* (London: Wishwa Prakashan, 1994); Kuzuo Inamori, *A Passion for Success: Practical, Inspirational, and Spiritual Insight from Japan's Leading Entrepreneur* (New York: McGraw Hill, 1995); Yamamoto Shichihei, "A Protestant Ethic in a Non-Christian Context," *Entrepreneurship: The Japanese Experience* (PHP Institute, Kyoto, Japan, 1986): 1–9; E.E. Williams, "Entrepreneurship in the People's Republic of China," in *Frontiers of Entrepreneurship Research 1989*, ed. Robert H. Brockhaus (Wellesley, Mass.: Babson College, 1989), 495–508.

[7] John E. Tropman and Gersh Morningstar, *Entrepreneurial Systems for the 1990s: Their Creation, Structure and Management* (New York: Quorum Books, 1989), 7.

[8] Rosabeth Moss Kanter, *The Change Masters: Innovation & Entrepreneurship in the American Corporation* (New York: Simon & Shuster, 1983).

[9] Drucker, *Innovation and Entrepreneurship.*

[10] Charles Handy defines spirituality as a "taste for the sublime," the lifting of our hearts to "something bigger than ourselves and of the infinite possibilities of life." He quotes the official definition of the Department of Education in Britain: "The valuing of the non-material aspects of life, and intimations of an enduring reality" (Charles Handy, *The Hungry Spirit: Beyond Capitalism—A Quest for Purpose in the Modern World* [London: Hutchinson, 1997], 108).

[11] Max Weber, *The Protestant Work Ethic and the Spirit of Capitalism*, trans. Talcott Parsons (New York: Charles Scribner's Sons, 1958), 42.

[12] Weber, quoting Richard Baxter, notes, "Waste of time is the first and in principle deadliest of sins" (Weber, *Protestant Work Ethic*, 157).

[13] Adrian Furnham, *The Protestant Work Ethic: The Psychology of Work-Related Beliefs and Behaviours* (London: Routledge, 1990), 13; Robert Banks, "Work Ethic, Protestant," in *The Complete Book of Everyday Christianity*, ed. Robert Banks and R. Paul Stevens (Downers Grove: InterVarsity Press, 1997), 1129–1132.

[14] The Reformation was essentially for Luther a matter of soteriology (salvation) and not ecclesiology (church structure). It is often noted that Luther, and for that matter Calvin, did not provide the ecclesiology to contain the "new wine."

[15] Poggi, *Calvinism and the Capitalist Spirit*, 41, 60–61. Weber points to Luther's many statements against usury or interest in any form as evidence that Luther had a more traditionalist approach: a person does not by nature wish to earn more and more money (Weber, *Protestant Work Ethic*, 60, 82). Weber argues that the Bible, and the Old Testament in particular, actually favours this traditionalist view. It is exemplified in the words of Jesus: "Give us this day our daily bread" (Ibid., 83).

[16] Poggi, *Calvinism and the Capitalist Spirit*, 61.

[17] Guy Oaks, "The Thing That Would Not Die: Notes on Reflection," in *Weber's Protestant Ethic: Origins, Evidence, Contexts*, ed. Harmot Lehmann and Guentor Roth (Washington: Cambridge University Press, 1993), 241.

[18] Weber argues that predestination was the most characteristic doctrine of Calvinism, which was the centre of the great political and cultural struggles of the sixteenth and seventeenth centuries in the Netherlands, England and France. But in support of this Weber quotes the Westminster Confession of 1647: "By the decree of God, for the manifestation of His glory, some men and angels are predestined unto everlasting life, and others foreordained to everlasting death" (ch. III). Milton's well-known opinion of this "double predestination" (arguably not from Calvin) was, "Though I may be sent to Hell for it, such a God will never command my respect" (Weber, *Protestant Work Ethic*, 101). The novelist Charles

Williams expressed a more scriptural interpretation of the matter, maintaining that no one is ever sent to hell, but rather people insist on going. In a note on the subject Weber carefully explains that "we are not studying the personal views of Calvin, but Calvinism, and that in the form to which it had evolved by the end of the sixteenth and in the seventeenth centuries in the great areas where it had a decisive influence and which were at the same time the home of capitalistic culture" (Ibid., 220, note 7). Weber argues that both Luther and Calvin had a double God: the fearsome God of the Old Testament and the loving Father of the New. With Luther, so Weber argues, the New Testament kept the upper hand; with Calvin, the transcendent God of the Old won out (Ibid., 221, note 12). While offering an attractive explanation for the cultural events that followed the Reformation, Weber lacks support from the Reformers themselves for this view.

[19] Poggi, *Calvinism and the Capitalist Spirit,* 65. Weber notes that in Islam the related doctrine is not predestination but predetermination "and was applied to fate in this world, not in the next. In consequence the most important thing, the proof of the believer in predestination, played no part in Islam" (Weber, *Protestant Work Ethic,* 227, note 36).

[20] Weber, *Protestant Work Ethic,* 70.

[21] Ibid., 66.

[22] Ibid., 172.

[23] On this point Weber observes, correctly, that the Reformation recovered the holiness of everyday life (in contrast to the contemplative life), though he makes the case as a matter of church control: "The Reformation meant not the elimination of the Church's control over everyday life, but rather the substitution of a new form of control for the previous one. It meant the repudiation of a control which was very lax, at the time scarcely perceptible in practice, and hardly more than formal, in favour of a regulation of the whole of conduct which, penetrating to all departments of private and public life, was infinitely burdensome and earnestly enforced" (Weber, *Protestant Work Ethic,* 36).

[24] Poggi, *Calvinism and the Capitalist Spirit,* 56.

[25] Ibid. Poggi's own critique of Weber raises the question of whether the "spirit of capitalism" was the necessary precondition for the development of modern capitalism (48).

[26] Weber, *Protestant Work Ethic,* 172.

[27] We are to gain all we can without compromising our life (food and sleep), health (especially in mind) or hurting our neighbour: "We cannot devour the increase of [the neighbour's] lands, by gaming, by overgrown bills...We cannot, consistent with brotherly love, sell our goods below the market price; we cannot study to ruin our neighbour's trade in order to

advance our own…sell anything that tends to impair health…by minister-ing, suppose, either directly or indirectly, to his unchastity or intemper-ance…Gain all you can by honest industry. Use all possible diligence in your calling. Lose no time. If you understand yourself, and your relation to God and man, you know you have none to spare. If you understand your par-ticular calling, as you ought, you have no time that hangs upon your hands. Every business will afford employment sufficient for every day and every hour" (John Wesley, "The Use of Money," in Stackhouse, et al, *On Moral Business,* 194–197.)

[28] Poggi, *Calvinism and the Capitalist Spirit,* 79. While Poggi argues that the set of conditions Weber described were not *sufficient* to account for the rise of capitalistic entrepreneurship, Weber described "a *necessary* part" in these phenomena. The multiple factors essential for a capitalistic economic system to emerge from feudalism are considered in Brian Griffiths, *The Creation of Wealth* (London: Hodder and Stoughton, 1984), 94.

[29] Griffiths, *Creation of Wealth,* 31.

[30] James Champy and Nittin Nohria, *The Arc of Ambition: Defining the Leadership Journey* (Cambridge, MA: Perseus Books, 2000), 26.

[31] Ibid., 28.

[32] Of the many critiques of Weber, significant studies include Richard H. Tawney, *Religion and the Rise of Capitalism* (Harmondsworth: Penguin Books, 1938); Kurt Samuelson, *Religion and Economic Action* (London: Heinemann, 1961); and Gianfranco Poggi, *Calvinism and the Capitalist Spirit: Max Weber's Protestant Ethic* (London: Macmillan Press, 1983).

[33] In one endnote, where Weber does refer directly to Calvin's writings, he remarks, significantly, "Calvin himself most emphatically denies that works were indications of favour before God, although he, like the Lutherans, considered them the fruits of belief (*Inst.*, III, 2, 37, 38). The actual evolution to the proof of faith through works, which is characteristic of asceticism, is parallel to a gradual modification of the doctrines of Calvin. As with Luther, the true church was first marked off primarily by purity of doctrine and sacraments, but later the *disciplina* came to be placed on an equal footing with the other two" (Weber, *Protestant Work Ethic,* 228, note 41).

[34] Weber finds the smaller participation of Catholics in the modern business life of Germany all the more remarkable in that, generally, minorities are driven to economic activity by their disadvantaged state, a factor he observes among the Poles in Russia, the Huguenots in France under Louis XIV, the Nonconformists and Quakers in England and the Jews for two thousand years (Ibid., 39).

[35] David Landes, "Religion and Enterprise: The Case of the French Textile

Industry," in *Enterprise and Entrepreneurs in Nineteenth-Century France*, ed. Edward C. Carter II, Robert Forster and Joseph Moody (Baltimore: John Hopkins University Press, 1976). Landes explores the phenomenon of the relatively slower development of industry in France, in comparison with England, and claims that this was due not so much to Catholicism but to the fact of family firms, whose primary concerns were safety, continuity and privacy. It can be argued, however, that even these were an expression of Catholic culture. Samuelson also critiques Weber on this point, showing that his statistical assessment of the relation performance of Protestants and Catholics were flawed (*Religion and Economic Action*, 141). Indeed Samuelson notes that Catholic Belgium was second after England to begin industrialization (Ibid., 121).

[36] Weber acknowledges his dependence on Baxter's *Christian Directory* in an endnote in which he summarizes: "This recommendation of worldly activity as a means of overcoming one's own feeling of moral inferiority is reminiscent of Pascal's psychological interpretation of the impulse of acquisition and ascetic activity as a means to deceive oneself about one's own moral worthlessness. For him the belief in predestination and the conviction of the original sinfulness of everything pertaining to the flesh resulted only in renunciation of the world and the recommendation of contemplation as the sole means of lightening the burden of sin and attaining certainty of salvation" (Weber, *Protestant Work Ethic*, 229, note 47).

[37] Weber notes: "The name in itself shows what impressed contemporaries as characteristic of its adherents: the methodical, systematic nature of conduct for the purpose of attaining the *certido salutis*" (Weber, *Protestant Work Ethic*, 139). Wesley's "methodism" was primarily pragmatic, a way of implementing practical Christianity through the class system rather than a way of achieving certainty of salvation.

[38] Ibid., 50, 53, 180. In support of the alleged Protestant "duty of the individual toward the increase of his capital which is assumed as an end in itself," Weber quotes Franklin: "He that loses five shillings, not only loses that sum, but all the advantage that might be made by turning it in dealing, which by the time that a young man becomes old, will amount to a considerable sum of money" (Ibid., 50–51). Later Weber argues that in answer to why money should be made, Franklin quotes Proverbs 22:9 "See it thou a man diligent in his business?" [NIV: "skilled in his work"] "He shall stand before kings," a matter Weber maintains was drummed into Franklin by his Calvinist father (Ibid., 53). Bob Goudzwaard's definition of deism is worth noting: "the conception that God has created the world in such a perfect manner that immediately afterwards he could afford to go into early retirement" (*Capitalism &*

*Progress: A Diagnosis of Western Society,* trans. Josina Van Nuis Zylstra [Grand Rapids: Eerdmans, 1979], 20).

[39] Banks, "Work Ethic, Protestant," 1129. As is well known, Adam Smith accounted for the economic process in a typically deist manner by attributing the harmony created when each person pursues their own ends but unwittingly serves a general good because of an "invisible hand." As Goudzwaard says, "the invisible hand is the deistic version of the role of God's providence" (*Capitalism & Progress,* 22). Deism provided the philosophical basis for the science of economic activity since it envisioned the economic cosmos as controlled by natural laws that could be subjected to human analysis.

[40] Weber, *Protestant Work Ethic,* 115. It is this thought that becomes central in the famous "self-help" books of Samuel Smiles (Tim Travers, *Samuel Smiles and the Victorian Work Ethic* [New York: Garland Publishing, Inc., 1987]).

[41] Weber, *Protestant Work Ethic,* 128.

[42] *Inst.,* II, 12, 7.

[43] Martin Luther, "Treatise on Good Works," in *Luther's Works,* trans. W.A. Lambert, ed. James Atkinson (Philadelphia: Fortress Press, 1966), 26–27. Calvin reflects this idea as well: "We have not an uncertain God of whom we have created a confused and indistinct apprehension but one of whom we have a true and solid knowledge" (Comm. Ps 4:2). Salvation for Calvin was knowing God and knowing ourselves. This double knowing was the work of the Spirit—the *testimonium internum*—and internal persuasion (*Inst.,* III, 2, 14–16).

[44] Keynes, quoted in Handy, *Hungry Spirit,* 31.

[45] Ibid., 157.

[46] Oden, 45.

[47] Authors taking up this challenge include L. Bolman and T. Deal, *Leading with the Soul: An Uncommon Journey of Spirit* (San Francisco: Jossey-Bass, 1995); Denis Breton and Christopher Largent, *The Soul of Economics: Spiritual Evolution Goes to the Marketplace* (Wilmington, Delaware: Idea House Publishing Co., 1991), which reinterprets the law, beatitudes and Lord's prayer as a mythical structure for rethinking economics; Jack Canfield and Jacqueline Miller, *Heart at Work: Stories and Strategies for Building Self-Esteem and Reawakening the Soul at Work* (New York: McGraw Hill, 1998); Gilbert Fairholm, *Capturing the Heart of Leadership: Spirituality and Community in the New American Workplace* (Westport, CT: Praeger, 1997); Charles Garfield, Michael Toms, et al, *The Soul of Business* (Carlsbad, Calif.: Hay House Inc., 1997); Emilie Griffin, *The Reflective Executive: A Spirituality of Business and Enterprise* (New York: Crossroad, 1993); Os Guinness, *Winning Back the Soul of American Business* (Washington, D.C.: Hourglass Publishers, 1990); Ian Percy, *Going Deep* (Toronto: MacMillan Publishing Co.,

1998); John Renesch, ed. *New Traditions in Business: Spirit and Leadership in the 21st Century* (San Francisco: Berrett-Koehler Publishers, 1992).

[48] Handy, *Hungry Spirit.*

[49] Renesch, *New Traditions in Business,* 16.

[50] My thesis student, Jeff Sellers, has helpfully summarized this mixture of New Age and traditional religious spiritualities under three aspects: 1) the corporate aspect (higher purpose more than higher profit, ecological sensitivity); 2) the personal aspect (self-actualization, autonomy, creativity, spiritual motivation); 3) the cosmic aspect (cooperation, harmony, spiritual evolution and global synergy).

[51] Renesch, *New Traditions in Business,* 66.

[52] Handy, *Hungry Spirit,* 78.

[53] Noteworthy are the stunning examples of creativity (they call it ambition) in Champy and Nohria, *The Arc of Ambition.*

[54] Renesch, *New Traditions in Business,* 15.

[55] Ibid., 141–156.

[56] One issue is anthropology, the implicit view of the human person. Much of the New Business Spirituality deifies the person in speaking of "the limitless potential of the individual," and the "Divinity that is at our deepest core" (William Miller, quoted in Renesch, *New Traditions in Business,* 71). "Human transcendence" is an oxymoron—the extension of the tree of the knowledge of good and evil into the twenty-first century. Authors in the field of business spirituality use "transcendence" for the Buddhist experience of transcending all distinctions so that emptiness equals fulfillment (Maynard, quoted in Renesch, *New Traditions in Business,* 42). Second, there is the issue of soteriology or redemption. The New Business Spirituality appeals to the intrinsic goodness of humankind without dealing with human brokenness, disorder (sin). Original sinfulness, it has been suggested, is the only biblical doctrine that can be empirically verified. Theory X and Y wrestle with these double truths about humankind (see Lee Hardy's *The Fabric of This World*). While human beings cooperate with God in the process of redemption, ultimately humankind cannot save itself. Third, there is the issue of epistemology and ontology. The acceptance of the subjective principle of epistemology—we invent what we know; what we believe is what is—leads to a multiverse. So there is new life without new birth, repentance without turning to God, hope without a substantial worthy end for the whole human story, god without God, faith without God.

[57] Novak believes that the deepest moral justification for a capitalistic system "lies in its promotion of human creativity" (*Catholic Ethic and the Spirit of Catholicism,* 235).

[58] Michael Novak, *Business as a Calling: Work and the Examined Life* (New York: The Free Press, 1996), 37.

[59] Dorothy Sayers, *Christian Letters to a Post-Christian World* (Grand Rapids: Eerdmans, 1969), 77–79. In contrast, see my critique of the New Business Spirituality in footnote 56.

[60] Stackhouse, et al, *On Moral Business,* 113.

[61] One significant difference that John O'Del discovered in his comparison of Polish and American entrepreneurs was that the Polish ones (in their new market economy) were prepared to take greater risks (John N. O'Del, *Polish Entrepreneurs and American Entrepreneurs: A Comparative Study of Role Motivations* [New York: Garland Publishing, Inc., 1997]).

[62] Don Flow, "Profit," in *The Complete Book of Everyday Christianity*, ed. Robert Banks and R. Paul Stevens (Downers Grove: InterVarsity Press, 1997), 809–813.

[63] Champy and Nohria, James Champy and Nittin Nohria, *The Arc of Ambition,* 236.

[64] Handy, *Hungry Spirit,* 86ff.

[65] Bruce Barton, *The Man Nobody Knows: A Discovery of the Real Jesus* (New York: Triangle Books, 1924), 89.

[66] Ibid., 177. In contrast, see Edmund F. Byrne, *Work, Inc.: A Philosophical Inquiry* (Philadelphia: Temple University Press, 1990), 66. Byrne claims that Jesus is not a good role model for work.

# TOWARD A TRINITARIAN WORK ETHIC

*From* Vocatio, *vol. 1, no. 1 (February 1998)*

A work ethic answers three questions: 1) Why work at all? 2) What kind of work should we do? 3) How should we go about our work? In this article we are attempting to answer these questions from the timeless truths of Scripture. We see various approaches to the idea of the work ethic. The Protestant work ethic (really post-Protestant) encourages people to work to prove they are saved. The traditional Catholic work ethic proposes that work is a means of atonement. In *All You Who Labour*, Stefan Cardinal Wyszynski says, "work done with love helps to achieve man's redemption...When we undertake work from love of God, this merciful God lets us share in a task of great honor and efficacy—that of atonement."[1] The Confucian work ethic (in its simplest form) proposes that people should work to bring honour to their family and not to bring shame. But what does the Bible say about all of this?

## Work in the Bible

The first image we see in the Bible is God working—speaking, fashioning, designing, crafting. God makes light, matter, space, time, sea and land and, most beautiful of all, human beings. Later in Scripture, God is pictured as an architect, weaver, potter, king, teacher, shepherd and homemaker. The Bible also opens with a parallel vision: human beings made in God's image to "work [the garden] and take care of it" (Gn 2:15). Contrary to what most Christians think, the world was not made for human beings; human beings were made for the world. We do this work in spectacular ways—town planning, serving in parliament, sending a rocket into space and splicing a gene—as well as the most mundane—collecting the garbage, keeping financial accounts, putting a meal on the table and selling paint. All work "keeps stable the fabric of the world" (Eccl 38:25–32, 34).[2]

Summarizing the contribution of the Old Testament, we find that work is (1) mandated by God (Gn 1:28), (2) energized, blessed and instructed by God, (3) meant to be a form of communion with God, and (4) has become laced with frustration and toil through sin (Gn 3:17). The Sabbath is a reminder that we live by God's work, not our own (Gn 2:3; Mt 11:29; Heb 4). Humankind is created in the image of God (Gn 1:26) not simply in being a worker, but specifically in having a rhythm of work and rest, like God (Gn 2:2).[3]

In the New Testament work is a subordinate theme. "Work" is largely used as a metaphor for "ministry." The New Testament does not, by itself, give us a comprehensive grasp of the significance of human work for two reasons. First, it assumes the Old Testament and cannot be understood without it. Second, the primary purpose of the apostles was to witness to Jesus, the resurrection and the gospel. So there are sparse references to work in the usual sense of energy expended. The New Testament does, however, start with the stunning truth that Jesus was an artisan—either a carpenter or a mason, since *techton* can be translated in more than one way. Jesus might have made houses, boats, cradles or ox-yokes, perhaps all of them.

Summarizing the contribution of the New Testament we find that (1) work is used to describe the salvation work of Jesus and the kingdom work of Christians (Jn 6:29; Phil 2:12; 2 Thes 1:11; 1 Cor 3:6-9; Jn 4:34–38; 2 Cor 5:20–6:1); (2) this, however, does not exempt believers from ordinary work (Eph 4:28; 1 Thes 4:11-12; 2 Thes 3:7–12); (3) indeed, even slave-work becomes a ministry to the Lord when one's heart is right with God (Col 3:22–4:1); (4) there is not a single instance in the New Testament of a person being called to be a religious professional—the professional ministry as a career (the "work" of the ministry is essentially voluntary, an amateur "for-love" activity); (5) there is not a single instance in the New Testament of a person being called to a societal occupation,[4] though all worthy occupations, paid and unpaid, become a means of service in and to the kingdom of God (Acts 18:3); (6) work can be pleasing to God not because of its religious character (or even its public character in advancing the kingdom), but because it is done with faith, hope and love (Col 3:23–24; Eph 6:5-8); (7) work will transcend this life and continue in the new heaven and new earth (Rv 21–22); (8) finally, our work lasts and counts in the final day in view of the full coming of the kingdom of God, the proof of this certainty being the resurrection of Jesus, and so is "not in vain" (1 Cor 15:58). Normally this text is applied to the "work of the ministry," but there is another perspective.

**What Kind of Work is God-Work?**

When Christians speak of "doing the Lord's work," they normally mean doing the work of a church minister: preaching, sharing the good news and caring for souls. But the Bible provides another answer. Human work embraces the full scope of God's interests: creation, preservation, redemption, consummation. The biblical answer to the question, "What is the work of God?" is all-encompassing: making, adorning, separating, organizing, cultivating, beautifying, improving, fixing, redeeming, renovating, informing, announcing, revealing outcomes, healing breaches, making peace, helping, sustaining, bringing to conclusion, being with, communicating worth, celebrating, expressing joy and beauty artistically, imagining, dealing with evil, designing, planning, enlisting, empowering, consummating, entertaining, welcoming, providing a context, showing hospitality and serving.

The great themes of the Bible are evocative of the work of God (and the God-work of God-imaging creatures). God, the creator, forms, fabricates, maintains and finishes. God, the Lover, does relational work, bringing dignity, health and meaning. God, the Saviour, does redemptive work, mending, uniting and saving. God, the Leader, does people work. Every legitimate human occupation (paid or unpaid) is some dimension of God's own work. God's work is done by the whole people of God (the *laos*) and (without their knowing it) most not-yet-believers. Where is God's work done? It is done both in the world and the church.

Here a Trinitarian perspective is transformative. Godly work is Father-work (creational and covenantal), Son-work (as furthering the kingdom of God) and Spirit-work (expressing the empowering presence of God through giftedness and ethical action). Further, it is more than the sum of all three: work is an expression of the ecstatic (out of oneself/beyond oneself) relational life of the Triune God, who goes beyond himself, extending and expressing himself through love-work. Human work is a participation in God's outgoingness. In this way human work is God-inundated, God-mandated and God-glorifying.

Why work? Because God does, and God-imaging creatures share in God's ongoing and outgoing purposeful activity.

**How Then Shall We Work?**

The triad of theological virtues (faith, hope and love) appears so often in the New Testament, sometimes together and often singly, that we cannot miss their central significance. They are what makes the Christian worker "tick."

For example, Paul says, "We always thank God for all of you, mentioning you in our prayers. We continually remember before our God and Father your work produced by faith, your labour prompted by love, and your endurance inspired by hope in our Lord Jesus Christ" (1 Thes 1:2–3).

## Working in Faith

Working in faith means being so directed to God (Lk 11:33–36) that one's service is gratuitous. This is the exact opposite to what is commonly thought of as the "Protestant work ethic." Drivenness derives from a non-gospel orientation. One is trying to justify herself or himself by works and performance. In contrast, Martin Luther, in his "Treatise on Good Works," shows how gospel confidence delivers people from workaholism—spiritual, religious or occupational:

> Thus a Christian man who lives in this confidence toward God knows all things, can do all things, ventures everything that needs to be done, and does everything gladly and willingly, not that he may gain merits and good works, but because it is a pleasure for him to please God in doing these things. He simply serves God with no thought of reward, content that his service pleases God. On the other hand, he who is not at one with God, or is in a state of doubt, worries and starts looking for ways and means to do enough and to influence God with his many good works.[5]

The key insight of the disturbing parable of Matthew 25:31–46 is the surprise factor. The righteous are surprised that they had actually ministered to Jesus; the unrighteous protest that if they had known it was Jesus, they would gladly have done it. It is precisely because it was not done for reward, not done as a means of growth or anything contrived that the work is rewarded. Faith, as Job learned, is not for anything, in spite of the devil's insinuation that Job had ulterior motives for being so good (Jb 1:9).

On that day, the Lord will say to a mother, "You changed my diapers!" She will protest, but the Lord will say, "Inasmuch." Someone will say, "I made electronic widgets; most of them broke before long." "But you made me happy, along with a thousand children." The Lord will say, "You prepared invoices for me." "For you? Your invoices!" "Yes, you helped to make my world work."

## Working in Love

Believers have the privilege of being drawn into the love of God. The Scripture "God is love" (1 Jn 4:16) is not merely descriptive, but a statement that reveals both the identity and work of God. God works by loving. The world runs on love. Every human being is a love-child. God's work arises from love. God is lover, beloved and love itself.

Work in the end will be evaluated by what it does to relationships—between ourselves and God, our companions and the earthly resources we are called to treasure and develop. Significantly, in Paul's letters, work is never mere provision for ourselves (2 Thes 3:10–13) and our families (1 Tm 5:8), but also to have something to "share with the needy" (Eph 4:28). So work is one of the basic ways we fulfill the second great command—to love our neighbour as ourselves. There are many ways of doing this, including designing, connecting and facilitating transportation and interaction. Work is a ministry to the commonwealth (the common good). It is practical social love, even when the work does not involve us in direct relationships with the people we are serving.

But work is meant to be a form of love for God—thus fulfilling the first commandment. This is behind Paul's exhortation to the slaves in Colossae to "work at it with all your heart, as working for the Lord...It is the Lord Christ you are serving" (Col 3:23–24).

Simply put, work is a context in which we are loved by God and, in turn, we love God and neighbour. In this way we participate in the life of the Triune God.

## Working in Hope

Romans 8:19–21 pictures a continuum of the present in which creation "groans" with hope of a future without groaning. As John Haughey puts it, "Creation's hopes will not be mocked by annihilation any more than ours will be."[6] The present will be factored into the future. The God who created with no materials will one day recompose the first creation with the materials of that creation over time, including the work of human beings.

Miroslav Volf argues,

if the world will be annihilated and a new one created *ex nihilo* then mundane work has only earthly significance for the well-being of the worker, the worker's community, and posterity—until the day when "the heavens will pass away with a loud noise, and the elements, will be dissolved with fire." Since the results of the cumulative work of humankind throughout history will become naught in the final apocalyptic catastrophe, human work is devoid of direct ultimate significance.[7]

As Volf shows, eschatological annihilation and responsible social involvement may be logically compatible but they are theologically inconsistent.[8] He offers several arguments for the *transformatio mundi* (transformation of the world): (1) the earthly locale of the kingdom of God in Revelation 21–22 fulfills the earthly hopes of the Old Testament prophets (Is 11:6–10; 65:17–25); (2) the Christian doctrine of the resurrection of the body makes little sense in a non-earthly future eschatological existence; (3) the New Testament explicitly promotes the vision of a liberation of the world—animate and inanimate—which could not be accomplished through its destruction (Rom 8:21); (4) finally, the Bible shows that ultimately creation is good, even though polluted with sin.[9] Volf stresses that this is not merely projecting the survival and transformation of individual works but the cumulative work of the race and that human work creates a home in the environment that is permanent. Further, he posits that the statement in Revelation that the saints "rest from their labors, for their deeds follow them" (Rv 14:13; cf. Eph 6:8) "could be interpreted to imply that earthly work will leave traces on resurrected personalities."[10]

How this will be done is not told to us, but we are invited to consider which of our works will last (1 Cor 3:12–15). In view of the scope of re-creation envisioned, these works cannot simply be ecclesial (or religious). Ironically, Paul envisions a situation in which a person's works are burned in the final fire, but the person himself is saved (1 Cor 3:14).

This brings new meaning to those who toil in so-called secular work in arts, education, business and politics. They, too, are shaping the future of creation in some limited way, just as missionaries and pastors are. Most people think that only religious work will not be in vain (1 Cor 15:58), but if Christ is the first-born of all creation and the first-born from the grave, then all work has eternal consequences, whether homemaking or being a stockbroker. We look forward to a time of exquisite transfiguration. We are invited to leave beautiful marks on creation, on the environment, family, city, workplace and nation. And when we cannot do this, and cannot undo the violence we have committed against the cosmos, we have faith in Jesus that one day he will transfigure even the environmental, social, cultural and political scars we have left through our work.

### Conclusion

Why work? The biblical work ethic proposes that we work to share in God's own work as God-imaging creatures and stewards of creation. We work with faith, love and hope—with passion, compassion and promise—not to prove we are among the elect, or to gain God's approval, but because in the gospel we are profoundly accepted. God's achievement in Christ not only relativizes our work achievements, but God's work revolutionizes ours, turning toil into a ministry. The gospel is both subversive and revolutionary. Even the slave can work with all his heart "as working for the Lord" (Col 3:23) and in the long run can never be underpaid (Col 3:24).

Years ago I heard the poem, "Only one life, t'will soon be passed/ Only what's done for Christ will last." It was quoted to underline the importance of "the work of the ministry." But the poem has a deeper meaning: only what is done for Christ in faith, love and hope (whether wallpapering or preaching) will last. William Tyndale once said, "There is no work better than another to please God; to pour water, to wash dishes, to be a souter [cobbler], or an apostle, all are one, as touching the deed, to please God."[11]

## Endnotes

[1] Stefan Cardinal Wyszynski, *All You Who Labor: Work and the Sanctification of Daily Life* (Manchester, NH: Sophia Inst. Press, 1995), 187.

[2] Revised Standard Version.

[3] See Alan Richardson, *The Biblical Doctrine of Work* (London: SCM Press, 1952), 55.

[4] Ibid., 36–37.

[5] Martin Luther, "Treatise on Good Works," in *Luther's Works,* vol. 44, trans. W.A. Lambert, ed. James Atkinson (Philadelphia: Fortress Press, 1966), 26–27.

[6] John Haughey, *Converting Nine to Five: A Spirituality of Daily Work* (New York: Crossroad, 1989), 104.

[7] Miroslav Volf, *Work in the Spirit: Toward a Theology of Work* (New York: Oxford University Press, 1991), 89.

[8] Ibid., 90.

[9] Ibid., 94–96.

[10] Ibid., 97–98.

[11] William Tyndale, "A Parable of the Wicked Mammon" (1527), in *Doctrinal Treatises and Introductions to Different Portions of the Holy Scriptures,* ed. Henry Walker (The Parker Society, Cambridge: Cambridge University Press, 1848), 98.

## For Further Reading

R. J. Banks and G.R. Preece, *Getting the Job Done Right* (Wheaton: Victor Books, 1992).

Karl Barth, *Church Dogmatics III/4: The Doctrine of Creation,* ed. G.W. Bromiley and T.F. Torrance (Edinburgh: T&T Clark, 1961).

Dietrich Bonhoeffer, *Life Together,* trans. John W. Doberstein (New York: Harper and Row, 1954).

Robert Farrar Capon, *An Offering of Uncles: The Priesthood of Adam and the Shape of the World* (New York: Crossroad, 1982).

Jacques Ellul, *The Ethics of Freedom* (Grand Rapids: Eerdmans, 1976).

T.W. Engstrom and D. J. Juroe, *The Work Trap* (Old Tappan: Fleming H. Revell, 1979).

David Falk, "Call in the New Testament" (unpublished MCS Thesis, Regent College, Vancouver).

Thomas Green, *Darkness in the Marketplace: The Christian at Prayer in the World* (Notre Dame: Ave Maria Press, 1981).

Stanley Hauerwas, "Work as Co-Creation—A Remarkably Bad Idea," in *Co-Creation and Capitalism,* ed. J. Houck and O. Williams (Washington, DC: University Press of America, 1983).

Joe Holland, *Creative Communion: Toward a Spirituality of Work* (New York: Paulist Press, 1989).

Pope John Paul II, "Laborem Exercens," in *Proclaiming Justice and Peace: Documents from John XXIII–John Paul II,* ed. M. Walsh and B. Davies (Publications Mystic, 1984).

Martin Luther, *Werke Kritische Gesamtausgabe,* vol. 51 (Weimer: Hermann Bohlaus, 1883).

———, "Treatise on Good Works," in *Luther's Works,* vol. 44, trans. W.A. Lambert, ed. James Atkinson (Philadelphia: Fortress Press, 1966), 15–29.

Jürgen Moltmann, *God in Creation: A New Theology of Creation and the Spirit of God* (San Francisco: Harper and Row, 1985).

———, "The Right to Meaningful Work," in *On Human Dignity* (Philadelphia: Fortress Press, 1984).

G.R. Preece, "The Threefold Call," in *Faith Goes to Work,* ed. R. J. Banks (Washington DC: Alban Institute, 1993).

Charles Ringma, "A Theology of Work: Some Preliminary Considerations," *Phronesis* 1 (August 1994): 13–36.

R. Paul Stevens, "Drivenness," in *The Complete Book of Everyday Christianity,* ed. Robert Banks and R. Paul Stevens (Downers Grove: InterVarsity Press, 1997), 312–317.

J. Stott, *Issues Facing Christians Today* (Basingstoke, UK: Marshals, 1984).

Hans Walter Wolff, *Anthropology of the Old Testament,* trans. Margaret Kohl (Philadelphia: Fortress Press, 1974)

Nicholas Wolterstorf, "More on Vocation," *Reformed Journal* 29, no. 5 (May 1979): 20–23.

C.J.H. Wright, *An Eye for an Eye* (Downers Grove: InterVarsity Press, 1983).

# BEING KEPT BY SABBATH

*From* Vocatio, *vol. 7, no. 1 (Winter 2003)*

Sabbath is what our stressed-out, leisure-hungry and work-addicted culture desperately needs. But the very word seems to bring to most minds negation, absence and all the restrictions that well-meaning Christians over the years have placed on Sunday. We will explore the biblical meaning of rest, the theological meaning of Sabbath, and Sabbath as a life-giving discipline. In the end we will see that we do not keep Sabbath so much as Sabbath keeps us!

## The Ultimate Rest

The negative view of Sabbath has some foundation. The Hebrew word *shabath* means "to stop, to desist, to cease from doing." The first formalized reference to Sabbath in the Ten Commandments clearly requires desisting from labour one day a week, though it does not legislate six days of labour: "Remember the Sabbath day by keeping it holy. Six days you shall labour and do all your work, but the seventh day is a Sabbath to the Lord your God. On it you shall not do any work" (Ex 20:8–11). As Witold Rybczynski notes, viewing the weekend as a day or two in which one is not required to work, and viewing it as a period in which one is required not to work are not the same thing.[1] Sabbath, however, is more, but not less, than a twenty-four-hour day of enforced rest. A weekly experience of rest is fundamental to our regaining perspective and entering the rest that is essential to personal, social and creational survival. Of all the Ten Commandments, being neglectful of this one has resulted in more deaths than even the prohibition against murder. Heart disease and other stress-related ailments have taken their toll. Especially in the postmodern Western world, we are killing ourselves by neglecting Sabbath.

But Sabbath rest is more than keeping one day a week. Rest is not merely cessation but appropriation. There is a positive meaning to Sabbath that takes us beyond the simple etymology of the word. Israel was commanded to enjoy the day! To enjoy rest. Rest is a state of body, mind and soul that is essential for health, both physical and spiritual. It involves restoring balance, rejuvenating energies, regaining perspective, allowing our emotional energies to recover, being in harmony with our own bodies and, especially, enjoying God. Rest is a multifaceted blessing including sleep, vacation, play and leisure. But Sabbath is rest in its purest and most complete form, probably because it involves gaining the three-fold harmony of God, humankind and creation.

Harmony with God means that we have peace with God, enter God's own rest and enjoy God. Tragically, some people do not even like God, let alone enjoy God! Harmony with humankind means that our own persons are rejuvenated and given perspective. Unlike leisure, which is concerned primarily with cultivating oneself, Sabbath ministers to the self indirectly by recovering our focus on God, renewal being a byproduct. Harmony with creation suggests that God's desire is not only that people have rest but even animals and, and every seven years as well as one day a week, the land (Ex 20:10; Dt 15:1–12). This three-fold harmony can also be expressed in terms of prayer (God-humankind harmony), play (harmony with oneself) and peacemaking (humankind-creation/social harmony): enjoying God, enjoying ourselves and celebrating creation.

To show how fundamental Sabbath is to the life of faith, Scripture describes the creation of Adam and Eve on the sixth day as the penultimate creation, the climax coming the next day, the Sabbath. Nothing is closer to God's mind and heart than the creation of Sabbath. Adam woke up from his unconscious sleep not to start his work of caring for God's world but to experience rest. Adam and Eve's first vocational experience was to waste time for good and for God. Only if we do the same can we understand why we are to take care of God's world, build community and pray.

### No Trivial Pursuit

There is a theology of leisure in the Bible, but it is secondary to the great and extensive material on Sabbath. What we find from Genesis to Revelation is not the cultivation of a perfect balance of work and leisure but of work and Sabbath. There are deep theological reasons for this.

### Sabbath Reveals the Heart of God

God rested on the seventh day (Gn 2:2) but this was not mere cessation; it was refreshment (Ex 31:17). God literally put aside the work of creation both to enjoy rest ("It is good") and to put creation in its place (it is good but not god). So the people that were first called to bear God's image on earth—Israel—were given two archetypal images of salvation to proclaim good news to others and to be refreshed in their own faith: the Exodus (symbolized in the festival of Passover) and the Sabbath (their weekly reminder that God is in charge).[2] Both Exodus, a dramatic rescue accomplished by the mighty hand of God, and Sabbath, a period that implies trusting in God's provision enough to set aside one's work, are tangible signs of having faith in a God of grace. The kind of God we actually worship is revealed by whether we keep Sabbath.

This was not to be an experience of multiple restrictions; rather Israel was "to call the Sabbath a delight" (Is 58:13). Delight in the Sabbath was not eliminated by the coming of Christ, but rather wrenched up a notch as we wait for the manifestation of Christ and the kingdom when full rest will be attained. Jesus claimed to be Lord of the Sabbath (Mk 2:27–28) and declared that he fulfilled rather than annulled it. Being Sabbath's lord did not mean Jesus could break it at will; rather it meant that the Lord fulfilled Sabbath's meaning and intent. Therefore Jesus healed and gleaned in the fields (as a poor man) on Saturday, the Jewish Sabbath. More important, he embodied Sabbath by restoring people to God through forgiveness of sins, healing the sick and bringing unmitigated joy, the first stage of the three-fold harmony of God, creation and humankind that will receive its final fulfillment when Christ comes again. In the New Jerusalem (Rv 21–22) the Lamb is everywhere (we enjoy God in uninterrupted communion); creation is renewed (not only the new heavens but even a new material earth!); and people are released for permanent creativity and exquisite joy. So there is a rich Sabbath overtone in the invitation of Jesus: "Come unto me and I will rest [Sabbath] you and you will find Sabbath for your souls" (Mt 11:28–30).

### Sabbath Reveals God's Intentions for the World

Sabbath is the celebration of creation. Jürgen Moltmann speaks of this as the "feast of creation." Put differently, Sabbath involves the redemption of both space and time, the re-harmonizing of God, humankind and creation in both spatial (and material) as well as temporal terms.

On the first, Sabbath brings both the enjoyment and stewardship of creation. This positive delight is witnessed in God's own word of praise, "It is good" (Gn 1:31) and echoed in Adam's first burst of praise at the creation of Eve, "At last!" (Gn 2:23).[3] This celebration of creation is also found in the book of Job, which contains an African safari for the purpose of viewing two really untamable animals (probably the hippopotamus and the crocodile) and a voyage in a weather satellite to show Job that God really enjoys influencing the climate, much of which is not for our benefit or even experienced by human beings. In this profound contemplation, God reveals that he enjoys being God! In light of this, Job—and the rest of humankind—can join God as co-workers and co-creators, "playing god" with God by making things. That is part of the joy of hobbies and crafts. We are recovering Sabbath when we are creative, a matter that illuminates the edifying effect of healthy recreation. But it is not only space that gets rejuvenated by Sabbath.

First and foremost Sabbath is the redemption of time. To the unreflective and the religiously dutiful, Sabbath might appear to be a waste of time. Nothing is accomplished, or so it seems. But in reality something indispensable is taking place: time is being recovered as a gift from God rather than a resource to be managed. The first mention of holiness in the Bible refers to time: "And God blessed the seventh day and made it holy" (Gn 2:3). In contrast, humankind seems preoccupied with making holy places. In his brilliant exposition of Sabbath, Rabbi Abraham Heschel observes that all pantheistic religions are religions of space and sacred places, in contrast to the faith of Israel, which is concerned with the redemption of time.[4] The prophets maintained that the Day of the Lord was more important than the house of the Lord. Not only religion, but also technology, has been concerned primarily with the conquest of space. In the process we have forfeited experiencing holiness in time. Heschel says, "There is a realm of time where the goal is not to have but to be, not to own but to give, not to control but to share, not to subdue but to be in accord."[5] The great cathedrals, he maintains, are cathedrals in time. And Sabbath is the holy architecture of time.

Surprisingly God's work in creating the world is presented in Scripture as play. Wisdom describes herself as "the craftswoman at (God's) side...filled with delight day after day, rejoicing always in his presence, rejoicing in the whole world and delighting in mankind" (Prv 8:30–31). Sabbath and play have much in common.

### Sabbath Reveals the Playfulness of God

Sabbath for humankind is playing heaven. The best way to learn to work is to play at it! Children do this naturally before the dreadful process of growing up drives a wedge between work and play. They "play house" and so fit themselves for being grown-ups in their own homes. When we "play heaven"—by co-creating with God, delighting in creation, making things fit a heavenly model and worshipping—we are anticipating the joys of being full "grown-up" men and women in Christ in heaven (where we will truly become children again!). Once again Rabbi Heschel is eloquent on this subject: "Sabbath is an example of the world to come."[6]

## Having the Time of Our Lives

We have been exploring Sabbath as a lifestyle, something that informs and transforms all the facets of everyday life: work, leisure, family life, vacations and even sleep. We have good scriptural warrant for universalizing Sabbath in a way that makes it an everyday reality rather than a one-day-a-week affair. The apostle Paul said, "One person considers one day more sacred than another; another considers every day alike. Each one should be fully convinced in their own mind" (Rom 14:5). This opens up the possibility of every day being regarded as such. "He who regards one day as special, does so to the Lord...for none of us lives to himself alone" (Rom 14:6–7).

### Sabbath Lifestyle

Paul was not original in expressing this idea but was merely expounding the words and deeds of Jesus. In Jesus' day, many had reduced Sabbath-observance to a task, a work to be performed. The religious people of his day were hedging the day with myriad prohibitions either to make it happen or to protect it from impiety. So the day came to be served both for its own sake and for the merit people obtained in "doing it just right." In contrast, Jesus viewed Sabbath as something given by God for people's benefit, not bondage: "The Sabbath was made for man, not man for the Sabbath" (Mk 2:27). Jesus regarded himself Lord even of the Sabbath. He enjoyed the day by doing what his Father loved to do on the Sabbath: creating and recreating, resting and bringing rest to others.

It is hard to resist the conclusion, given the number of miracles Jesus worked on the Sabbath, that Jesus deliberately chose to do most of his healings on Saturdays! He had a point to make: Sabbath is not the absence of work but experiencing the joy of God and entering into God's work. The author of the letter to the Hebrews had this same thought when he called us to "make every effort to enter that rest...for everyone who enters God's rest also rests from his own work, just as God did from his" (Heb 4:10–11). This author hints that entering Sabbath is, ironically, hard work for us, because we are so driven to make Sabbath a personal performance, a thing we make happen, rather than a delicious relaxation in God. So Sabbath becomes the model and metaphor of salvation.

Having considered the universalization of Sabbath in a lifestyle, we must now address the question of Sabbath as one day a week.

### Sunday Sabbath

The emergence of the Jewish Sabbath in the context of societies that did not have a seven-day week is a fascinating study in itself. The further emergence of the Christian Sunday in relation to the Jewish Sabbath is a complicated matter. Obviously early Jewish Christians celebrated both the Sabbath (sundown Friday to sundown Saturday) and the Lord's Supper on resurrection day (Sunday) before returning to work on Sunday. In time, Sabbath observance diminished, normally without having the Christian Sunday take on all the characteristics of Jewish Sabbath.[7] But the Christianization of the Roman Empire had its effect on Sunday. Formal law relating to Sunday observance was first enacted in 321 by Emperor Constantine, who forbade people to work on "the venerable day of the Sun." But it was not until the twelfth century that the term, "Christian Sabbath," was used, marking as it does the grafting of the Sabbath tradition, especially in its negative restrictions, onto the Lord's Day.[8] Needless to say, in North America, the Lord's Day is almost gone, though some businesses still observe a weekly holiday on Sunday.

Some form of weekly or regular Sabbath is not an optional extra for the New Testament Christian. It is fundamental to spiritual health and even to emotional health, as some medical studies have shown. But keeping one day as a special day of reflection on the meaning of the other six is increasingly more difficult in a secularized society that now exploits Sunday as the ultimate day for shopping and leisure activities. But, as Eugene Peterson has suggested, if we cannot take a weekly Sabbath, if we cannot put our work down and truly rest, we are probably taking ourselves too seriously. And probably we are not taking God seriously enough. Truly we do not "keep" Sabbath but Sabbath "keeps us"—keeps us focused on the really real, on God's purpose, on God's priorities for our lives and on God himself.

*Reprinted with permission from* The Complete Book of Everyday

Christianity, *ed. Robert Banks and R. Paul Stevens (Downers Grove: InterVarsity Press, 1997).*

## Endnotes

[1] Witold Rybczynski, *Waiting for the Weekend* (New York: Viking Penguin, 1991), 60.

[2] Jürgen Moltmann, *God in Creation,* trans. Margaret Kohl (London: SCM Press, 1985), 287.

[3] Revised Standard Version.

[4] Abraham Heschel, *The Earth Is the Lord's and The Sabbath* (New York: Harper and Row, 1950), 4–6.

[5] Ibid., 3.

[6] Ibid., 73.

[7] Rybczynski, *Waiting for the Weekend,* 66.

[8] Ibid., 70–71.

## Further Reading

Samuel Bocchiochi, *From Sabbath to Sunday: A Historical Investigation of the Rise of Sunday Observance in Earliest Christianity* (Rome: Gregorian University Press, 1977).

Marva J. Dawn, *Keeping the Sabbath Wholly* (Grand Rapids: Eerdmans, 1989).

Tilden Edwards, *Sabbath Time* (New York: Seabury, 1982).

Alan D. Goldberg, "The Sabbath as Dialectic: Implications for Mental Health," *Journal of Religion and Health* 25, no. 3 (Fall 1986): 237–244.

Elizabeth O'Connor, *Eighth Day of Creation: Gifts and Creativity* (Waco: Word, 1971).

Eugene Peterson, "The Pastor's Sabbath," *Leadership* (Spring 1985): 55–56.

Hugo Rahner, *Man at Play* (New York: Herder and Herder, 1972).

W. Rordorf, *Sunday: The History of the Day of Rest and Worship in the Earliest Centuries of the Christian Church* (London: SCM, 1968).

# STRESS, SABBATH AND SERENITY

*From* Vocatio, *vol. 1, no. 2 (July 1998)*

Most stress workshops explore the flight and fight alternatives. And there certainly is a right time to do one or the other. Joseph *ran* from seductive Potiphar's wife (Gn 39); Moses *confronted* Pharaoh (Ex 5–11). But there is a third alternative: *lean into the stress!* Don't run away from it. Don't even try to "resolve it" (it probably cannot be harmonized). Maybe it shouldn't be smoothed out. There is no such thing as a "balanced Christian life." We live it on the cross—with God's strength made perfect in weakness—with rhythms of work and rest/reflection. Tension is a spiritual discipline. God is most likely inviting us in the tensions to know him and to know ourselves—that combination of knowings that Calvin said is the essence of true religion. Luther said there is a cross to be taken up in the workplace (hardly a symbol of tranquillity, like folded hands). So one way of growing through tension is really to get into the work, not to seek religious escapes or neatly compartmentalized protective zones for yourselves. But that is not all.

## Keeping Sabbath

Critical to growing through stress is keeping Sabbath. As I will show, in reality we do not keep Sabbath; Sabbath keeps us—keeps us focused on the really real, keeps us being renewed in holy priorities, keeps us from defining ourselves by what we do, keeps us looking toward heaven. Indeed, taken together, work and Sabbath are a way of playing heaven; they are a foretaste of the new heaven and new earth (Rv 21–22).

The idea behind Sabbath is that we cannot really get into our work in a healthy and holy way unless we get out of it. The word "Sabbath" simply means "to stop" or "to cease." Sabbath is full of rich meanings in Scripture.[1] It means rest from work (i.e., to rest in God—Gn 2:3), celebration of creation (i.e., to restore your relationship with creation—Ex 20:8–11), celebration of redemption (i.e., to remember how and why you were saved—Dt 5:12–15), renewal (i.e., so even your servants, employees and animals will be refreshed—Ex 23:12), a sacrament to renew your relationship with God ("This will be a sign between you and me for the generations to come, so you may know that I am the Lord, who makes you holy"—Ex 31:12–13, 17). It is also, along with our work, a foretaste of the new heaven and new earth, where the true three-fold Sabbath rest of God, creation and humankind will be consummated.

Rabbi Abraham Heschel notes that the first mention of holiness in the Bible refers to time (Gn 2:3). "There is a realm of time where the goal is not to have but to be, not to own but to give, not to control but to share, not to subdue but to be in accord."[2]

Six days a week we live under the tyranny of things in space; on the Sabbath we try to become attuned to holiness in time. It is a day on which we are called upon to share what is eternal in time, to turn from the results of creation to the mystery of creation, from the world of creation to the creation of the world.

So daily Sabbath (Rom 14:5), weekly Sabbath and a Sabbath lifestyle are essential to putting work in its proper place—as a piece of the whole, but not everything. Some people supposedly die from overwork, but they really die from failure in Sabbath-keeping. In addition to the physical death that often results from stressful work without Sabbath is the equally devastating spiritual death of those who fail to experience the Sabbath: they are dead to life, dead to family, dead to friends, dead to self and dead to God.

In *One Minute Wisdom,* Anthony de Mello relates the following conversation:

> Said the Master to the businessman: "As the fish perishes on dry land, so you perish when you get entangled in the world. The fish must return to the water, you must return to solitude."
>
> The businessman was aghast. "Must I give up my business and go into the monastery?"
>
> "No, no. Hold onto your business and go into your heart."[3]

Walter Hilton, a fourteenth-century Augustinian canon, said something similar in *Letters to a Layman:*

> You ought to mingle the works of an active life with spiritual endeavours of a contemplative life, and then you will do well. For you should at certain times be busy with Martha in the ordering

and care of your household, children, employees, tenants, or neighbours…

At other times you should, with Mary, leave off the busyness of the world and sit down meekly at the feet of our Lord, there to be in prayer, holy thought and contemplation of him, as he gives you grace. And so you should go from one activity to the other in maintaining your stewardship, fulfilling both aspects of the Christian life. In so doing, you will be keeping well the order of charitable love.[4]

How can you keep Sabbath? Every way you can!

By keeping a weekly Sabbath—dedicating one day not to religious activism but to contemplation.

By keeping a daily Sabbath—starting the day with reading the Bible and praying. Only then do we see the moral content and spiritual value of even the smallest deed.

But what about a continuous Sabbath, keeping Sabbath on the job—or, as I now suggest, with serenity?

## Serenity

One of the greatest joys in parenting and grandparenting is reading to one's children. I remember reading to our children one of the Arch children's stories from the Bible. What I recall is a single picture, a powerfully evocative image: Jesus in the middle of a storm totally enclosed in an enveloping calm. That is serenity—calmness, quietness within, a holy calm in the soul even while "taking up the cross" that comes from faith in the one who "for the joy set before him endured the cross."

Almost twenty years ago James Houston wrote a *Crux* article on "The Serenity of Christ." He showed how the eight beatitudes are the true principles of Christian serenity, revealing a penetration of God-given light into our souls that is timeless, imperishable, ordered, appropriate and invincible.[5] This is the true meaning of the term "happy" or "blessed," not the superficial happiness that depends upon circumstances, such as too much alcohol, or too little sorrow, or a too superficial life.

The poor in spirit recognize their inadequacy before God and look to God in everything. Those who mourn discover that serenity "actually comes through sorrow, pain and distress, and not just in spite of them." The meek are not weak, but those who yield to the grace and will of God in all things and so have more real power than the "elbow-pushers and go-getters."

Serenity does not come from evading the tension, or succumbing to it. Rather it is comes from a hearty trust in the God who can make all things work for the good of those who love him (Rom 8:28). It is the holy perspective for the one who has truly found the treasure in the field and "sold all" (Mt 13:44). For the loss of money, career, prestige and position ultimately will not be unsettling. Serenity comes from knowing that our identity is not in what we do but in Whose we are. Our vocation is not simply a call to do something but to be someone. We are loved. Held. Purposed. We are safe in the everlasting arms of God. God is at work in our lives to will and work his own good pleasure (Rom 8:28). It is God's work that makes sense out of our work and brings serenity even in the thick of it all.

## Endnotes

[1] See Robert Banks and R. Paul Stevens, *The Complete Book of Everyday Christianity* (Downers Grove: InterVarsity Press, 1997), 862–870.

[2] Abraham Heschel. *The Earth is the Lord's and The Sabbath* (New York: Harper and Row, 1951).

[3] Anthony de Mello, *One Minute Wisdom,* cited in Elizabeth A. Dryer, *Earth Crammed with Heaven: A Spirituality of Everyday Life* (New York: Paulist, 1994), 89.

[4] Walter of Hilton, *Towards Perfect Love* (Portland: Multnomah Press, 1985), 8–9.

[5] James Houston, "The Serenity of Christ," *Crux* XV, no. 1 (March 1979): 3–7.

## Further Reading

Robert Banks, "Stress, Workplace," in *The Complete Book of Everyday Christianity* (Downers Grove: InterVarsity Press, 1997), 970–974.

# FOUR DAYS ON THE MOUNTAIN OF SILENCE:

## MOUNT ATHOS

*From* Crux, *vol. 40, no. 4 (December 2004)*

I am a pilgrim. So I lean forward to embrace the icon of Christ harrowing hell through his resurrection—"The Anastasis." Christ moves toward the right, raising Adam with his right hand and holding a closed scroll in his left. Christ is flanked by two groups. On the right are the righteous, headed by the supplicant Eve. On the left are the kings and prophets of the Jews, headed by John the Baptist. Theophanis, the Cretan iconographer, has placed behind the two groups "beetling cliffs [that] converge on the central figure of Christ. The whole foreground is occupied by the rocky cavern of Hades, with its smashed doors and empty sarcophagi. In the middle of the cavern are the figures of Hades and Satan, crouching together in dread of Christ, who has vanquished death." [1]

This is the icon of the day in Holy Monastery Stavronikita. But as I lean forward, along with the other pilgrims in the exquisite sanctuary of the main church (*katholikon*), reflected in the glass cover of the icon, I see an image of Christ from the cupola of the church. There, in the centre of the dome, is Christ *Pantokrator* (all-powerful), representing Christ bending down Heaven and descending. [2] This is my prayer: Lord, may I know you better and know your resurrection life. Maximus the Confessor pondered the implications of Christ's victory over the forces of disunity: "Christ is the center where all lines converge." [3] But why am I here, of all places, in this only monastic state in the world, Mt. Athos, where there are no women, no meat, no singing, not even any female dogs?

### Stavronikita Monastery

"And just what do you think a pilgrimage on Mt. Athos will actually do to your personal relationship with Christ?" This probing question was asked by a good friend.

"Well, I'll be praying for four days," I replied.

"You could do that just as well at home."

"But..."

Tongue-tied at the moment, I later reflected on my real reason. The late Harvard sociologist Pitirim Sorokin claimed we can know reality in three ways: through the eye of the senses (empirical science), through the eye of the mind (rational theology and philosophy) and through the eye of contemplation. The Western church has, by and large, concentrated on the senses and reason while the Eastern Church has focused on contemplation. Kyriacos Markides, a Cypriot Orthodox drawn to his own roots though educated in the West, maintained that "Mount Athos has, in its quiet way, preserved the 'eye of contemplation.'"[4] If, as is alleged, the church has two lungs—West and East—then I have been breathing mainly through one lung. I am intellectual and my theology is in large measure based on intellectual constructs. What I long for is a deeper direct experience of God, to breathe from both lungs.

For more than ten centuries men have lived here on this slender peninsula in northern Greece, many in directed communities (*coenobitic*), some in independent farm houses (*sketes*), some in small communities attached to a monastery and under its discipline (*kellias*) and some in tiny hermit cells (*hesychasteria*) dotted like peppers over the austere and wild beauty of this mountainous terrain, which is clothed in the lower regions with pine, acacia, chestnuts and wild flowers and on the higher with the grey-white crystalline limestone peak of Mount Athos, which crowns the fifty-six kilometer peninsula. Since normal development has been prohibited for ten centuries this is a virtual paradise, a wilderness, a desert, untouched except for the majestic, cliff-hanging, multi-storied monasteries, which have been pieced together over the centuries stage by stage since 835 AD like medieval cathedrals.

Stavronikita, like the other monasteries, is under constant reconstruction. Though it is the newest (tenth century) of the twenty remaining active monasteries, housing some 1,400 monks in total, it is the smallest and the only one with a view of the mountain of silence itself. I pray sitting under an arcade of grapes just outside the massive steel fortress doors at the entrance (which will be closed irrevocably at sundown), while beside me a building crane whirs away, the twenty-first century equivalent of a hundred monastic labourers bearing blocks of stone to add to the fortress tower that easily dwarfs the *katholikon*.

In the sanctuary, as I lean over to touch the icon of the resurrection and cross myself in the Orthodox way, I see that the main church itself is a dark room—or so it seems at first when entering from the blazing sun outside—encrusted with centuries of candle smoke, oil lamps and incense. The great chandelier in the middle, lined up exactly under the *Pantokrator*, is not electrified, but it is laden with a hundred or so candles. And as my eyes adjust to the darkness, I see that every square inch of the walls and ceiling is covered with evocative images that speak to my heart. Like the ambassadors of Vladmir, the Prince of Kiev, who journeyed to St. Sophia in

Constantinople, I could exclaim, "We knew not whether we were in heaven or on earth, for surely there is no such splendour or beauty anywhere on earth."[5] There is St. Nicholas, the patron saint of the monastery, in a fading icon at the entrance, and there are images of prophets, apostles, saints and John Climacus's Ladder of Perfection, with Christ at the top receiving those who ascend virtue on virtue to perfection. (There is half-truth here. There is progress in godliness but Christ also comes down Jacob's ladder to meet us just where we are). But Christ's welcome seems a sharp contrast to the welcome I received on entering.

Walking from Karyes, the administrative centre of the peninsula, reached by a two-hour ferry ride (there is no overland entrance to the monastic peninsula), I walked for two hours, mainly downhill, stitching back and forth—alone but not alone—breathing the prayer, "Lord Jesus Christ, Son of God, have mercy on me" (and, as the Russians add), "a sinner." This Jesus prayer, the heart of Orthodox spirituality, is a practice that dates back to the remotest antiquity and is embodied in *The Way of the Pilgrim* (linked with the name of Hesychius)[6], and it remains alive in the Orthodox way today. Theodore the Recluse proposed that by thus praying without ceasing "will be exactly like holding an object in the sun, because this is to hold yourself before the face of the Lord, who is the Sun of the spiritual world."[7] Communion is the goal of prayer itself, summarized frequently in the tradition as three stages: first, asking God for what is fitting; second, an ascent of the spirit to God and finally the spirit's colloquy with God.[8]

Spiritual theology in the orthodox tradition is simply prayer. It is "lived dogma"[9] or, as Vladimir Lossky has noted, a theology that has no sharp distinction between mysticism and theology in contrast to the Kantian turn, which pushes authentic Christian experience back "into the realm of objects of faith."[10] A real theologian is someone who has reached intimate communion and perception with God. John the Evangelist is called "the theologian" (*theologos*) in the icons because, in the opening passages of his Gospel, he witnesses to the divinity of the Logos and thus introduces us to the mystery of the Holy Trinity. Evagrian says, "If you are a theologian, you will pray truly. And if you truly pray, you are a theologian."[11] Spiritual theology holds together three things dear to the pilgrim: Spirit, God (*theos*) and Christ (*logos*), so that we might participate in the divine fellowship through prayer. John says, "our fellowship is with the Father and with his Son, Jesus Christ."[12] This, then, is the mystery, essential to Orthodox spirituality and too easily missed by the flip casual spirituality of Western evangelicalism. Not surprisingly, the Eastern Church has often been compared to Mary and the Western church to Martha.

The mystery of God in the conventions of iconography is represented by a cloud-encircled mountain with a schematized jagged peak, not unlike the sharp, rocky irruptions along the shore that I saw as we made our way by boat from the last port—Ouranopoli—where I left my wife for her own private retreat. But now, as I am sitting under the grape arbour at Holy Stavronikita, I can see that resemblance in Mount Athos itself rising majestically 2,039 meters from the sea, with its jagged ridge and hovering clouds, tethered to the peak like kites in the lee of the wind. Mount Athos has inspired many of the icons of the transfiguration of Jesus on another mountain, provoking the desire, sometimes spoken of as an *eros,* dynamic love for God and a passion for the Tabor light. Paul's prayer is mine: "And we, who with unveiled faces all reflect the Lord's glory, are being transformed into his likeness with ever-increasing glory, which comes from the Lord, who is the Spirit."[13] The all-powerful death-plunderer and life-giver is within, above, below, around. The Orthodox term for this metamorphosis is deification. The church fathers say that God became man so that he might make us gods.[14]

Tomas Spidlik summarizes the tradition usually attributed to Irenaeus in these words: "For it was for this end that the Word of God was made man, and he who was the Son of God became the Son of Man, that man [*sic*], having been taken into the Word, and receiving adoption, might become the son of God."[15] While the Western church has stressed sanctification and holiness (and often as a human accomplishment), the Eastern Church has stressed what Peter proposes in his letter, that we "may participate in the divine nature"—true godliness.[16]

I was speaking earlier about the reception here. The doorman is a lean, ageing monk with a stovepipe hat and a beard that plunges like a cataract to his waist. He was, truth to tell, occupied with a bus load of day visitors, who had whipped in for a glass of cold mountain water, a Turkish delight, a five-minute visit to the *katholikon* to kiss several of the icons, and then they were off to "do" another monastery. There was no silence, no contemplation, no embrace of God, if one may judge another on pilgrimage, if indeed a roulette wheel monastic immersion can be called a pilgrimage at all. But that crowd of spiritual tourists did allow me, as a heretic, to come into the inner part of the *katholikon* and to be confronted again with the Lord. I continued to breathe, "Lord Jesus Christ, Son of God, have mercy on me, a sinner." The doorman (whom I mistook for the guest master, the *arhondaris*) was a rather austere figure without a smile. He motioned for me to put down my tiny knapsack, crammed with all I needed for four days of hiking, and to produce my *diamonitirion*—the precious permit that allowed me access and that took me weeks of phoning, writing, e-mailing, snail-mailing and faxing to obtain. He did not speak any English except the word, "Telephone?" asking thereby whether I had arranged for the overnight visit by telephone, which I had, weeks ago. But perhaps I misunderstood the ancient virtue of monastic hospitality. Barsanuphius advised, "Receive your guest; after you greet him ask, 'How are you?' Then remain seated with him in silence."[17] So this is the mountain of silence, as it is called.

Even my companion in room 19 of the guest house, a man my own age, speaks only Greek "*et un peu française.*" We are foot to foot in a small, Spartan, but clean room, obviously rebuilt a few years ago with a new slate roof that shines like mica in the late-afternoon sun.

The bell rings for the liturgy. A monk walks through the courtyard banging the talanton, a long plank that sends a reverberating sound through the stone walls of the monastery calling people to prayer. We all enter, crossing ourselves, and find a seat in stations surrounding the inner part of the church—the first and central sanctuary. An icon is brought in and placed on the stand. It is Anastasis—the Resurrection.

Icons are not religious paintings. They are symbols to be venerated but not worshipped. The Iconodules insisted, in the controversies that revolved around icons, that the Incarnation has made representational religious art possible. The whole of creation is to be redeemed. Nicholas Zernob (1898–1980) claimed "the icons were pledges of the coming victory of a redeemed creation over the fallen one…The icons were part of the transfigured cosmos."[18] They are windows on eternity. Leonid Ouspensky says,

> Christianity is the revelation not only of the Word of God but also the Image of God…The ways of iconography, as a means of express-ing what regards the Deity, are here the same as the ways of theology. The task of both is to express that which cannot be expressed by human means…There are no words, no colours or lines, which could represent the Kingdom of God…Both theology and iconography are faced with a problem which is absolutely insoluble—to express by means belonging to the created world that which is infinitely above the creature…Therefore the methods used by iconography for pointing to the Kingdom of God can only be figurative, symbolical, like the language of the parables in the Holy Scriptures.[19]

I am interrupted in my meditation by an embarrassing question.

"Are you Orthodox?" The youngest monk, obviously a novitiate (*dhokimos*) and probably the only English-speaker in the room, has sidled up to me.

"I am Church of England," I answer.

"Orthodox?"

"Almost!" I attempt a conciliatory thrust.

"You must remain outside."

So I retreat to the outer sanctuary. To my surprise, some of the monks have chosen this as their place to pray. Afterwards, as this young man and I share the fading glow on a cloudless Athos—now with deep rills of light and dark green on the lower wooded part of the mountain beneath the sheer and stubborn peak—I discover that the novitiate's name is Demetrius, an architect from Thessalonika who, after fourteen years "in the world," came here to stay just five months ago.

"What time is breakfast?" I ask, having eaten a simple supper of potatoes and zucchini with the other pilgrims in the refectory (*trapezaria*).

"Tonight is special—Ascension Day. We have an eight-hour liturgy, all night. It starts at midnight, your time." (For they go by a different clock as well as a different calendar.) "The meal after is not really breakfast. We have fish at 8:30 a.m. your time, 11:30 a.m. our time."

As I hear this gracious invitation, I think privately that I will have to leave before the meal in order to walk to Karyes and take the bus to the port, Daphni, and a boat to Gregoriou monastery, for we are only allowed one night at each place. As the last amber bathes the Athos peak I thank God for a truly wonderful day. "Dusk and dawn take turns calling, 'Come and worship.'"[20]

The kerosene lamp burns all night in the hall outside my guest room. There is no electricity in this monastery—only candles, oil lamps, wood-fired stoves and heaters. Early in the morning, the *katholikon*, to which I make my way, is very dark. There are dimly burning wicks by each of the icons at the entrance of the inner church, from which I have been banned. Black-robed monks, barely distinguishable from their standing chairs, are shuffling in and out as the all-night liturgy comes to a conclusion behind the royal doors in the iconostasis (the icons screen separating the table from the rest of the sanctuary). The doors are open and I can see into the mystery. The church itself, as Scripture says, is a mystery, once hidden but unveiled and partly realized today, and the building itself communicates this. Abbot George describes this: "The moment we enter an Orthodox Church and witness the beautiful

*A view of Mt. Athos*

iconography, then and there we have an experience: we learn what God's undertaking for humanity is, and what the purpose of our life is."[21] I am discovering that liturgy enables one to maintain attentiveness to God, to pray continuously, which surely is the essence of Orthodox spirituality.

## On the Way

Dawn is breaking on a cloudless Athos. I must be on my way, foregoing the fish meal that waits for the conclusion of the liturgy. I am moving. The monks are stationary. Perhaps they are on a journey while staying still. The morning is exquisite. Athos is bathed in a pinkish glow—that great rock finger pointing, as it were, to God. I am not into fasting yet. I have carried a supply of nuts and dried fruit "just in case" and along the way, having missed breakfast, I stop to eat by the roadside privately and discreetly. A special fault among monks was *latrophagia,* eating in secret, and I am guilty already on the second day!

Actually the monks are moving now, too, but not on foot. I have yet to see a monk walking any distance except between the refectory and the sanctuary. I trudge along the dirt road, step by step, prayer by prayer, being engulfed in clouds of dust as the monks speed by in their new Datsun pick-ups. One has whizzed by me in a new Mercedes truck, another in a Land Rover, going perhaps to Karyes to buy the Husqvarna chain saw I spotted in the window of one of the shops yesterday in the administrative centre of this strange state. No women here, but the latest chain saws. Karyes, the capital, is a meeting place. It is now laden with shops, but in the days when the Saturday market was the main event, a Russian monk, Vasily Gregorovic Barsky, described the event in a way that still happens in the streets.

> And this somber-hued spiritual spectacle is marvelous to behold: pious, long-bearded elders with stovepipe hats and clad in humble cassocks, some from neighbouring districts in sandals and others from far off in shoes of hemp, some girdled and laden and others unencumbered, embrace each other and kiss each other courteously, either because they have not seen each other for a long time or out of great love for God. Some are emaciated from fasting and pale from attending vigils, others are grimy from lack of washing and have calloused hands from their prostrations and manual labour, some are fat and rubicund from easy living, some are beardless and some carry a staff, while others do not. And they are of different races, and converse in different languages: Greek, Serbian, Bulgarian, Turkish, Vlach, Albanian and other tongues. And it is truly wonderful to see, and to hear the exchange of different pieces of news and the endless talk about spiritual and secular matters.[22]

The bus ride from Karyes to Daphne is uneventful, except where the mountainous switchbacks bring us to the unprotected edge of a precipice with dizzying verticals. The driver is careful. Waiting for St. Anna (*Agios Anna*), the local monastery boat to the south shore, is a discouraging immersion in sounds, mostly Greek, though one French Canadian waits behind me in the line for a ticket. Beer, smokes and icons are being hawked.

On the trip down the south coast, we round a craggy bluff, and I suddenly see, a thousand feet up, Simonos Petras, a multi-storied monastery clinging to a cliff like a giant bird's nest. Then we travel on to Gregoriou Monastery, where I get off at the *arsanas*, the landing ramp and wharf of the monastery by the shore. This monastery rises from the sea rather than

*Simonos Petras*

descending from the sky. The guesthouse is separate, and I am berthed with three Greeks who do not speak a word of English. In the reception room (*arhondariki*), the doorkeeper serves a Turkish delight (*loukoumi*), a glass of *rakia* (home-made Ouzo, which is to be tossed down in one gulp), a cup of Greek coffee (to be sipped slowly) and a glass of cool water. I begin exploring this fascinating complex, especially the *katholikon*, which has exquisite wall paintings of Gabriel, Michael, Solomon, Ezekiel, David and an unusual icon of Paul and Barnabas. Usually the icons are of Paul and Peter holding up the church (one to the Gentiles and the other to the Jews), but this icon recognizes the strategic partnership of Paul and Barnabas. Mount Athos has preserved the largest collection of Christian art in the world, a heritage amassed over many centuries through the successive donations of Byzantine, Russian and Slav emperors. Each monastery has a treasure and the monks are proud to show their visitors the icons and paintings.

## Gregoriou Monastery

"Are you Orthodox?" a man asks. I recall William Dalrymple's dilemma in nearby Lavra Monastery when he was tracking down the original manuscript of John Moschos's *Spiritual Meadows* in the monastery library. "Forgive me," the guest master asked him, "but are you Orthodox or heretic?"[23]

But this time, the man asking me is a long-term guest puffing one cigarette after another in the guesthouse lounge.

"Yes," I say, "I do have icons. Yes, I believe, as Peter says, that we can partake of the divine nature. Yes, I believe in the communion of saints. Yes, I believe we come to know God mainly through prayer rather than reason."

Later, at Vespers, I enter the first and second of the three sections of the church, thinking I have reserved the third part for the Orthodox, but once again the guest master asks the vexed question. I feel like saying, "Almost." Or, "I am not a heretic." But I say, "The Church of England." How can I explain non-denominational, free, unaffiliated, part-Baptist, part-Brethren, part-Anglican and part-community church? Can I say simply, "Christian?"

"Then you must move back to the narthex," he says.

After vespers we all move into the *trapezaria* (refectory) for a meal of beans, eggs, feta and bread, served with retsina wine and water. We eat silently, while there is reading from the pulpit, but at lightning speed. I am still wolfing down the last beans when the abbot (*igoumenos*) rings the bell. Seventy monks and thirty-six guests leap to their feet, and the abbot prays and leads a brief Eucharist. Unlike the meals, the refectory is beautiful. Every square inch is covered with wall paintings—saints, biblical scenes and, over the head table, the Last Supper. We are all ushered back into the church, this time into all three parts, except, of course, behind the iconostasis. The attending priest brings out four silver boxes, variously shaped, and thirty-five guests, myself excepted, kiss each of the boxes—the skull of St. Gregory, a piece of the hand, the skin of a saint and, yes, a piece of the true cross of Christ. I cross myself and leave, only to be found in the monastery courtyard by the guest master, Father Damian.

Father Damian is the monk who excommunicated me to the narthex, but he offers me a CD and envelope as a "souvenir." Sitting outside in the quadrangle I open the envelope—it is the story of Naaman and the story of Samuel and Saul.

*Gregoriou Monastery*

The Jordan river of healing that springs from these two sources, the Jor and the Dan, symbolically stand for truth and obedience, and is named orthodoxy…Your faith in obedience to the truth will become the joy of your salvation. There is only one church—the Orthodox. There hasn't been true spirituality in the West for 1000 years. The scholasticism of the West has destroyed true faith.

Later Father Damian takes me to the graveyard on the east side of the monastery at the edge of the bluff with an awesome prospect of the next two headlands. Dionysiou Monastery, my next visit, is hidden behind the last headland. One of the graves bears a cross indicating that the monk died at the age of 103. "His mind was still sharp. Monks here never suffer dementia," Damian assures me.

"Do you know Jesus?" I ask him.

"I am getting to know him," he replies.

"So am I."

"Greek," Damian continues, is the most powerful language. It is impossible to translate into English *psyche* and *nous*. We have kept the tradition since the first council in Jerusalem. There is only one church and it is the Orthodox Church—not that we can restrict the work of the Holy Spirit in other so-called churches."

I try another tack. "What have you found most helpful in growing in Christ?"

"I can't answer that question," he replies.

"Do you like being a monk?" I ask. Father Damian has told me that he is an English-born Greek who returned to England after a brief visit to Athos and then came here to spend his life.

"'Like' is not an appropriate word. It is the way for me. Do you have children?" he asks.

"Yes, three married children and eight grandchildren."

Damian responds, "I pray the Lord's blessing on them."

"Indeed," I say, "that is part of what I am doing on Mt. Athos."

"What do you do?" he asks.

"I teach marketplace theology."

"What's that?"

"It is the integration of Christian faith with service and work in the world."

"It is not possible," he responds. "That's why I am a monk. It is very, very difficult to be a Christian in the world."

"But," I counter, "it is not easy being a monk. The demons are everywhere."

"Yes," continues Damian, "but it is much easier here when you have left the world."

Monasticism is a form of martyrdom, laying down one's life intentionally. In the past, and even at Athos, this has led to a variety of eccentric forms. There were grazing and browsing monks with no fixed abode, dendrites who lived in trees, statics who remained standing in open air, stylites on pillars and recluses locked in cells. Athos has developed largely through *lavras*, hermit colonies established around a church under the direction of a spiritual elder and monasteries under the direction of an abbot. One saying applies to all forms: "Keep to your cell, and your cell will teach you everything! Only in his cell is a monk in his element, like a fish in water."[24]

The monks work. Indeed, for the monk, work is spiritual. John Chrysostom elaborated the various aspects of this vocation of work: it creates a bond between people; it is a way of loving your neighbour; it helps the poor. Spidlik says, "The ideal model would be the work of monks. It is performed in an atmosphere conducive to prayer, accompanied by explicit prayers; it becomes in itself a prayer, because its motivation is charity."[25]

I ponder the business and professional person in the world that I serve. Perhaps the same advice holds. Do not leave and join a monastery (or become a pastor). Go deep where you are. Keep to your business and your business will teach you everything. It is your monastic cell. My cell on Athos, however, seems not so fruitful.

### A Night from Hell on the Holy Mountain

The Hebrew people began the day with nightfall: "the evening and the morning were the first day." The logic is persuasive. Just as Adam and Eve woke into God-consciousness on the sixth day to experience, first of all, not work but Sabbath, so we begin the day by resting, by trusting God enough to do nothing, to let God run the world while we sleep. Sleep is an act of faith. It was especially so last night, or I should say, the beginning of today. The sign inside the guest room door says not to leave money or valuables in the room lest they be stolen. Little did I guess that what would be stolen from me was my sleep.

I was placed, once again, across from the washroom with three young Greek men. The monastery doors, steel-clad and of fortress quality, are closed and locked at sundown. So it is good to turn in early, which I did at nine o'clock, but I did not anticipate the people factor. What I find so strange in this "mountain of silence" is that I am continuously running away from people to have silence. Spidlik deals with this perceptively. "A person is alone when he runs no risk of meeting another human being in his habitual living area. This is flight in the material sense. He is still alone as long as he does not converse with anyone. This is the solitude of silence. Finally, he is alone when his mind at its utmost depth has no interlocutor, when *logismoi* (thoughts) do not trouble his mind. This is the solitude of the heart."[26] For the Hesychasts, one could not have stillness (*hesychia*) without material solitude. But last night I could not flee even in the material sense.

Across the hall in a smoke-filled room men laughed and guffawed until midnight. Down the hall another cluster talked noisily like crows on a summer morning. Two of my roommates came in and out, in and out, each time turning on the light (there is electricity here powered by a small hydro station and solar panels) and fidgeting with their bags. The third, already under the thick wool blanket when I entered, got up every fifteen minutes or so throughout the night, put on the hard plastic sandals kept next to each bed and steamed to the washroom across the hall, returning with a slam of the door.

"On my bed I remember you; I think of you through the watches of the night."[27] I am thinking about the Incarnation: God really dwelling with us, sleeping foot to foot with the disciples, with all the irritations of thoughtless people. "Have I been with you so long... O foolish... Could you not watch with me one hour?" This reality is captured evocatively by a wall painting by the famous fourteenth-century iconographer Manuel Panselinos in the Protaton, the oldest church on the peninsula, located in Karyes. It shows the disciples graphically sleeping in the Garden of Gethsemane while Christ wages war in the Spirit.[28] The Incarnation is the miracle of miracles and the greatest mystery: God in a roomful of imbeciles whom he loves and promises never to leave.

At 6:00 a.m. the huge Caterpillar bulldozer underneath our window surged into life, huffing and puffing to get started at the day's work moving a pile of gravel somewhere else.

Later, when Damian asked how I slept, I suggested that he put up a sign asking for silence between ten and six. He replied, "It wouldn't work. This is Greece."

Prince Charles was here last week at Vatopedhiou Monastery and I am sure he did not have to endure this. He arrived with thirty cases, including a satellite phone and his own food. The U.K. paper explained why: "The food is vile here."[29] Perhaps that is a little too strong, but the food does sit on one's stomach late into the night until, finally and reluctantly, the digestive system capitulates. I try to imagine Charles in a room with two transient men and one beating an all-night trail to the water closet. The water closet is a strange, stand-on-the-floor device with a huge handle for flushing, which releases a noisy cataract like the throat of Foz de Iguaçu or the Niagara Falls, an almost deafening roar that can be heard in every room, or at least certainly mine.

Before breakfast Damian takes me out to the balcony overlooking the sea. We discussed several books we have both read and the mystical life. Meanwhile we watch a supply ship bringing in hardware and materials. There is no road to this isolated monastery; it can only be reached by ship and donkey trail.

"Technology!" quips Damian with a cynical touch.

The monastery was built in 1300 with monks carrying stones in packs on their back up the hill.

"In some monasteries," Damian continues, "there are original supporting timbers that are a thousand years old. And today we can only build for a hundred years—or less. Look at these stones. The pointing is new, but behind the cement is a mortar that withstands the pounding

*Dionysiou
Monastery*

of the sea. We know what the ingredients are but can't reproduce this waterproof cement. And the long horizontal timbers inserted in the courses of stones"—I could see they were original and very weathered—"are shock absorbers in this earthquake prone area.

"But the end is near. All of the monks on Athos have a sense that the time has come—a war that will make the Second World War seem like a tea party—an antichrist and then the Lord's second coming. It will be awesome, wonderful and glorious. But there will be no evacuation."

We say goodbye with mutual blessing. I have appreciated this soul friendship. Damian presses into my hand some postcard icons and a sermon on deification by the abbot of the monastery. It includes a prayer: "Merciful Lord, also guide the steps of heterodox Christians towards an awareness of Your Truth, so that they are not left outside Your bride chamber, deprived of the Grace of Deification. Merciful Lord, have mercy on us, and on Your creation. Amen."[30] I am on my way again, this time to Dionysiou.

## Dionysiou Monastery

The journey to Dionysiou takes me over one of the most difficult vertical parts of Athos. While the total elevation is less than a thousand feet, this is scaled several times as I make my way around headlands, going up and down on rough rocks placed strategically and in an angular way to provide footsteps for the donkeys that carry in supplies and people. I make my way slowly and carefully, knowing that one badly twisted ankle could shut me down. The scenery is stark: jagged rocks protruding as one sees in the icons, a hanging waterfall a thousand feet above, wild flowers and an occasional rustling in the brush—there are poisonous snakes on Athos. This is the desert—not of sand, but the absence of the addictions of civilization, the seductiveness of signs and advertisements, the Internet and, for the most part, cars—creation, raw and resplendent. No wonder some took to the trees and the pillars. The first monastic foundation in Athos was established by St. Euthymius of Salonica in the ninth century. At the tender age of eighteen he took to moving around on all fours and eating grass. Sometime later he became a stylite and berated his brethren from the top of a pillar.[31] I feel the absence of women especially. It is mandated by an imperial edict after, so the story goes, "the monks were in the habit of debauching the daughters of the shepherds who came to the mountain to sell milk and wool."[32] It is relatively easy to be free of lustful thoughts when there is no temptation. But it is a strange world with only one sex, perhaps not what God intended at all, perhaps not even spiritually healthy. "Basil, by contrast, believed that in monasteries there was a need to converse with women for the sake of personal edification or to take care of business matters."[33]

Nothing could have prepared me for the first sight of Holy Monastery Dionysiou. The sweat has drenched my hat, face, shirt and trousers. Rounding the last bend, I see it, gleaming in the morning sun like the Meteori monasteries perched on the top of huge rocks, a sanctuary castle built on an almost impregnable natural fortress, approached by stairs leading to a small opening capable of being fortified and locked against attack, with the inner doors clad in thick iron.

Upon arrival I discover the sixteenth-century icons of the Revelation that I have seen in books. They are gloriously evocative, though sadly now in poor repair, with many of the faces defaced by the damp. I take three photographs, then am asked to desist. Scripture is everywhere here. Spidlik notes, "St. Basil in particular affirmed an immutable principle: that every word and action must be checked against the witness of Scripture…Seraphim of Sarov, for example, read the entire New Testament once a week."[34] But

*Hermit Cell*

the fathers also distinguished two sources of faith: Scripture and "the mysteries of the church"—or tradition, which connects dogma and devotion. It is tradition, so it is said, that is a progressive incarnation of the divine life in the concrete humanity of various cultures, accomplished by Christ through the Spirit, what amounts to a "progressive and dynamic deification."[35]

The welcome, however, is delightful, in spite of the photographic excommunication. The guesthouse is renovated and spotless. After signing the register and showing my *diamonitirion* to the doorkeeper, I am served the customary glass of cold water, Turkish delights, liquor and Greek coffee. Then to my room: a private room, a cell—actually, the guest master's former cell. After last night's sleepless trial I am ecstatic. It is only six feet by seven feet with an archer's slit for a window, but it is private. I am alone. In silence and solitude my soul waits for God. "My soul finds rest in God alone."[36]

After vespers and dinner—a simple plate of rice—Father Ionnikos, who speaks excellent English, takes the three English-speaking guests under his wing. There are three of us—Barry from London and Pierre from Switzerland. He leads us through the church dedicated to John the Baptist, where there is a fourteenth-century icon of the Baptist rescued from a hermit on Mt. Athos. Then he takes us upstairs to the main office, an immaculately embellished room with fine wood everywhere. One of the monks, a photographer, photographed the hundreds of wall paintings in the monastery and composed a thick volume that has been published. We went through the volume page by page: the life of Christ, John the Baptist, Mary, the saints and the martyrs. Walking through the church and adjoining buildings is tantamount to reading both Testaments and the lives of the saints, the latter actually being read out loud from a text daily during meals in the refectory.

The day begins (at 9:00 p.m.) with a magnificent sleep in my monk's cell. "He gives sleep to his beloved"[37] as the Lord builds the house and guards the city. Sleep is a ministry—trusting God and renewing the soul.

Breakfast is Spartan—two slices of hard bread and three olives, consumed without a bell demanding that we leave the refectory immediately, finished or not. The previous night my new traveling companion, Pierre from Switzerland, a medical doctor, barely got halfway through his meal. But this morning we eat without a bell on the guesthouse balcony, a cantilevered apparatus several hundred feet above the sea. The sun rises exquisitely on the other side of *Agios Oros* (the holy mountain), tossing slashes of light on the craggy ridges where just yesterday I hiked.

We decide to take the morning boat, *Agios Anna*, all the way to the end of the peninsula to see St. Paul Monastery (*Agiou Pavlou*) and the Skete of St. Anna. Approaching the edge of the peninsula, which rises from the sea at gravity-defying angles, the mountain emerges from the sea to over 6,000 feet without foothills or subsidiary landings. In the first thousand feet there are dozens of sketes and hermit cells, some clinging tenaciously to the edge of a cliff, inspiring the question of how the monks get there, how they get water and, more particularly, how they got the building materials there. These are, by and large, not temporary buildings but rock-built structures meant to last and built for solitude. St. Anthony, the founder of Eastern monasticism, has had a lasting influence on the Holy Mountain. His icon is everywhere and his life is read while monks subsist on the simplest of fare.

Ascetics, those who deny the world, or "love it not," to use John's phrase, or "mortify the flesh," to use Paul's phrase, are the models copied everywhere here. Asceticism is a training that involves perseverance, tolerating no rest and no inattention. This is the praxis of the desert. Abbot George explains, "Without ascetic endeavour, there is no spiritual life, no struggle and no progress. We obey, fast, keep vigil, labour with prostrations, and stand upright during prayer; all of this we do in order that we may be cleansed of our passions."[38] The purpose is a quest for God and the growth of the soul. Spidlik explains the essential link: "the union of asceticism and mysticism is the doctrinal foundation of all forms of monasticism."[39]

A travel brochure says that the monks of Mt. Athos live the ideal Christian life. I ponder this, knowing that only four days of deliverance from the media, the Internet, the lust of the eye, the lust of the flesh and the pride of life have been instrumental for centering on God, without distraction, wholly and directly. Significantly the dedication of Holy

Monastery Dionysiou to John the Baptist is, as a concluding coda to my pilgrimage, a true beginning. On the fresco at the entrance of the monastery, John holds a scroll with the words (in Byzantine script): "Repent for the kingdom of heaven is at hand." John reminds me that repentance is not a once-for-all conversion, but a life of continuing conversion. But there is another pole of spiritual patterning in Scripture.

Ascetic practice, as Eugene Peterson says, "sweeps out the clutter of the god-pretentious self, making ample space for Father, Son, and Holy Spirit; it embraces and prepares for a kind of death that the culture knows nothing about, making room for the dance of the resurrection."[40] But alongside the ascetic is the aesthetic, God's yes to match God's no. Peterson notes this theme in the story of the transfiguration:

> "Peter, James and John see Jesus transfigured before them on the mountain into cloud-brightness in the company of Moses and Elijah, and hear God's blessing…Everything fitting together, the luminous interior of Jesus spilling out onto the mountain, history and religion beautifully personalized and brought into deep, resonating harmony, the declaration of love."[41]

The world drains the beauty out of people, as Peterson says, but so does a lot of religion. There certainly is beauty on the Holy Mountain with its wall paintings and icons— thousands of them. It is effulgent with the glory of God just as Ezekiel foretold it: "the land was radiant with his glory."[42] The Apocalypse with its luminous presentation of the lion and the lamb in heaven ruling with the mighty angels, serving, implementing, protecting, the icon of the harrowing of Hades (the *Anastasis*), the icon of the ascension and the *Pantokrator* ruling over all the principalities and powers—all of these reveal beauty, but I perceive little joy here, especially in the liturgy, which often seems like a protracted moan. It is hard to hold together both world-denial and world-love, God's no and God's yes, the ascetic and the aesthetic, hard to hold all of this within the love that is before and above all loves, the love of God.

I have learned much by coming to the Holy Mountain—the need for simplicity, the call to continuous repentance, moment by moment trust in God, contemplation as the normal Christian life, the mystery of God, the communion and modeling of the saints, the long and fruitful tradition of the church, intercession and the absolute centre of spiritual theology in prayer. ("Do you teach your students to pray?" asked Father Damian.) But to deepen my journey in aesthesis, I must return to my work, to my world and to my wife. As the preacher said, "Enjoy life with your wife, whom you love."[43] But

I will take with me what I have learned from the mountain of silence.

"Together with all the saints," Paul says, we can "grasp how wide and long and high and deep is the love of Christ"[44]—African, Eastern European, American, Orthodox, Catholic and Protestant. We, in the West, need our Orthodox brothers and sisters—and they need us, too, though it appears that they do not see this need. Mary needs Martha and Martha needs Mary. We need both lungs, West and East, for proper breathing.

## Endnotes

[1] Athanasios A. Karakatsanius, ed., *Treasures of Mount Athos* (Thessaloniki: Museum of Byzantium Culture, 1997), 133.

[2] Archimandrite George, Abbot of the Holy Monastery of St. Gregorios, Mt. Athos, "Deification: The Purpose of Life," (unpublished), 12.

[3] Tomas Spidlik, *The Spirituality of the Christian East: A Systematic Handbook* (Kalamazoo, Mich.: Cistercian Publications, 1986), 37.

[4] Kyriacos C. Markides, *The Mountain of Silence: A Search for Orthodox Spirituality* (New York: Doubleday, 2001), 8.

[5] Timothy Ware, *The Orthodox Church* (Harmondsworth, UK: Penguin Books, 1983), 269.

[6] Helen Bacovcin, trans., *The Way of the Pilgrim and The Pilgrim Continues His Way* (Garden City, NY: Image Books, 1978).

[7] Spidlik, *The Spirituality of the Christian East,* 317.

[8] Ibid., 308.

[9] Ibid., 37.

[10] Ibid., 72.

[11] George, "Deification: The Purpose of Life," 38.

[12] 1 Jn 1:3.

[13] 2 Cor 3:18.

[14] George, "Deification: The Purpose of Life," 8.

[15] Spidlik, *The Spirituality of the Christian East,* 355.

[16] 2 Pt 1:4.

[17] Spidlik, *The Spirituality of the Christian East,* 214.

[18] Ware, *The Orthodox Church,* 42.

[19] Leonid Ouspensky and Vladimir Lossky, *The Meaning of Icons,* trans. G.E.H. Palmer and E. Kadloubovsky (Crestwood, NY: St. Vladimir's Seminary Press, 1983).

[20] Ps 65 (*The Message*).

[21] George, "Deification: The Purpose of Life," 12.

[22] Kriton Chryssochoidis, *Mount Athos: The Kellia of Karyes* (Thessaloniki: Hagioritiki Hestia, 2004).

[23] William Dalrymple, *From the Holy Mountain: A Journey in the Shadow of Byzantium* (London, UK: HarperCollins, 1998), 9.

[24] Spidlik, *The Spirituality of the Christian East*, 213.

[25] Ibid., 168.

[26] Ibid., 212.

[27] Ps 63:6.

[28] Manuel Panselinos, *From the Holy Church of the Protaton* (Thessaloniki: Hagioritiki, 2003), 197.

[29] Geoffrey Levy, "Charles and a most unorthodox visit," *Daily Mail* (Thursday, 13 May 2004): 13.

[30] George, "Deification: The Purpose of Life," 5.

[31] Dalrymple, *From the Holy Mountain*, 4–5.

[32] Ibid., 5.

[33] Spidlik, *The Spirituality of the Christian East*, 223.

[34] Ibid., 5.

[35] Ibid., 8.

[36] Ps 62:1.

[37] Ps 127:2.

[38] George, "Deification: The Purpose of Life," 22.

[39] Spidlik, *The Spirituality of the Christian East*, 180.

[40] Eugene Peterson, "Saint Mark: The Basic Text for Christian Spirituality," in *Exploring Christian Spirituality: An Ecumenical Reader*, ed. Kenneth J. Collins (Grand Rapids: Baker Books, 2000), 335.

[41] Ibid., 335–6.

[42] Ez 43:2.

[43] Eccl 9:9.

[44] Eph 3:18.

THEOLOGY OF EVERYDAY LIFE

# LIVING THEOLOGICALLY:

# TOWARD A THEOLOGY OF CHRISTIAN PRACTICE

*From* Crux, *vol. 30, no. 3 (September 1994)*

I believe in Christianity as I believe that the Sun has risen not only because I see it but because by it I see everything else.
—*C.S. Lewis*

L iving theologically—my title—is an oxymoron like black light, constructive criticism or servant leadership—two ideas that normally do not belong together. What has theology to do with everyday life?

Theology is usually considered an abstract discipline. It is rational, reducible to propositions, and capable of being categorized (liberal, conservative, evangelical, Reformed, liberation). It is not usually thought of as practical. People in business, law, the professions and the trades often regard the study of theology as a process of becoming progressively irrelevant. The hardest words of critique are offered by insiders. For example, Lesslie Newbigin says:

> Christian men and women who are deeply involved in secular affairs view theology as the arcane pursuit of professional clergymen. This withdrawal of theology from the world of secular affairs is made all the more complete by the work of biblical scholars whose endlessly fascinating exercises have made it appear to the lay Christian that no one untrained in their methods can really understand anything the Bible says. We are in a situation analogous to one about which the great Reformers complained...[1]

Theology! God-words. God-study. God-thought.
Then there is life! Everyday life. Getting-up-in-the-morning life.

137

Paying-the-bills life. Watching-a-hockey-game life. Trying-to-find-a-job life. Trying-to-say-"I love you"-to-your-spouse life. Raising-a-family-in-a-postmodern-culture life. Computers, credit cards, freeways, gridlock, virtual reality, running a small business, movies, the economy, racial tension, sexual appetite, recession, radar imaging from satellites, fashion, television, ambition, workaholism, debt, prayer, Bible study, theological discourse—what do these have in common?

It should be obvious that I am pleading for a different definition of theology than what is commonly thought, one closer to the Bible.² Such is supplied by the Puritan William Perkins, who said, "Theology is the science of living blessedly forever."³ J.I.Packer, in the same tradition, says that "theology is for achieving God's glory (honour and praise) and humankind's good (the godliness that is true humanness) through every life-activity."⁴ If these definitions come close to capturing the biblical approach to theological education, then the only theology that is truly Christian is one being applied. I would not want to be a professor of unapplied theology! One reason is that the movement of the Bible is always from the indicative to the imperative, from doctrine to duty, from *kerygma* to *didache*, from theology to ethics, from revealed truth to extraordinary living. Francis of Assisi once said that humankind has as much knowledge as it has executed. That means that what you really know—in the fully biblical and Hebraic sense—is what you live. You may have passed some examinations and written some academic papers. But these are trivial tests compared with life itself. For example, James Houston recently suggested at a pastors' conference that the *curriculum vitae* of a pastor is usually written on the face of his wife. There was a stunned silence among the predominantly male audience.

In this paper I will explore the life-theology connection by looking through three lenses, each providing a way of looking at the rich connection designed by God but largely fragmented in contemporary theological education.

## Orthodoxy

Orthodoxy is made up of two words that mean "straight" or "right" (from which we get the English word "orthodontist," the person who makes straight teeth) and the Greek word for "glory" or "worship"—*doxa*. Doctrine that lines itself up (*orthos*) with Scripture is designed to be a blessing to everyday life and, at the same time, to bless God (*doxa*) in life itself. It aims, as Packer says, at true godliness that is true humanness.

### Redeeming the Routine [5]

The whole of our life has the glorious prospect of living out the great doctrines of the faith. The doctrine of the Trinity, for example, directs God-imaging creatures to live relationally. Those who proclaim that God is love are invited to be included in the love-life of God and so become lovers themselves (Jn 17:21). To believe in God the creator is to accept trusteeship of the earth. The incarnation revolutionizes our attitude to things and promotes a radical Christian materialism. The atonement equips us to live mercifully. Ecclesiology evokes the experience of peoplehood, living as the *laos* of God rather than a bouquet of individual believers. Eschatology teaches us to view time as a gift of God rather than a resource to be managed.

All of this involves straight thought. Far from denigrating thought, the Bible invites us to love God with our minds (Mt 22:37) by thinking comprehensively (taking the whole into consideration, including paradox, ambiguity and the aesthetic), thinking critically (not allowing our minds to be conformed to this age) and thinking devotedly by taking captive every thought to make it obedient to Christ (2 Cor 10:5). The fruit of such thinking should be a blessing for everyday life. Thinking Christianly is part of the "science of living blessedly forever."

### The Danger of Unapplied Theology

But orthodoxy involves more than merely speaking correctly about God. We could do that and still be damned, like the friends of Job—Eliphaz, Bildad and Zophar—who spoke with impeccable correctness about God but in the end received God's judgment: "I am angry with you [Eliphaz] and your two friends, because you have not spoken of me what is right, as my servant Job has" (Jb 42:7). Remarkably, God judged Job as orthodox and his friends were regarded as heretics. Why? It is not only a fascinating question but a vital one.

A careful study of the book of Job reveals that the only authentic theologian in the book was Job himself. The reason is sublimely simple: while the friends talked *about* God, Job talked *to* God. P.T. Forsyth says that "the best theology is compressed prayer."[6] While Job's friends delivered their lectures about God, Job talked to God, and in so speaking—with all his holy boldness—he spoke well of God. His theology was orthodox. We will return to this later.

The danger of mere intellectual orthodoxy is that we are tempted to think we can manage God. Our doctrines then become idols–static, fixed and inflexible. According to Psalm 115:8, "those who make [such idols] will be like them." They will become people who are static, inflexible and unsurprising. In contrast the Lord "does whatever pleases him" (115:3). And those who worship the Lord become free and spontaneous. God can never be contained by the human mind. If he could then God would be too puny a God to be worshipped. The point of theology is to understand God (to stand *under* God in reverent awe), not to over-stand God by attempting to control him through theological discourse. Much that passes for theological education is the extension of the tree of knowledge of good and evil through history offering the temptation to transcend our creatureliness. True worship is the opposite invitation. Orthodoxy welcomes mystery and confesses with Job, "these are but the outskirts of his ways" (Jb 26:14 KJV). As Robert Capon says: "The work of theology in our day is not so much interpretation as contemplation...God and the world need to be held up for ooh's and ahh's before they can be safely analyzed. Theology begins with admiration, not problems."[7] So orthodoxy is about worshipful living.

### Truthful Living for God's Glory

Doctrine that does not lead to doxology is demonic (Jas 2:19). That is why those who set out together on a theological education-experience are on a dangerous journey. We must make sure we are heading in the right (orthodox) direction. The goal of biblical theological education is to increase our love for God and to make us more human. For this reason the academy must work in partnership with the church and the marketplace since there is in these real life ministry and life situations a built-in reality check. More important there is a built-in love check. We cannot learn to love the church as Christ does (Eph 5:25) without being in both Christ and the church. The church cannot be loved in *absentia* the way some people get their degrees. The congregation is essential for our God-given goal of forming people who will worship God through preaching, examining a balance sheet, preparing a family meal, praying with a friend, pruning their rose bushes and equipping the saints.[8] According to Ephesians the purpose of congregation- and life-based education is that the saints will live for the praise of God's glory (1:12,14)—that is, to live doxologically.

So, looking at the theology and everyday life connection through the lens of orthodoxy, we see that the great doctrines of the faith beg for application. They bless everyday life. They point us simultaneously to the adoration of God and to the possibility of living a genuinely human existence. But we must now look through a second lens—orthopraxy—to discover what is involved in the connection of theology and daily life. "Orthopraxy" literally means right or straight practice.

### Orthopraxy

We are in desperate need today of a theology of good works, especially we evangelicals. We are saved by grace and not of works—that is the gospel. Further, faith without works is dead—and that is the gospel too. But how can people saved by grace work? What is right practice? When is a work "Christian?"

### Humanizing Theological Living

Is "Christian Work" evangelism, preaching, pastoral care, counselling— all the subjects loosely called "applied theology" or "ministry division" courses? I can only point in passing to the fine piece of analysis done on right practice by Craig Dykstra.[9] Dykstra notes the ubiquitous tension between the so-called academic fields of theology—Bible, history, ethics (disciplines in which practice is thought to have no intrinsic place)—and the applied theology division, which is often relegated, in some people's minds, to "how to" techniques for clergy. It is now widely recognized in theological circles that we must break out of the dichotomy of practical skills and theoretical knowledge. Perhaps we will never resolve the tension. Indeed, we may better speak of useful and fruitful tension as we work on integration. As we do this we can put the question differently along these lines: what is theological about praxis and what is practical about theology?

In contrast to the dichotomizing of theology and practice in the theological academy today, the New Testament presupposes a community in which every person is a theologian of application, trying to make sense out of his or her life in order to live for the praise of God's glory.[10] On the most basic level, orthopraxy is about practices that are in harmony with God's kingdom in the church and world, that bring value and good into the world. It is not obvious, however, that one cannot do the doctrine fully in a classroom or library, or learn the doctrine in the classroom and do it later. Instead of training for ministry and then going into it, we assume you should not "go into the ministry" unless you are already "in it." The best education is education *in* ministry and not just *for* it. It is transformative, not preparatory.[11] Behind this is an important principle of spiritual theology: any attempt to know God apart from the activities of life is unreal.[12] My own experience is illustrative. After two years as a student in theological college I was suffering from academic burn-out. My wife and I moved into the slums of Montreal and tried to serve God in an inner-city church while I continued my MDiv part-time. This rejuvenated my theological education. I engaged every course with questions that came out of daily ministry and our immersion in the poverty of the city. This points to a truth we must explore: that there is more to orthopraxis than application. There is revelation and illumination.

### Knowing Through Doing

There is a growing critique of the traditional linear, cause-effect approach in theological education: first you get the theology and then you apply it. In contrast we must aim at a circle of learning: theory expressed in practice, which leads to deeper theoretical/theological reflection, which leads to praxis again, and on it goes. We should speak of this as a spiral of learning as we keep re-entering each phase at a deeper level.[13] Obviously by relegating praxis to the post-academy experience, we are short-changing learning. Perhaps this is easier to grasp in Africa or Asia than in the West. The orthodoxy-orthopraxy tension in the West reflects the intrinsic dualism of Western civilization and the lingering effects of the Enlightenment.

In contrast, the Bible invites us to holistic living that embraces propositional truth, as well as truth learned through image, imagination and action, all a seamless robe. For example, the apostle Paul hammered out his doctrine of justification by faith in the context of the Gentile mission. He was a missionary theologian. Ray S. Anderson notes, "Paul's theology and mission were directed more by the Pentecost event which unleashed the Spirit of Christ through apostolic witness rather than through apostolic office. This praxis of Pentecost became for Paul the 'school' for theological reflection."[14]

The Gospels point to the same unity of knowledge. Many of the commands of Jesus link revelation with obedience. "If you obey my commands, you will remain in my love" (Jn 15:10). "If you hold to my teaching, you are really my disciples" (Jn 8:31). "If anyone keeps my word, he will never see death" (Jn 8:51). Sometimes Jesus invited people to "believe this"; more often, Jesus said, "do this and you will live" (Lk 10:28; see also Mt 19:21). Especially in the Gospel of Luke Jesus teaches that obedient action is the organ of further revelation. If people do not obey the law and the prophets, he said, "they will not be convinced even if someone rises from the dead" (Lk 16:31). He put these words on the lips of Abraham in the parable of Lazarus and the rich man and proclaimed that even his resurrection from the grave will have no evidential apologetic value if they were not acting on the light they had. We know more through doing what we already know.

Biblical theological education is not inert theology and unreflective action but "praxis-laden theory" and "theory-laden praxis."[15] Immanuel Kant said something similar when he offered the maxim that experience without theory is blind, but theory without experience is mere intellectual play.[16] What we can learn by doing is much more than simple technique. Every action has implicit theory just as every theory has implicit action. So theological reflection *in* ministry or a societal occupation is essential to living theologically. But in these things we are not trying to squeeze blood from a rock. Daily life is bursting with theological meaning just as theological truth is laden with blessing for daily life. God can be known and loved through praxis in the realities of everyday life. It would be a strange psychology that required one to love one's spouse fully and only then to kiss in order to love! What a strange perversion of the Christian life that would forbid one to act until one knows, and not act in order to know! We are formed theologically not only by reading and reasoning, but by action and by service.

My own story may be illustrative. I abandoned professional ministry at thirty-eight years of age, took up the trade of carpentry for five years and planted a church. It proved to be a theological education immersion experience. I learned theology through that.[17] I prayed as much as a carpenter as I did as a pastor, possibly more, because I was so frequently beyond my comfort zone. But the experience deepened my theology and spirituality. Indeed, as Eberhard Jüngel said, "Everything can become the theme of theology on the basis of its relation to God."[18] In this we have a clue to our basic question—what makes practice Christian?

### Inside Christian Practice

What makes an activity Christian is not the husk but the heart. Preaching, caring for the flock and equipping the saints can be profoundly secular. Listening to a child, designing a software package and examining a balance sheet can be profoundly Christian. What makes a work Christian is faith, hope and love. This is a crucial point. Orthopraxy is not merely accomplished by the skilful performance of ministerial duties like leading Bible studies, praying for the sick and doing acts of justice. This misunderstanding has seduced many non-clergy laity to aspire to ministerial duties in order to be "doing ministry." They become paraclergy instead of regarding their ordinary service in the world as full-time ministry. It is not the religious character of the work that makes service Christian but the interiority of it. William Tyndale said, "There is no work better than another to please God; to pour water, to wash dishes, to be a souter [cobbler], or an apostle, all are one, as touching the deed, to please God."[19] I can preach a sermon to impress people; I can fix our shower door at home for the glory of God. I have probably done both. The difference is faith.

Luther deals with this brilliantly in his *Treatise on Good Works*. He uses the analogy of husband and wife as an example of the Christian practices that spring from gospel confidence. Where the husband is confident of his acceptance he does not have to do big things to win his wife's favour. In the same way the person who lives by the gospel "simply serves God with no thought of reward, content that his service pleases God. On the other hand, he who is not at one with God, or is in a state of doubt, worries and starts looking for ways and means to do enough and to influence God with his many good works."[20] Faith defines orthopraxy. Faith by definition cannot be calculating, or even self-evaluative, just as the eye cannot look at itself, designed as it is for looking at another. When the eye is single or sound, the whole of one's bodily life is filled with the light of Christ (Lk 11:34–36). Life centred on God transforms the ordinary into the extraordinary so we discover what Alfons Auer describes as "the sense of transparency in worldly matters."[21]

The unselfconsciousness of such faith is the matter raised by the disturbing parable of the sheep and goats (Mt 25:31–46). The unrighteous protest that if they had seen Jesus in the poor, hungry or stranger, even if they had known Jesus was disguised in the poor, they would gladly have done a service directly to the Lord. So the unrighteous are surprised that their failure to love their neighbour was a failure to love Jesus. They would have gladly done Christian practices for Jesus but not for others! Apparently that is not enough. In contrast the righteous found to their exquisite surprise that what they did not regard as a ministry to Jesus (but just loving their neighbour) turned out to be a Christian practice approved by the Lord. They too protest, "Lord, when did we see you, hungry, naked and thirsty, and feed you?" Jesus says, "Whatever you did for one of the least of these my brothers of mine, you did for me" (Mt 25:40). We onlookers are caught up in the parable and are surprised also by the implication that compassionate actions (surely intrinsically Christian practices) are Christian precisely because they did not have a spiritual reward in view! They are Christian, Luther would say, because they arise from gospel confidence, from the generosity of a heart set free by acceptance in Christ. It is this element of surprise for which we are least prepared when we ponder the parable. Perhaps the purpose of theological education is to set us up to be surprised as the righteous on the day of judgment to discover we acted in love without knowing it was for and to Jesus.

True Christian action—orthopraxy—is gratuitive, free from a contrivance, free from a calculating spirit, free from a contractual, "I do this for God and he does that for me." Orthopractic living is essentially spontaneous. With Jesus in our hearts we love because there is someone in need, not to gain approval by God or to receive the benefits of Christian action.

This is the issue behind the question that dominates the book of Job. Satan said, "Does Job serve God for nothing?" (Jb 1:9). In the end our own service to God can be tested by the same probing question. One of the great lessons of the book of Job is this: Job proves that faith is not for the this-life benefits of having faith—not for healing (indeed he never even prays for healing); not for the restoration of his fortunes (this only comes after he meets God again). Faith is for the glory of God. Christian practice, whether developing a compensation package for a business or empowering the poor, is for God's glory. The South American liberation theologian Gustavo Gutierrez comments on this insightfully (and remarkably in view of his theological orientation):

> The truth that [Job] has grasped and that has lifted him to the level of contemplation is that justice alone does not have the final say about how we are to speak of God. Only when we have come to realize that God's love is freely bestowed do we enter fully and definitively into the presence of the God of faith... God's love, like all true love, operates in a world not of cause and effect but of freedom and gratuitiveness.[22]

Orthopraxy is action in harmony with God's purposes in which one can discover God and his truth. Orthopraxy is not necessarily clerical, though it includes the work of the pastor. Whether washing dishes or preaching, being a cobbler or an apostle, "all is one, as touching the deed, to please God." Orthopraxis is not measured by excellence, by efficiency or by its religious character but by faith, hope and love. We must cultivate the heart and not merely the husk of such action. But that points to a third lens through which to investigate the theology-life connection: orthopathy.

## Orthopathy

Orthopathy literally means "right passion"—an expression coined by Richard Mouw. There is also a hint in the writings of the Jewish author Abraham Heschel, who says that the prophets proclaimed a theology of the divine pathos, that is, what God cares for. Jürgen Moltmann develops the idea of the pathos of God as a "free relationship of passionate participation."[23]

The cultivation of the heart—a more holistic way of knowing—is the very thing our postmodern culture is inviting.[24] But the biblical response to the postmodern challenge is not to abandon reason but to allow God to evangelize our hearts as well as our heads, to care for what God cares for. As Micah said, "He has showed you, O man, what is good. And what does the Lord require of you? To act justly and to love mercy and to walk humbly with your God" (Mi 6:8). How can theological education cultivate these? Such orthopathic education would require healing the fragmentation of theological knowledge and recovering the view promoted in the Middle Ages that theology is a *habitus*,[25] a disposition of the soul. As a practical knowledge of God unifying head and heart, theology has the character of wisdom. But where do we get wisdom?

### Educating the Heart

It is often conceded that the academy cannot be a solo educator, but there is little evidence that the academy needs the home, the congregation and the marketplace, though all four are linked by God in a daily life system for learning. The first school, of course, is the home. The congregation and the academy are poor substitutes when it comes to the education of the heart. I refer to my own orthopathic education in a story I develop in *Disciplines of the Hungry Heart.*

Though my parents never intended it, their spiritual nurturing included exposing me to the ministry of the poor to the rich. They built our lovely family home on a three-acre plot next door to a one-room shack without water, electricity, indoor plumbing or a furnace. Albert Jupp lived with his aged and ill mother in that smelly, dank shack.

As he was occupied with the care of his mother, Albert was unable to hold down a steady job. Somehow he eked out an existence beside the Stevens, his rich next-door neighbour. Today the rich hardly see the poor except on television or from an air-conditioned tour bus.

Each night Albert would get a pail of water at our outside tap, which was always kept running, even in the dead of winter when our neighbours had their taps safely protected from freezing. My mother was one of the most generous souls on earth, and her sensitive conscience would not allow her to set a fine meal before our family without thinking of Albert and his mother. So night after night I was asked to make a pilgrimage up the hill to the shack with two portions from our table for our poor neighbours. I confess that as a teenager I usually resented doing this. But what I think was bothering me was how that nightly visit to the Jupps made me think about my own existence as a rich young man. Daily I was confronted existentially with the truth that the rich cannot know God well without relating to the poor. My neighbour made an evangelical invitation to my heart.

In a remarkable series of seven sermons on the parable of the rich man and Lazarus, the fourth-century church father, John Chrysostom, addressed the illusions of wealth. In these prophetic sermons, Chrysostom argued that the rich are not owners of their wealth but stewards for the poor.[26] Appealing to the prophets of the Old Testament (Mal 3:8–10), Chrysostom warns about the spiritual dangers of the rich. "The most pitiable person of all," he says, "is the one who lives in luxury and shares his goods with nobody."[27] In contrast, "by nourishing Christ in poverty here and laying up great profit hereafter we will be able to attain the good things which are to come."[28] In this last quotation Chrysostom hints that ministering to the poor simultaneously heals the hearts of the rich and nourishes Jesus. What should be observed is the truth that God has provided for the education of our hearts in love and compassion through our everyday family experiences and through our neighbours. Both are a means of grace.

### Neighbour as Educator

As we have already seen the neighbour becomes a means of grace precisely when the neighbour is taken seriously as a neighbour and not as a means of grace! We cannot simply deal with the poor, the stranger and the outsider in principle, or engage in theoretical or strategic considerations of how to care for our global neighbours. It is in the context of actual neighbour relationships that we are invited to live the life of faith. It is precisely in the unplanned and uncontrollable circumstances of our lives that we can find God and be found by him. Bonhoeffer spoke to this with great depth in a conversation he reports he had with a young French pastor.

> I discovered later, and I'm still discovering right up to this moment, that it is only by living completely in this world that one learns to have faith.

> ...By this worldliness I mean living unreservedly in life's duties, problems, successes and failures, experiences and perplexities. In so doing we throw ourselves completely into the arms of God.[29]

We find God (and get our hearts educated) in the centre of life rather than the circumference. This was the case for Job.

### Passion for God

Job is a stunning example of orthopathy. His school was his life. He, like David, was a man after God's own heart. As he went through test after test, sometimes with obvious weariness, Job began to want God more than he wanted health. Indeed—and this is seldom noted—Job never asked for healing. What he wanted was the friendship of God (Jb 29:4). So most of Job's speeches are directed to God, inquiring of God, challenging God, exploring God, demanding of God, confronting God with holy persistence (Jas 5:11). At times I think his orthodox friends may have hid under the table expecting, God to liquidate him for his impertinence. But in the end the God-talkers were condemned and Job was justified, being blessed with a first-hand experience of God (Jb 42:5). Was this because Job spoke well of God (the primary theological task) by speaking to him boldly, with passionate faith (the primary theological method)?

Job used his experience of the absence of God in order to know God better. P.T. Forsyth once said, "Prayer is to the religious life what original research is for science—by it we get direct contact with reality."[30] Job was not a half-hearted researcher. He took God on, like Abraham pleading, like Jacob refusing to let God go until he had blessed him, like the Syrophoenician woman begging for crumbs under the table, like Paul asking three times for the thorn to be removed, like—dare we say it?—Jesus in the garden exploring his own heart options with the Father until he could freely do the Father's will through submission rather than compliance. Job withstanding God, wrestling with God, extracting revelation from God and in the end knowing God—is this orthopathy? Is this proof-positive that the kingdom of God is not for the mildly interested but the desperate? God-knowers (orthodox, orthopractic theologians) will "take" the kingdom by violent, passionate (orthopathic) faith (Mt 11:12). Luther described the qualifications of a theologian this way: "living, or rather dying and being damned make a theologian, not understanding, reading or speculating."[31] By undergoing the torment of the cross, death and hell, true theology and the knowledge of God comes about. Job, the Old Testament theologian, would say, Amen. Caring for what concerns God, caring for God's concerns in daily life and caring for God above all—this is orthopathy.

Orthodoxy. Orthopraxy. Orthopathy. All three point to the marriage of theology and everyday life: theology and life linked in praise (orthodoxy), practice (orthopraxy) and passion (orthopathy). What God therefore has joined together let no theological institution put asunder.

Might not the most pernicious heresy in the church today be the disharmony between those who claim to be theologically approved but live as practical atheists? Is the greatest challenge not graduating from Regent College, but in the end, at the conclusion of our life-long theological education, having the Lord say, "I know you?" Would not the most fearful failure be to have God say, "I never knew you" (Mt 7:23; 25:12)?

One of the desert fathers[32] was approached by an eager young student who said, "Abba, give me a word from God." The wise mentor asked if the student would agree not to come back until he had fully lived the word.

"Yes," the eager young student said.

"Then this is the word of God: 'You shall love the Lord your God with all your heart, soul strength and mind.'" The young man disappeared, it seemed forever.

Twenty-five years later the student had the temerity to come back. "I have lived the word you gave. Do you have another word?"

"Yes," said the desert father. "But once again you must not come back until you have lived it."

"I agree."

"Love your neighbour as yourself."

The student never came back.

## Endnotes

[1] Lesslie Newbigin, *Foolishness to the Greeks: The Gospel and Western Culture* (Grand Rapids: Eerdmans, 1986), 142–143.

[2] The working definition of theological education developed within the Coalition for the Ministry in Daily Life is as follows: "Theological education

for all the people of God is the life-long, life-based (rooted in life and not abstracted), and life-oriented (directed toward the totality of life) process of forming and transforming persons, communities, organizations and institutions into Christian maturity for the purpose of serving God and God's purposes in the world." "Consultation on Ministry in Daily Life: Task Group Report" (November 14, 1992).

[3] William Perkins, *The Golden Chain* (1592), in *The Work of William Perkins*, ed. Ian Breward (Appleford, England: Courtney Press, 1970), 177.

[4] From an unpublished lecture delivered at Regent College (September 1992, Vancouver, BC).

[5] This is the title of the excellent book authored by my friend Robert Banks (Victor Books, 1993).

[6] P.T.Forsyth, *The Soul of Prayer* (London: The Independent Press, 1916/1954), 11.

[7] Robert Farrar Capon, *An Offering of Uncles: The Priesthood of Adam and the Shape of the World* (New York: Crossroad, 1982), 163.

[8] A strand of witness through the Old and New Testaments points to education in the thick of life and in the context of daily ministry: the family as the primary educational unit; the reinforcement of public festivals; structured patterns of instruction through creeds and stories; the schools of the prophets; congregational instruction in the synagogue; the disciple community around Jesus engaged in action as well as withdrawal for reflection; Paul's travelling seminary with his missionary co-workers (Timothy, Gaius, Tychicus and Trophimus); the Hall of Tyrannus as education in the marketplace (Acts 19:9–10); and the local household churches, undoubtedly the primary place for the education of the whole people of God.

[9] Craig Dykstra, "Reconceiving Practice," in *Shifting Boundaries,* ed. Barbara Wheeler and Edward Farley (Louisville, KY: Westminster/John Knox, 1991), 35–66. Dykstra defines a Christian practice (as distinct from activities) as inherently cooperative (not a solo action), inherently good (generates value) and inherently revelatory (bears epistemological weight). Unfortunately he then lists as Christian practices those activities that could appear obviously to be done in the name of Jesus: interpreting Scripture, worship and prayer, confession and reconciliation, service, witness, social criticism and the mutual bearing of suffering (45, 48).

[10] While the Bible offers several models of and contexts for theological education, there are some consistent themes: (1) it is community-oriented rather than individualistic; (2) it is cooperative rather than competitive; (3) it

is life-centred rather than school-based; (4) it is transformational rather than exclusively informational; (5) it is life-long rather than seasonal, packaged and concentrated; (6) it is available to all the people of God rather than to a clerical elite; and (7) it is concerned with equipping the people of God both for service in the church (the *ecclesia*) and for societal service to God (the *diaspora*).

[11] Extensive research and theological reflection on the congregation as the centre for spiritual and theological formation has recently taken place. Representative of this are the following: Craig Dykstra, "Reconceiving Practice," in *Shifting Boundaries,* ed. Barbara Wheeler and Edward Farley; Edward Farley, *Theologia: The Fragmentation and Unity of Theological Education* (Philadelphia: Fortress Press, 1983); Joseph C. Hough and Barbara Wheeler, eds., *Beyond Clericalism: The Congregation as a Focus for Theological Education* (Atlanta: Scholars Press, 1988).

[12] I attribute this thought to a formative paper delivered by Dr. F. W. Waters in 1962, "Knowing God Through Thinking and Service," a presentation that started my own journey of integration.

[13] See Max Stackhouse's discussion of *theoria, praxis* and *poesis* in Max Stackhouse, *Apologia: Contextualization, Globalization, and Mission in Theological Education* (Grand Rapids: Eerdmans, 1988). His approach does not negate the importance of straight thinking. Indeed he critiques liberation theology for its faulty *theoria* on pages 84–105.

[14] Ray S. Anderson, *The Praxis of Pentecost: Revisioning the Church's Life and Mission* (Downers Grove, IL: InterVarsity Press, 1993), 196.

[15] Philip S. Keane and Melanie A. May, "What Is the Character of Teaching, Learning, and the Scholarly Task in the Good Theological School?" *Theological Education* 30, no. 2 (Spring 1994): 40.

[16] Quoted in Ludwig von Bertalanffy, *General System Theory* (New York: George Braziller, 1968), 101.

[17] The reflection that was inspired by this practice is documented in R. Paul Stevens, *Liberating the Laity* (Downers Grove, IL: InterVarsity Press, 1985).

[18] Eberhard Jüngel, *The Freedom of a Christian: Luther's Significance for Contemporary Theology* (Minneapolis: Augsburg Press, 1988), 22.

[19] William Tyndale, "A Parable of the Wicked Mammon" (1527), in *Treatises and Portions of Holy Scripture* (Cambridge: Parker Society, 1848), 98, 104.

[20] Martin Luther, "Treatise on Good Works," in *Luther's Works*, vol. 44, trans. W. A. Lambert, ed. James Atkinson (Philadelphia: Fortress Press, 1966), 26–27.

[21] Alfons Auer, *Open to the World: An Analysis of Lay Spirituality*, trans.

Dennis Doherty and Carmel Callaghan, (Baltimore: Helicon Press, 1966), 230 (italics mine).

[22] Gustavo Gutierrez, *On Job: God-Talk and the Suffering of the Innocent*, trans. Matthew J. O'Connell (Maryknoll, NY: Orbis Books, 1987), 87.

[23] Jürgen Moltmann, *The Trinity and the Kingdom*, trans. Margaret Kohl (Minneapolis: Fortress Pres, 1993), 25.

[24] See Stanley J. Grenz, "StarTrek and the Next Generation: Postmodernism and the Future of Evangelical Theology Today," *Crux* 30, no. 1 (March 1994): 24–32.

[25] Farley, "Interpreting Situations," 18.

[26] St. John Chrysostom, *On Wealth and Poverty*, trans. Catherine P. Roth (Crestwood, NY: St. Vladimir's Seminary Press, 1984), 50.

[27] Ibid., 57.

[28] Ibid., 55 (emphasis mine).

[29] Dietrich Bonhoeffer, in a letter from Tegel prison in 1944, quoted in Melanie Morrison, "As One Who Stands Convicted," *Sojourners* (May 1979): 15.

[30] Peter T. Forsyth, *The Soul of Prayer* (London: The Independent Press, 1916; reprint 1954), 78.

[31] *D. M. Luthers Werke,* Kritische Gesamtausgabe (Weimer, 1993— ), 5. 163: 28–29, quoted in Alister E. McGrath, *Luther's Theology of the Cross: Martin Luther's Theological Breakthrough* (Oxford: Basil Blackwell, 1985), 152.

[32] This story was cited by Dr. James Houston in a public lecture. The source is unknown.

# ON THE ABOLITION OF THE LAITY:

# TOWARD A TRINITARIAN THEOLOGY OF THE

# PEOPLE OF GOD

From Crux, *vol. 31, no. 2 (June 1995)*

George Bernard Shaw once said that every profession is a conspiracy against the laity. But there is a problem with this cynical remark when it is applied to the church. It is utterly pointless to launch a conspiracy against something that no longer exists. The New Testament does not reveal two peoples: the professional clergy (those who are superior, gifted and powerful) and the laity (those who are inferior, untrained and powerless). Rather there is one people: the laity, the Greek word being *laos*. And *laos* includes the leaders. Moreover the leaders, like the led, are first and foremost members of the laity and share the exquisite honour of the people of God (1 Pt 2:9–10). Indeed the cultivation of professionalism by leaders of the church—a matter not considered in this paper—is incongruous with the essentially amateur nature of all Christian service. It is the work of love, as proposed by the root meaning of "amateur." To recover a biblical perspective on the people of God we may need to abolish both the words laity and clergy. We may also need to reinvent language to express the dignity and duty of the ordinary Christian. In preparation for this we must first examine the biblical data, then reflect theologically on the identity and vocation of the people of God and finally consider what this all means.

## Biblical Data: A People Without Laity or Clergy

New Testament authors rejected two down-putting "laity" words available to them when describing the people of God under the newly reconstituted covenant:

1) The word *laikos*—"belonging to the common people"—is not used at all in the New Testament. It was first used to describe Christians by Clement of Rome at the end of the first century. He used "layman" (*laikos*) in his epistle to the Corinthians to describe the place of laity in worship when the presbyters were being deprived of their functions.[1] Alexandre Faivre notes both the military comparison—commander-in-chief—and the allusion to the Old Testament cultic hierarchy,[2] two obvious sources of the clergy-lay distinction that would be later institutionalized in the church. This first use of "layman" by a Christian passed largely unnoticed and it was not until much later, with Clement of Alexandria and Tertullian, that the term emerged again.[3] The term does not appear either in the writings of Justin Martyr (AD 150)—for whom the title "Christian" was sufficient[4]—or Irenaeus (AD 180).[5]

2) The word *idiōtēs*, root of the English word "idiot," means "layperson in contrast to an expert or specialist." This pejorative word is much closer to Bernard Shaw's use of the term "laity." But this term is never used by an inspired apostle to describe Christians.[6] In Acts 4:13 members of the Jewish Sanhedrin expressed their amazement that these "unschooled, ordinary men" (in this case the *idiotai* were Peter and John) could preach with eloquent power. The word is also used in 1 Corinthians 14:23 to describe the person from outside the church who comes into a Christian meeting totally uninitiated and cannot understand what is going on. Here *idiōtēs* refers to people who are not yet Christians. So neither of the two available negative words—*laikos* and *idiōtēs*—is used to describe ordinary Christians. Instead two other words are employed.

The Greek word *laos* originally meant "the crowd" and "the people as a nation." It was eventually employed in the Greek translation of the Old Testament (LXX) as the universal designation for "the people of God," translating the Hebrew *'am*.[7] This word may be properly translated "laity" but to do so we would need to reinvent the word. It does not mean "untrained" or "ordinary" but "the people of God"—a truly extraordinary people. It is fundamental to note that while we observe in the church today two classes of people separated by education, ordination[8] and intonation—the "laity" (who receive the ministry) and the clergy (who give the ministry)—we discover in the New Testament one ministering people with leaders, also members of the *laos,* serving them to equip the people for the work of the ministry (Eph 4:11–12).[9]

Remarkably, the second word used to describe the whole people of God is the Greek word *kleros,* the word from which our English "clergy" is derived. The word means "assigned by lot or inheritance" and is used for the privileges and appointment of all the people of God (Col 1:12; Eph 1:11; Gal 3:29). With the exception of Ignatius of Antioch (who used *kleros* to describe the martyr), the term was not used for "clergy" until the third century. Simultaneously, the term "laity" reappears. As Alexandre Faivre shows, laypersons can only exist when they have an opposite against which they can define themselves and, until the second century, there simply was no such opposite![10] Of considerable interest to us is the reflection of a Jewish scholar, Reuven Kimelman, who argues that the reality of being away from the Temple during the exile and the ultimate fall of Jerusalem provided the Jewish community with the social and theological opportunity to "appropriate the original divine charge to become a kingdom of priests."[11] The rabbis attempted not to make the Jewish community into a democracy (thereby levelling the clergy) but to raise all the people to become priests and rabbis together. This Jewish vision of every-member ministry was still something less than the vision of the New Testament.

The church in the New Testament has no "lay people" in the usual sense of that word and is full of "clergy" in the true sense of that word. A biblical theology of the laity must communicate this. As Alexandre Faivre says:

> One searches the New Testament in vain for a theology of the laity. Neither laymen [*sic*] nor priests can be found in it, at least in the sense in which we understand those words today. The inheritance was a joint inheritance, shared equally between all the heirs. The people experience their vocation as believers collectively. The lot which God had promised since the time of Abraham and distributed in Christ was not divided unequally. The elders, those presbyters who could not be called priests, were not in control of that lot as though they were masters. They had to take care to be models that would make it possible for the members of the *kleros* to identify themselves as chosen people.[12]

The church as a whole is the true ministerium, a community of prophets, priests and princes/princesses serving God through Jesus in the power of the Spirit seven days a week. All are clergy in the sense of being appointed by God to service and dignified as God's inheritance. All are laity in the sense of having their identity rooted in the people of God. All give ministry. All receive ministry. That is the constitution of the church. But when we step into the modern church we see something quite different.

Deeply ingrained in the culture of the modern church is the belief that the "full-time ministry" is the highest human vocation. From the perspective of the New Testament, however, a part-time option has never been available! If, it is thought, one is not able to "go into the ministry," a second-best alternative is to spend one's discretionary time in church-related activities. Equipping thus gets reduced to making para-clergy out of the rest of the members of the church in order to assist "the minister" instead of the pastor becoming an assistant to the people for their ministry in the church and world. Not surprisingly, few businesspeople, for example, think of themselves as full-time ministers in the marketplace. Fewer still are encouraged in this by their churches. Hardly anyone gets commissioned to their service in the world.[13] Christians in the first century would have found such a state of affairs anachronistic—a throw-back to the situation before Christ came when only a few in Israel knew the Lord, when only one tribe was named as priests, when only a select few heard the call of God on their lives. Nothing but a Copernican revolution of the mind and heart can change this state of affairs.

## Toward a Trinitarian Theology of the Laity

To accomplish this transformation a theology *of* the laity that is also a theology *by* the laity[14] must be written, articulated and embodied. But this theology must not merely explore the identity and vocation of the non-clergy portion of the people. As such it would be a compensatory theology attempting to overcome seventeen centuries of clericalism. Reactionary theology is neither life-giving nor peaceable, and it is the recovery of the unity of God's people that is at stake. The apostle Paul was faced in his own day with something roughly parallel to clericalism, namely performance of the law as a means of gaining righteousness and defining membership. Paul's approach to the problem gives us an important clue. Paul went behind discussions of the law to rediscover something that *preceded* the law and gave it meaning—namely, the promise (Gal 3:15–18). In a biblical theology of the laity we must get behind the clergy-lay problem that has plagued the church since the third century and find out what God originally intended for his people.[15] To do this we must explore, first, the meaning of the Trinity and, second, the original intention of God for his creatures on earth. We will take up each of these two matters in turn.

A fully trinitarian approach is needed since the identity and ministry of the *laos* is shaped by the God whose people we are. God has called out "a *laos* for himself" (Acts 15:14), or as the KJV puts it, "a people for his name." If the identity of the *laos* comes from the Trinity, the vocation of the *laos* comes from God's original mandate to his creatures so that becoming *laos* will mean fulfilling the human vocation on earth. This human vocation, which I have elsewhere called "the covenant mandate,"[16] is substantially restored by Christ's salvation and constitutes the ministry of the people of God. In this way both the being and the doing, both the identity and the vocation of the *laos* will be considered.

The ministry of the *laos* is not generated exclusively by the people, whether from duty or gratitude. All ministry is God's ministry. God continues his own ministry through his people, a matter Roy Bell clearly expounds in his unpublished paper.[17] This ministry begins not when we "join the church" to help God do his work but when we join God (Jn 1:12) and have "fellowship with the Father and with his Son" (1 Jn 1:3). *Laos* ministry is participation in the in-going ministry of God (relationally among God the Father, Son and Holy Spirit), and simultaneously participation in the out-going (sending) ministry of God. On this latter point Jesus prayed in the high priestly prayer, "As you sent me into the world, I have sent them into the world" (Jn 17:18). On the first (the in-going) God is "lover, the beloved and the love itself," as Jürgen Moltmann puts it.[18] On the second, God is sender, sent and the sending.

So there was ministry before there was a world, that ministry taking place within God himself (Jn 17:5, 24). This pre-creation ministry was neither curative nor redemptive. There was nothing broken or fallen to restore even though "the lamb slain from the foundation of the world" (Rv 13:8) is an evocative hint of God's redemptive willingness. God's ministry is creative and unitive (Rv 17:21–23) and not only curative and redemptive, thus constituting a broader definition of service and relationship than is normally ascribed to the term "ministry." Like their God, the people of God have ministry that is both restorative and creative, both curative and unitive—thus challenging the common evangelical preoccupation with the Great Commission (Mt 28:19–20) as the exclusive definition of ministry, as important as that mandate is.

To this rich understanding of peoplehood and ministry each of the three persons of the Godhead contributes. The Father creates, providentially sustains and forms a covenantal framework for all existence. The Son incarnates, transfigures and redeems. The Spirit empowers and fills with God's own presence. But each shares in the others—coinheres, interpenetrates, cooperates—so that it is theologically inappropriate to stereotype the ministry of any one. But that is exactly what is done.

Christians tend to "play favourites" when it comes to describing peoplehood and ministry.[19] For order, providence, and sustaining the structures of society, we appeal to the Father. The Son is associated with redemption and winning the lost. The Holy Spirit is the favourite of those seeking renewal, empowering charisms and direct religious experience. Churches and denominations tend to form around one of the three: Father-denominations emphasize reverent worship and stewardship; Son-denominations stress discipleship and evangelism, thus furthering the work of the Kingdom of God; Spirit-denominations promote gifts and graces. The implications of this specialist approach for peoplehood, vocation and leadership in the church can be expressed in the following diagram:

|  | PEOPLEHOOD | VOCATION | LEADERSHIP |
| --- | --- | --- | --- |
| **FATHER** | Covenant Community | Creational Stewardship | Hierarchical |
| **SON** | Kingdom Community | Christocratic Service (continuing works of Jesus) | Servant |
| **SPIRIT** | Charismatic Community | Exercising Gifts Empowerment | Charismatic |

A rich and full doctrine of the Trinity avoids such stereotypical designations. God is more than the sum of the three. God is not God apart from the way the Father, Son and Holy Spirit give and receive from each other what they essentially are. "One God"—the primary confession of Islam—is ironically the Christian's deepest praise. We affirm that God is more one *because* he is three. Within the limitations of rational discourse, and recognizing that if we could fit God into our puny minds he would be too small a God to worship, we respectfully confess that the unity of the Holy Trinity is neither a homogenized unity that blurs the distinctions nor a collective. As is often noted in the history of theological reflection, the Orthodox church started with the diversity and made the unity of God a matter of doxology, while the Western church started with an abstract notion of unity and struggled to grasp rationally the possibility of diversity. The net result of this latter effort is that God appears to be one in spite of being Father, Son and Holy Spirit. A biblical approach reverently affirms the opposite. God is one *because* he is three.

In the same way Paul affirmed that diversity and unity thrive together in the people who bear God's name. Paul's point in 1 Corinthians 12 contradicted the Corinthian preoccupation with one

Spirit-manifestation—tongues—as the litmus test of true spirituality. Instead Paul affirmed that diversity is what the body is about.[20] The *laos* does not have a "mashed potato" unity as is sometimes alleged but a rich social unity in which each member becomes more himself or herself through experiencing an out-of-oneself (*ek-static*) community life. Unity is not the means to the end—a practical necessity to get the church's work done. Unity is the end, the goal, the ministry itself.[21]

Three biblical metaphors expound this: the body of Christ, the family of God and the covenant community.[22]

## The Recovery of a Trinitarian Identity

To be *laos* then is not merely to be a bouquet of Christians or a cluster of saints.[23] To be *laos* means simultaneously to be communal and personal. In the long history of trinitarian reflection this supreme idea of the personal and interpersonal within God forms the true basis for the identity and vocation of the God-imaging people. One insight in particular is illuminating.

The Cappadocian Fathers (Basil, Gregory of Nyssa and Gregory of Nazianzus from the fourth century) taught that the essence of God is relational, that God exists in a plurality of distinct persons united in communion. They avoided the twin dangers of collectivism and individualism by speaking of *perichoresis* (reciprocity, interchange, giving and receiving without blurring). *Perichoresis* involves a relatedness that is both static and dynamic. As Edwin Hui notes: "The three persons of the Trinity [are] 'being in one another'—drawn to the other, contained in the other, interpenetrating each other by drawing life from and pouring life to each other—as the communion of love."[24]

Colin Gunton speaks of "reciprocity, interpenetration and *interanimation*" since he finds the Latin derivative, "co-inherence," less satisfactory, suggesting as it does a more static conception.[25] The heart of the matter is the sociality of the Triune God, an elegant truth sometimes expressed through the metaphor of family: three Persons, one family.[26] The net effect of this recovery of perichoretic reflection is doxological reflection on the Triune God under the category of community rather than individuality. Commenting on John Damascene's doctrine of *perichoresis*, Jürgen Moltmann put the matter this way: "The doctrine of the *perichoresis* links together in a brilliant way the threeness and the unity, without reducing the threeness to the unity, or dissolving the unity in the threeness."[27]

The implications of this for peoplehood are substantial. Being *laos* means that members of Christ coinhere, interanimate and pour life into one another without coalescence or merger. It means belonging communally without being communistic or being a collective. Moreover, and pertinent to the clergy-lay dilemma, being a *perichoretic* people means being a community without hierarchy. The community of Father, Son and Holy Spirit finds its earthly reflection, as Moltmann says, "not in the autocracy of a single ruler but in the democratic community of free people, not in the lordship of man over the woman but in their equal mutuality, not in an ecclesiastical hierarchy but in a fellowship church."[28] Indeed, when trinitarian theology was adopted without *perichoresis*, as in the case of the Eastern church, there developed a thoroughly hierarchical approach to church life. A perichoretic community can have leadership and rich diversity without hierarchy;[29] it can be a community without superiors and subordinates; it can be a church without laity or clergy—in the usual sense of these terms.

Three conclusions may be drawn from this:

*First, there is no such thing as an individual layperson.* If, as I have proposed above, we live out the Christian life interdependently, "the individual Christian" is an oxymoron. Consistent with the Old Testament, the "saints" in Paul's letters is really a unit. "The saints" is the church, which is the body of Christ. As Ernest Best says, "it is this unit which is just as much in Christ as the individual believer."[30] Believers are held together in what can be conceived as a corporate, inclusive personality. It is biblically inconceivable for a person to be a believer in Christ and not a member of his community. And the body of Christ is not the local congregation but the whole church.[31]

Ernest Best summarizes Paul's thoughts aptly: "For Paul there is no such thing as a solitary Christian; the faith that unites a man to Christ unites him also to other Christians; the Church is more than an aggregate of Christians; it is a fellowship..."[32] He continues: "It is impossible to conceive of a Christian who is not a member of the Church, which is related to Christ as in him and as his body...Individual Christians consequently do not exist."[33]

This is remarkably in harmony with the message given to John Wesley by a "serious man" before Wesley was converted to Christ: "Sir, you wish to serve God and go to heaven? Remember that you cannot serve him alone. You must therefore find companions or make them; the Bible knows nothing of solitary religion."[34]

The believer's identity is corporate as well as individual. In Christ we can say, "I am us!" Within the granular individualism of Western culture, the basic unit of the church is the individual member. For Paul the basic unit of the church is the church!

*Second, there is no hierarchy of ministries.* In his seminal work on the theology of the laity, Hendrik Kraemer says, "All members of the *ecclesia* have in principle the same calling, responsibility and dignity, have their part in the apostolic and ministerial nature and calling of the church."[35] Incarnating our loving submission to Christ's lordship in every arena of life precludes saying that certain tasks are in themselves holy and others are sacred. *Laos* theology is not only concerned about the work of the ministry but also the ministry of work. William Tyndale, the English reformer, was considered heretical and executed for teaching, among other things, that "there is not work better than another to please God; to pour water, to wash dishes, to be a souter [cobbler], or an apostle, all are one; to wash dishes and to preach are all one, as touching the deed, to please God."[36] That is not simply saying that Luther's dairy-maid was called to milk cows[37] but that the call to live for God and his kingdom may come to us anywhere and be expressed anywhere (1 Cor 7:17, 20).[38]

*Third, supported Christian ministry is not the vocation of vocations but merely one way of responding to the single call that comes to all* (Eph 4:1). Most expositions about ministry are magnetically attracted to the supreme place of the ordained professional minister as the minister-par-excellence. It is small wonder that laypersons aspiring to ministry attempt to become amateur clergypersons or para-clergy. There is some reason for this. Work in the church is strategically more important than work in the world because the church is the prototype community and the outcropping of the Kingdom of God, but work in the church is only important in view of what its members will do and be in society. Church leadership must be evaluated not in terms of its priestly character but on whether the saints are equipped for the work of the ministry (Eph 4:11–12).

Until now we have been exploring the identity of the *laos* as a God-imaging people in its relationality. We turn now to the question of the vocation of the *laos* in restoring God's original purpose for humankind on earth. Not surprisingly the relational quality most characteristic of God and therefore also of his God-imaging people in both their identity and vocation is love.

## The Recovery of the Amateur Vocation

Meditations on the triune God take us inevitably to the profound revelation of John 17. In that chapter Christ reflects on the love the Father had for him even before the creation of the world (17:24) and prays that the Father's love may be in the disciples (17:26) while disciples and Master, disciple and disciple, and Son and Father all mutually indwell one another (17:22–23, 26). This gives new and deeper meaning to the well-worn text, "God is love" (1 Jn 4:16). Love is not merely an attribute of God, but love is who God is and what God does. That is what was affirmed by Jürgen Moltmann's reflection on a line by Augustine in the words quoted above, proclaiming that God is "lover, the beloved and the love itself."[39] This was also expressed by the trinitarian theologian John Duns Scotus (c. 1265–1308) when he affirmed that creation and redemption flow out of the love within God himself. The world was made by love, runs on love and will end with a glorious eternal love-in. In the same way love is the being and the doing of the *laos*.

Elsewhere[40] I have written about recovering the amateur status of the Christian in terms of the three full-time love-works of God's people. What Christ produces by his glorious redemption is not a new generation of angels but truly human beings and the beginnings of a renewed creation. In other words, the dignity of being *laos* is nothing more or less than becoming as substantially as possible in this life the people God originally intended his first human family to be. The first two chapters of Genesis are foundational to our understanding of this. Adam and Eve[41] are the prototype amateurs—those who work and serve for love. They are also the prototype Christians. They needed no commandment to love God with all their heart and their neighbour as themselves (Mt 22:34–40). That law was written on their hearts, as natural to them as breathing. Within that single love vocation they were given three full-time expressions—all of them for love: communion, community-building and co-creativity. Having all three is important. I share the un-ease of those who are not comfortable with reducing the salvation of Christ to this: the Great Commission invites people to become new creatures in Christ in order that they may now fulfil the original creation mandate of Genesis 1:27–29. As we are about to see, being Christians and being the *laos* of God is more than having dominion over fish, genetic engineering and the media—all part of the creation mandate but less than the full human vocation. Becoming Christian involves being restored to *all* that it means to be people and family on earth.

*First, there is the call to communion with God.* The first work of Adam and Eve is described rather than prescribed. Implicit in their humanity is the commission to work at communion with God. The man and the woman experienced the uninterrupted presence of God in a relationship of loving awe. The text suggests that the garden was not raw wilderness but a sanctuary-garden, a place of real meeting with God.[42] No activity was intended to take them away from their centre, though, like all relationships, there were seasons of special intimacy, as suggested by God's walking in the garden in the cool of the day looking for his creatures' fellowship (Gn 3:8). The practice of the presence of God is not the exclusive vocation of professional ministers and cloistered monks but every Christian's preoccupation.

*Second, there is the call to community-building.* This full-time work is also described but not prescribed. God's first negative statement in the Bible is that "it is not good for the man to be alone" (Gn 2:18). God judges man's solitariness. So God makes a "helper suitable for him" (2:18). God makes humankind innately social and inevitably sexual. "In the image of God he created him, male and female he created them" (Gn 1:27). The image of God is relational. We were built for community. Community-building is every person's vocation. Humankind is invited continuously to celebrate co-humanity, living in grateful awareness of the fact that neither male nor female can be the image of God alone. This brings new meaning to the affirmation that "God is love" (1 Jn 4:16), for it expresses the symmetry of the relational life within God as Trinity and the relational life of his creatures: "Whoever lives in love lives in God, and God in him." The family becomes God's prototype community on earth and is part of every person's vocational calling, whether one remains single or gets married. People-making (Gn 1:28) gives Adam and Eve the further privilege of making people in their own image (Gn 5:3) as God made them in his. With the birth of Seth and Seth's son, people "began to call on the name of the Lord" (Gn 4:26), thus becoming truly the people of God.

So humankind's duty and destiny is to build community, to express neighbourliness, to celebrate co-humanity—in a word, to love. We dare not relegate this to discretionary time activities. For example, it would be dangerous for me to think of myself as a part-time husband or a part-time grandfather. Some will earn their salary in community-building by being town planners or family counsellors, just as others will earn it by evangelism or carpentry. The way one earns one's living turns out to be incidental. The truth is that Christian vocation demands our all, all the time. The call of God that comes to every believer (Eph 4:1) embraces all of life: work, family, neighbourhood, politics and congregation.

*Third, there is the call to co-creativity.*[43] Adam and Eve were made regents, earthly rulers representing the interests of a heavenly king. They were to work not only *for* God but *with* God in making God's world work. In one sense they were made for the world, rather than the world for them, as suggested by the phrase, "there was no man to work the ground" (Gn 2:5). The human task of cultivating and enculturing the earth included everything from farming to genetic engineering, from landscape architecture to playing the flute (Gn 4:21). Eventually, Adam's children would do some of these things for a living. But, as I have said, that is incidental, because earth-keeping is everyone's full-time job.

Communion, community-building and co-creativity—this expresses the vocation and ministry of the *laos* of God. How is our sense of vocation enriched by a trinitarian understanding of God? First, we experience *communion* by becoming co-lovers of God. By the miracle of adoption we are drawn into the love-life within God himself. This is the heart of "loving God" and the essence of spirituality. Second, through *community-building* we become lovers of one another. To live *perichoretically* means to reject individualism and to live with a molecular identity—loving neighbour, family and friend. Many do not think of this as "ministry," "service" or "priesthood," but it is. It is holy ministry to play with one's children or to listen to a friend. Indeed, a theology of the laity must inform us of the theology and spirituality of our everyday relationships.[44] Third, *co-creativity* draws us into God's love for the world (Jn 3:16). The purpose of creation is the glorification of God.[45] Creation is expressive of God's character, an overflow of the love within God himself. The world was "created to be transfigured and glorified through the Spirit at the end."[46] Incarnation is the highest expression of nature and not only what God did to redeem the world. So a truly biblical theology of the laity is not only a rescue effort but lines up with God's purposes for the world. What is truly astounding is that humankind has, through the Spirit's irruption in our lives, the privilege of participating in the creative work of God.

"Only a layperson" is a phrase that must never be found on our lips. It is irreverent and demeaning. It denies that God has adopted, called, empowered and gifted us to receive the incredible privilege of being co-lovers of God, lovers of one another and those who share God's love for the world. This is our identity—a molecular social identity. The Duke of Windsor, recalling his upbringing in the royal house of King George V, claimed that every day his father would say, "Never forget who you are." Better yet, is never to forget *whose* we are. We are not *laikoi* or *idiōtēs*. We are *laos* and *kleros*. "Laity" in the popular sense no longer exists in Christ. It is useless to mount a conspiracy against it by promoting professionalism in ministry. It is equally ludicrous to liberate such a laity. Why try to liberate what is no longer alive? That people—segmented into higher and lower, subject and object of ministry, ministers and "their" people—no longer exists except as a tragic anachronism. Instead, there is the *laos* of the Triune God. We get our identity and our vocation from being the people of the Triune God. And the ministry of that people is to love and be loved. It is so sublimely simple that we could miss its reverent beauty and its life-giving potential.

## Endnotes

[1] Remarkably the only occasion I have discovered in the Old Testament where "lay people" is used in the NIV (2 Chr 35:5, 7) refers to this exact situation: the people of God who were not of the priestly tribe of Levi. In fact this English translation skews the meaning of the original towards a down-putting meaning and should be translated simply, "the rest of the people."

[2] Alexandre Faivre, *The Emergence of the Laity in the Early Church* (New York: Paulist Press, 1990), 15–24.

[3] Ibid., 22.

[4] Ibid., 26–35.

[5] Ibid., 35–40.

[6] I regret the unfortunate mistake in *Liberating the Laity* (Downers Grove: InterVarsity Press, 1995) on page 21 in which this word was used to describe the whole people of God.

[7] 1 Pt 2:9; Acts 15:14; Rom 9:25.

[8] Ordination as a rite or ceremony that conferred power or office simply did not exist in the New Testament. See Marjorie Warkentin, *Ordination: A Biblical, Historical View* (Grand Rapids: Eerdmans, 1982), 172. For a theological/philosophical defence of ordination, though not convincing to me, read Thomas F. Torrance, "The Ministry," in Ray S. Anderson, ed., *Theological Foundations for Ministry* (Grand Rapids: Eerdmans, 1979), 405–429.

[9] See Gordon D. Fee, "*Laos* and Leadership Under the New Covenant," *Crux* 25 no. 4 (December 1989) : 3–13.

[10] Faivre, *The Emergence of the Laity*, 23.

[11] Reuven Kimelman, "Judaism and Lay Ministry," *The NICM Journal* 5, no 2 (Spring 1980), 43.

[12] Faivre, *The Emergence of the Laity*, 7–8.

[13] See Jim Stockard, "Commissioning the Ministries of the Laity: How It Works and Why It Isn't Being Done," in *The Laity in Ministry: The Whole People of God for the Whole World*, ed. George Peck and John S. Hoffman, (Valley Forge: Judson Press, 1984), 71–79.

[14] The theologies of the laity to this date have been attempted from the academic viewpoint and normally do not express doing theology both "from above" and "from below" or express partnership between the professional theologian and the reflective person in the world. A brief summary is as follows: In 1958 Hendrik Kraemer authored his seminal prolegomena on *A Theology of the Laity*, partly to offer a Protestant equivalent to Yves Congar's *Laity, Church and World*, translated from the French in 1960. Mark Gibbs and T. Ralph Morton authored the revolutionary *God's Frozen People* in 1964. But little of substance was published until 1980, when Richard Mouw in *Called to Worldly Holiness* attempted a short sequel to Kraemer's volume. My friend Robert Banks authored *All the Business of Life* in 1987 (now reprinted in North America under the title *Redeeming the Routine*) with an important chapter on "A People's Theology." Greg Ogden in *The New Reformation* (1990) has summarized in popular form much of what has been said by many of us and has also advanced some practical applications. The Catholic William Rademacher has authored a truly penetrating critique of his church's neglect of the laity (in the old sense of the word) in *Lay Ministry: A Theological, Spiritual and Pastoral: Handbook* (1991). But there has not yet been written in the twentieth century a substantial theology of the laity, let alone one by the laity.

[15] Some of this discussion I owe to a conversation with Dr. Ray S. Anderson of Fuller Theological Seminary.

[16] R. Paul Stevens, "The Covenant Mandate" (unpublished lecture, Regent College, Vancouver, 1987).

[17] "Ministry is God's ministry as Father, Son and Spirit, arising out of His nature and being and not ours. It is ministry by Him, for Him and to Him. He is its source, its life, its goal and sustenance. It arises out of community and is service to the world. It recognizes that all ecclesiology is Christological and never an end in itself. That community is kenotic and ek-static. The ministry is of the entire community without class distinction. It expresses solidarity with the world and is lived transcendence in the world. The ministry becomes as a result, God's presence in the world seeking not only to model but be an Incarnational ministry seeking to bring reconciliation and grace, not simply in the narrow sense of personal reconciliation to God, but to bring genuine liberation in an alienated world that, because it is alienated in every aspect, needs God's Word in every aspect. Because it is God's ministry sustained by

His character and being, it is a ministry that must be Incarnational, kerygmatic and diakonal. When it is that kind of ministry involved in real proclamation in every dimension and open in its dialogue, matters like success and failure become irrelevant and viewed out of an entirely different perspective" (Roy D. Bell, "A Theology of Ministry" [unpublished manuscript, Carey Theological College, Vancouver, March 1984], 12).

[18] Jürgen Moltmann, *The Trinity and the Kingdom*, trans. Margaret Kohl (San Francisco: Harper and Row, 1991), 32.

[19] For example, Kraemer reduces the church to a Christocratic community, thus neglecting the full participation of Father and Son.

[20] See Gordon D. Fee, *The First Epistle to the Corinthians* (Grand Rapids: Eerdmans, 1987), 569–625.

[21] Eph 1:10; 4:13; Jn 17:22; Col 1:17,20.

[22] See Phil Collins and R. Paul Stevens, *The Equipping Pastor: A Systems Approach to Congregational Leadership* (Washington, DC: Alban Institute, 1993), 92–107. See also R. Paul Stevens, "Analogy or Homology? An Investigation of the Congruency of Systems Theory and Biblical Theology in Pastoral Leadership," *Journal of Psychology and Theology* 22, no. 3 (1994): 173–181.

[23] A great significance is the fact that "saints" (e.g., Eph 4:12) is always a corporate term, not merely a number of individual believers.

[24] Edwin Hui (unpublished notes, "Trinity and Christian Life," Regent College, Vancouver).

[25] Colin Gunton, *The One, the Three and the Many: God, Creation and the Culture of Modernity* (Cambridge: Cambridge University Press, 1993), 163 (emphasis mine).

[26] Jürgen Moltmann suggests that the analogy is not arbitrary since the divine image is person with person—which is exactly what family is all about. Indeed Gregory of Nazianzus saw Adam, Eve and Seth as an earthly parable because they were consubstantial persons (Moltmann, *The Trinity and the Kingdom,* 199).

[27] Ibid., 175.

[28] Ibid., viii.

[29] *Perichoresis* means that the submission of the Son to the Father is not subordination but the quality of the way the Son relates to the Father. No hierarchy is implied. In line with Athanathius we affirm that monarchy is in God not just the Father, and that *archē* in the Father does not mean hierarchy (Edwin Hui, "Perichoresis," [unpublished lecture notes, "The Trinity and the

Christian Life," Regent College, Vancouver, 1994]).

[30] Ernest Best, *One Body in Christ: A Study in the Relationship of the Church to Christ in the Epistles of the Apostle Paul* (London: S.P.C.K., 1955), 25.

[31] Ibid., 113.

[32] Ibid., 193.

[33] Ibid., 190.

[34] Quoted in Howard A. Snyder, *The Radical Wesley and Patterns for Church Renewal* (Downers Grove: InterVarsity Press, 1980), 148.

[35] Hendrik Kraemer, *A Theology of the Laity*, (Philadelphia: The Westminster Press, 1958), 160.

[36] Quoted in John A. Bernbaum and Simon M. Steer, *Why Work?: Careers and Employment in Biblical Perspective* (Grand Rapids: Baker Books, 1986), 21.

[37] See Dan Williams, "Was Luther's Dairy-Maid Called To Milk Cows?" *The Equipping Bulletin* 1, no. 2, 3 (Fall–Winter 1986–7).

[38] See Gordon Fee's brilliant reflection on how calling and situation interact in *The First Epistle to the Corinthians* (Grand Rapids: Eerdmans, 1987), 309–310.

[39] Moltmann is quoting these words from Augustine: "Thou seest the Trinity when Thou seest love...For the lover, the beloved and the love are three" (Moltmann, *The Trinity and the Kingdom*, 58).

[40] These thoughts were first published in *Disciplines of the Hungry Heart* (Wheaton: Harold Shaw, 1993), 15–17.

[41] Not surprisingly the trinitarian theologian Gregory of Nazianzus viewed Adam, Eve and *Seth* (the first to call on the name of the Lord) as the earthly parable of the divine Trinity (Moltmann, *The Trinity and the Kingdom*), 199.

[42] William J. Dumbrell *Creation and Covenant* (Nashville: Thomas Nelson, 1984), 38.

[43] Though the idea of co-creativity has been co-opted by such authors as Teilhard de Chardin, Gibson Winter, Matthew Fox, Chalene Spretnak, Brian Swimme and Thomas Berr, and fits the postmodern cultural framework of the day with its ecological-mystical reformulation of religious traditions, it would be tragic to label all thoughts of co-creativity as "New Age" or "postmodern." There are, however, some dangers. One Christian author, Joe Holland, seems to lose sight of the biblical perspectives of the transcendence and immanence of God and comes dangerously close to deifying human creativity and diminishing God's. But he makes the important point that "Jesus's gospel speaks to the work process not because he grew up in a carpenter family but because he proclaims a new creation" (Joe Holland, *Creative Communion:*

*Toward a Spirituality of Work* [New York: Paulist Press, 1989], 58).

[44] Moltmann expresses this beautifully. The unity of the triune God "only corresponds to a human fellowship of people without privileges and without subordinances. The perichoretic at-one-ness of the triune God corresponds to the experience of the community of Christ, the community which the Spirit unites through respect, affection and love. *The Trinity and the Kingdom,* 157–8.

[45] See Ibid., 209.

[46] Edwin Hui, "Trinity and Creation" (unpublished lecture notes "The Trinity and the Christian Life," Regent College, Vancouver, 1994).

LIVING IN THE WORLD, BUT NOT OF IT

# GRAPPLING WITH THE POWERS

*From* Vocatio *vol. 3, no. 1 (December 1999)*

L ife is not easy. Your boss requires you to do graphic art for a business with dubious connections. Your child watches television in a
neighbour's home, and you discover later that some of the material
was pornographic. Your church is denied the right to expand its building
because of a residents' lobby in the neighbourhood. The school system
teaches a godless approach to all subjects including the creation of the
world. Your money seems to purchase less and less because of global economic factors over which you have no power.

The reason for the complexity of life is not simply the perversity and
sin of individual human beings or even the cumulative effect of all the
sinners in the world, but something more systemic, more all-embracing.
For every visible foreground to a person's life—family, work, community
service, leisure, citizenship, and church—there is an invisible background
that is profoundly influential. What makes life difficult is systemic evil.

In this chapter I will look at the biblical evidence for an invisible world
that affects us both positively and negatively, consider how people interpret
and experience this world and suggest some approaches to living victoriously in the battle of life.

## Identifying the Powers

Paul deals with the trouble of living in this world though a cluster of terms:
power(s), thrones, authorities, virtues, dominions, names and thrones.
Interpretation of these terms has generally followed one of three lines:
(1) These powers are a mythic projection of the human disease onto the

cosmos; (2) these powers describe structures of earthly existence: tradition, morality, justice and order; (3) these powers are both socio-political and spiritual forces, both the outer and the inner structures of life, both the earthly and the heavenly. It is this last view that seems most persuasive.

A stunning example of how both the inner and outer realities of a "power" are intertwined and inseparable is the case of money. "Mammon" is an alternative god. The word "mammon" in Aramaic comes from the word *amen,* which means firmness or stability. It is not surprising that a common English phrase is "the almighty dollar." As Jacques Ellul shows, wealth has some of the pretended claims of deity.[1] It is capable of moving other things and claims a certain autonomy; it is invested with spiritual power that can enslave us, replacing singleminded love for God and neighbour with commercial relationships in which even the soul is bought (Rv 18:11–13). So money, "wicked mammon" (Lk 16:9), is a form or appearance of another power (Eph 1:21).

## Experiencing the Powers

Many authors understand our experience of resistance as primarily the fallen social structures of earthly life, structures that hold society together but have gone wild. We experience these as political, financial and juridical forces[2]—traditions, doctrines and practices that regulate religion and life,[3] dominant images and cultural icons like Marilyn Monroe, corporate institutions like GM or IBM, ideologies like communism, capitalism and democracy,[4] the power of money or mammon,[5] and the inner aspect of all manifestations of power in society.[6] If there are inadequacies in locating the powers exclusively in the human realm of structure and tradition, there are dangers as well in locating them exclusively in the angelic and demonic.

This latter approach assumes that at the heart of our experience of multilevel resistance is the presence of personal spiritual beings capable of purposeful activity. A number of popular novels and treatments of spiritual warfare, notably the works of Frank Peretti and David Watson, take this approach. Its strength is that without these powers we lack an adequate explanation of why structures so regularly become tyrannical. Its weakness is that too often it focuses energy only on prayer and "spiritual warfare" instead of also working to change structures, traditions and images in a concrete way.

Western society, and frequently the church, has rejected the spiritual interpretation of life. But Scripture witnesses to the complexity of systemic evil: structures, spiritual hosts, angels and demons, the devil and the last enemy, death (1 Cor 15:24–27)—all arenas in which Christians face resistance.

The complex vision of the last book of the Bible reveals multiple (and systematically interdependent) levels of difficulty, which can be pictured as concentric circles of influence: the red dragon (satan) at the centre of it all (Rv 12); the two beasts representing diabolical authority and supernaturalism (Rv 13); the Harlot representing the sum total of pagan culture (Rv 17) and Babylon as the world system (Rv 18). This elaborate picture shows that the Christian in the world not only encounters a multifaceted opposition, but one in which there are interdependently connected dimensions. This elaborate vision in Revelation shows us that the political power of Romans 13, then the good servant of God, has become the instrument of satan in Revelation 13 (in this case the same government but more colonized and corrupted)—thus showing the way in which supernatural forces and personages may influence and corrupt human institutions, structures and patterns of cultural and social life.

**Understanding the Powers**

Scripture shows that God has both visible and invisible servants. All were created by God. All have been corrupted. Paul claims that through Christ "all things were created: things in heaven and on earth, visible and invisible, whether thrones or powers or rulers or authorities; all things were created by him and for him" (Col 1:15). This, as Hendrik Berkhof brilliantly describes it, is the invisible background of creation, "the dikes with which God encircles his good creation, to keep it in His fellowship and protect it from chaos."[7] They were intended to form a framework in which we live out our lives for God's glory. Four such frameworks are marriage, family, nation and law, each ordained by God for our good.

Along with some supernatural beings (Jude 6:2; 2 Pt 2:4), these same structures have become broken, hostile and resistant to God's rule. Some of these powers have taken on a life of their own, making idolatrous claims on human beings: government, religion, culture, various "isms," symbolized in the names and titles that dominate the news (Eph 1:21; Gal 4:8–9). In Ephesians 6 Paul suggests these have been "colonized" (though this term itself is not used) by satan himself.

No Old Testament passage is quoted as frequently in the New Testament as Psalm 110:1, which declares that all the powers have been subjugated by the Messiah-Christ. Through the gospels Jesus is seen as supreme over the evil spirits. He casts out demons by the finger of God (Lk 11:20); he destroys the power of satan (Mk 3:23–26; Mt 12:26; Lk 11:18); he enters the strong man's house and plunders his goods (Mk 3:27). This extraordinary power of Jesus to overpower the powers is delegated to his followers (Mk 3:14f.; 6:7; Mt 10:1; Lk 9:1f.; 10:1). Paul further elaborates on the extensiveness of Christ's work now that he has died and been resurrected.

Paul uses several words to express how the hostile powers have been subjugated. They have been abrogated, stripped, led in triumphal procession or into captivity, made to genuflect, pacified or reconciled (1 Cor 15:24–26; Col 1:20; 2:15; Phil 2:10; Eph 1:22; 4:8–10). Drawing on the three phrases of Colossians 2:15, Berkhof points out how Christ made a public example of them. What once were considered fundamental realities are now seen as rivals and adversaries of God.[8] As divine irony the title "King of the Jews" was placed over the cross in the three languages that represent the powers that crucified Jesus: Hebrew, the language of religion; Latin, the language of government and Greek, the language of culture. By volunteering to be "victimized" by the power through his death, and "using" the powers to accomplish a mighty saving act, Jesus put them in their place as instruments of God rather than autonomous regents, showing how illusionary were their pretended claims. Christ triumphed over them in his resurrection, thus defeating even the power of death, and disarmed them by stripping them of the illusion that they were god-like and all-powerful.

Oscar Cullman compares the powers to chained beasts kicking themselves to death. Between the resurrection of Jesus and the Second Coming they are tied to a rope, still free to evidence their demonic character but nevertheless bound. Cullman uses a helpful analogy to explain the tension. D-Day was the day during the Second World War in which the beaches of Normandy were invaded and the battle was turned. One could say the war was "won" that day, even though there were months of battling ahead and many lives lost. V-Day was the day of final victory. Christ's coming and death is D-Day. But we must still live in the final consummation of the Kingdom at the second coming of Christ.[9]

### Grappling with the Powers

There are four historic approaches to the powers, all of which have their place in Christian mission: (1) exorcism and intercession, (2) suffering powerlessness, (3) creative participation and (4) just revolution. The church as a whole must engage in a full-orbed approach. But discernment is needed.

The Prayer Book of the Anglican or Episcopal Church provides a handy summary of our multi-faceted problem: "The world, the flesh and the devil." Each must be fought differently. We deal with the spirit of the world through nonconformity with it and conformity with the will of God

(Rom 12:2). We deal with our lower nature by mortification (identifying with Christ's crucifixion) and aspiration (breathing in the Spirit). We deal with the devil by resisting and fleeing (Jas 4:7; Rv 12:11). It is a multi-fronted battle. And our Lord meets us at each of these fronts by *transfiguring* us from within (Rom 12:2), *bearing Spirit fruit* through us (Gal 5:22, 25) and *overcoming the evil one*, the devil (Rv 12:10), as we put on Christ's armour through all kinds of prayer (Eph 6:13–18).

The first and most effective strategy against the false claims of the powers is preaching the gospel. However much we attempt to "Christianize" the powers, we must not bypass preaching the gospel and calling people to embrace the reign of Christ through repentance and faith.

Christ's complete victory over the principalities and powers, over satan, sin and death, assure us that there is nowhere in the universe so demonic that a Christian might not be called to serve there. We fight a war that is already won. Therefore as far as now possible, Christians should Christianize the powers, pacify the powers through involvement in education, government and social action, all the while knowing that the task of subjugating them is reserved for Christ alone (Eph 1:10; Phil 2:10.11). We work on the problems of pollution, food distribution, injustice, genetic engineering and the proliferation of violence and weaponry, knowing that this work is ministry and holy. In the short run, our contribution may seem unsuccessful, but in the long run it will be gloriously successful because we are cooperating with what Christ wants to do in renewing all creation. Jürgen Moltman speaks of eschatology or the "end times" as the most pastoral of all theological disciplines because it shows us that we are living at the dawning of a new day rather than at the sunset of human history.[10] Keeping end times in view is critical to grappling victoriously with the powers: it shows us that work done in this world is not resultless but, in some way beyond our imagination, contributes to a world without end. Eschatology also liberates us from a messianic complex (or inappropriate egoism) since the future is ultimately in God's hands. The kingdom will come to consummation in God's own way and time. Lesslie Newbigin comments on this with great depth:

> We can commit ourselves without reserve to all the secular work our shared humanity requires of us, knowing that nothing we do in itself is good enough to form part of that city's building, knowing that everything —from our most secret prayers to our most public political acts—is part of that sin-stained human nature that must go down into the

valley of death and judgment, and yet knowing that we offer it up to the Father in the name of Christ and in the power of the Spirit, it is safe with him and— purged in fire—it will find its place in the holy city at the end.[11]

*Reprinted with permission from* The Complete Book of Everyday Christianity *in* An A-to-Z Guide to Following Christ in Every Aspect of Life *(InterVarsity Press, 1997).*

## Endnotes

[1] Jacques Ellul, *Money and Power*, trans. LaVonne Neff (Downers Grove, IL: InterVarsity Press, 1984), 76–77, 81, 93.

[2] Markus Barth, *Ephesians*, 2 vols., Anchor Bible (Garden City, NY: Doubleday and Co., 1974).

[3] Ibid.

[4] William Stringfellow, *Free in Obedience* (New York: Seabury Press, 1964).

[5] Ellul, *Money and Power.*

[6] Walter Wink.

[7] Hendrik Berkhof, *Christ and the Powers*, trans. J.H. Yoder (Scottdale, PA: Herald Press, 1962), 28.

[8] Ibid., 38.

[9] Oscar Cullman, *Christ and Time: The Primitive Christian Conception of Time and History*, trans. F.V. Filson (London: SCM Press, 1951), 84.

[10] Jürgen Moltmann, *Theology of Hope*, trans. James W. Leitch (New York: Harper and Row, 1967), 31.

[11] Lesslie Newbigin, *Honest Religion for Secular Man* (Philadelphia: Fortress Press, 1966), 136.

## Further Reading

Peter L. Berger, *The Sacred Canopy: Elements of a Sociological Theory of Religion* (Garden City, NY: Doubleday and Co., 1967).

G. B. Caird, *Principalities and Powers: A Study in Pauline Theology* (Oxford: Clarendon Press, 1956).

Richard Mouw, *Politics and Biblical Drama* (Grand Rapids: Eerdmans, 1976).

Dan G. Reid, "Principalities and Powers," *Dictionary of Paul and His Letters*, ed. Kenneth DeRuiter (Downers Grove, IL: InterVarsity Press, 1993), 746–752.

Heinrich Schleir, *Principalities and Powers in the New Testament* (New York: Herder and Herder, 1996).

# WEALTH: BLESSING, TEMPTATION

# OR SACRAMENT?

*From* Vocatio, *vol. 5, no. 1 (August 2001)*

Hardly anyone wants to be poor; most would like to be rich. Wealth brings power, standing in the community, increased leisure and freedom from worry—so it is thought. Not surprisingly in the richest part of the world many Christians are preaching a "prosperity gospel"—that faithfulness to Jesus will lead to personal wealth. Tragically, this distorted message is now taking root in some of the poorest countries of the world. Is wealth a sign of God's blessing? Is money the main measure of wealth? Does the Bible endorse wealth, promote it or exclude it? How are we to respond in spirit and action? Our souls hang on our answers to these questions.

## Wealth as Power

Principalities and powers form an invisible background to our life in this world. One of those powers is money. *Mammon,* as it is sometimes called, comes from an Aramaic word, *amen,* which means firmness or stability. It is not surprising that a common English term is "the almighty dollar."

As an alternative god, mammon inspires devotion, induces guilt, claims to give us security and seems to be omnipresent—a godlike thing.[1] It is invested with spiritual power that can enslave us, replacing single-minded love for God and neighbour with buying-selling relationships in which even the soul can be bought (Rv 18:11–13).

We hear two voices of Scripture: one blessing the rich, the other cursing; one declaring that wealth is a sign of God's redemptive love to make us flourish on earth, the other declaring that "wicked mammon"

(Lk16:9), usually gained at the expense of the poor, is an alternative god. We need to look at each of these in turn.

### Wealth as Blessing

The idea that wealth is a sign of God's blessing (Dt 30:9; Prv 22:4) is illustrated by the lives of Abraham, Job and Solomon. In contrast to those who praised the Lord because they were rich (Zec 11:5) but were soon to be judged, it is noteworthy that each of these exemplars depended on God rather than their wealth (Gn 13:8–18; Jb 1:21). The wise person in the Proverbs is essentially a better-off person with servants—equivalent to our modern household machines—neither fabulously wealthy nor living in grinding poverty. Some wealth is a good thing; too much or too little would be alienating from God (Prv 30:9). So the wise person prays, "give me neither poverty nor riches, but give me only my daily bread" (30:8).

The "prosperity gospel" now being preached world-wide is not satisfied with a comfortable existence or merely praying for our daily bread. We can critique it on at least three grounds. First, it encourages perverted motives: focusing upon profitability. Second, it misinterprets God's deepest concerns for us: material well-being rather than total well-being. Third, it misinterprets God's promises to Israel as immediately applicable to Christians without being fulfilled and transfigured in Christ (compare 1 Tm 6:3–10). Nevertheless, the Old Testament clearly presents wealth as a means of God's grace.

### Wealth as Temptation

Even the Old Testament warns that the pursuit of wealth for its own sake is vain and harmful, leading to self-destructive autonomy (Prv 30:8; 23:4–5; 28:20; Ps 49:6–7; Prv 30:8–9; Hos 12:8). Wealth is an illusionary security and will not satisfy (Eccl 5:10; Ps 49:6–7).

Instead of becoming stewards of wealth for the benefit of the poor (Prv 31:5, 8, 9), we are tempted to use what wealth we have to dominate others (Am 2:6)—a subject taken up by John Chrysostom in his sermons on Luke 16. Just as the brothers of Joseph enjoyed their fine meal and did not "grieve over the ruin of Joseph" (Am 6:6; Gn 37:25), very few wealthy people have been able to resist becoming desensitized to the poor.

### Wealth as Sacrament

The Old Testament affirms that God is the true owner, proprietor and giver of wealth (Prv 3:16; 1 Sm 2:7–8; Eccl 5:19; Hos 2:8). We are merely stewards (Prv 3:9). But the fact that God gives wealth, indiscriminately it seems, produces what Jacques Ellul calls "the scandal of wealth." God sometimes gives wealth to the wicked (Ps 73:12–13; Ps 62:10; Jb 21:7–21). Why would God do this if wealth were a sign of being blessed? Contrary to the common argument that wealth is the result of "our hard-earned labour" or "our faithfulness," the Old Testament takes a more sacramental view.

Wealth is a free gift of God, a sign of God's grace given generously and without merit. Further, wealth points to the final consummation when our wealth will be taken into the Holy City (Is 60:3; Rv 21:24–26).[2]

## Wealth in the New Testament

When we turn to the New Testament we discover that "Jesus Christ strips wealth of the sacramental character that we have recognized in the Old Testament" (Lk 6:30; 12:33; Mt 6:24).[3] The rich fool trusts in his barns and investments and is not ready to meet God, nor is known by God. The rich already have their comfort (Lk 6:24); they have nothing to look forward to. The rich young man must give everything away and follow Jesus. True wealth is not the accumulation of houses, farms, jewels and money but something more.

Though these passages seem to argue for an anti-wealth New Testament ethic, it is not that simple. Jesus affirmed the extravagant and wasteful display of love when the woman poured perfume on his head: "She has done a beautiful thing to me" (Mk 14:1–11). And Jesus himself accepted the generous financial support of women with means (Lk 8:4). How are we to resolve this tension?

## Heavenly Wealth

Unquestionably many of Jesus' negative statements about the rich and the wealthy are addressed to the spiritual malady fed by material abundance. "Be on your guard against all kinds of greed; a man's life does not consist in the abundance of his possessions" (Lk 12:15; cf. Jas 5:1–6). As an alternative god, wealth must be repudiated, if necessary by giving it all away (compare Lk 16:13). Ultimate security and blessing cannot be found in the accumulation of things (compare Mt 6:19).

At this point Scripture now gives us a harmonious, though disturbing, single message. Possessions are solely and simply a matter of stewardship, not ownership, and this life's assets are to be used with a heavenly orientation. What are these heavenly treasures and how do they relate to everyday wealth, or the lack of it?

We gain an important paradigmatic perspective on this question from the Old Testament. There the inheritance received by Israel through the promise was a threefold blessing: the presence of God ("I will be with you"), the people ("you will be my people; I will be your God") and a place to belong ("the land will be yours"). What we are given "in Christ" more than fulfills the promises made to Abraham and his descendants. God is with us in an empowering way through the Spirit. In Christ we experience peoplehood, a new family with hundreds of brothers and sisters, fathers and mothers, children and lands (Mt 19:29; Mk 10:29–30). The promise of a place is fulfilled doubly: first in true fellowship here on earth through a full sharing of life with other believers and, second, in the place which Christ has prepared for us (Jn 14:2) in the new heaven and new earth, the city of God (Heb 11:13–16). Presence, peoplehood and a place—these are true wealth for the Christian. Money in the bank, ownership certificates of bonds and title deeds to properties are only an optional extra to this wealth. But, still, what are we to do with the temporal wealth God has entrusted to us?

### Stewards of Wealth

Stewardship is much more than giving money to the church or to charities. It is caring for God's creation, managing God's household, bringing God's justice. Old Testament social legislation pointed to the coming (and present) kingdom of God by principles that were economically gracious: the provision of gleaning for the poor by not harvesting everything one could (Ruth); the provision of the Sabbath for the land and for indebted people; the cancellation of debts with Israelites and resident aliens in the seventh year—thus stressing neighbour love (Dt 15:1–6); the command to lend without interest to one's neighbour (Dt 15:7–11); the release of Israelite slaves on the seventh year (Dt 15:12–18); the provision of Jubilee by which the hopelessly indebted could start again (Lv 25); the command that kings and leaders must not enrich themselves by that leadership but should live simply as brother-leaders (Dt 17:16–20).

While these commands are not to be slavishly followed under the circumstances of the New Covenant, they reflect a minimum standard for economic life for people "in Christ." Christian stewardship cares for the earth, releases debts, empowers the poor, brings dignity to the marginalized and equalizes opportunity. But there is also direct giving.

Probably no other single factor indicates our true spirituality more than what we do with the wealth we have, and in which spirit we share it. Christian giving is marked by hilarity (Lk 6:38; 2 Cor 9:7) that takes us beyond a calculated tithe and reflects the generosity of God. The Lord might well ask in this area as in others, "What more do you do than the pagans who know not God? And why?"

First, we are to invest primarily in people, especially the poor. The only treasure we can take from this life to the next is the relationships we have made through Jesus (Lk 16:9). The treasures in heaven are relationships that have been formed through the gracious use of money, the investment of the things of this life in a world without end, often in the context of everyday work.

Second, we are to give away wisely and carefully what we can. It was John Wesley who advised: "Gain all you can, save all you can, give all you can." But the giving must take us beyond merely relieving the symptoms of people's distress through giving alms. Almsgiving may be a perversion of giving because, as Ellul shows, it binds the recipient in an obligatory relationship, demands gratitude and does not usually address the reasons behind the person's poverty.[4] So individuals and churches should invest in people and causes that grapple with the systemic powers that hold people in bondage to a cycle of poverty. There may be no greater area of discernment needed for the Christian in everyday life than to decide when, where and how to give money away.

Third, some form of voluntary impoverishment is required of all followers of Jesus. It is not sufficient to say, as many do, "The rich young ruler (Mt 19:16–30) was a special case." We are all in need of profaning the false god of mammon and relativizing wealth in this life as something less than full treasure in heaven. There are several dimensions of voluntary impoverishment. We start by relinquishing ownership to God. We practise continuous thanksgiving, which is the only way to become content whatever our circumstances (Phil 4:12–13). We should pay our taxes with a generous heart, knowing that some of this is being used to provide services and care for the poor and disadvantaged. We should give directly to the poor with no strings attached as personally as possible (Lk 16:9).[5] We should give to God's global work (2 Cor 8–9). Finally we should be ready, if so commanded by Christ, to sell all.

Throughout the New Testament, writers emphasized the interiority of giving: freedom from manipulation and covetousness, motivated by true love for God and neighbour. As Jacques Ellul notes, "Ultimately, we follow what we have loved most intensely either into eternity or into death" (Mt 6:21).[6]

## Endnotes

[1] Richard Foster, *Money, Sex & Power* (San Francisco: Harper and Row, 1985), 28.

[2] Jacques Ellul, *Money and Power*, trans. LaVonne Neff (Downers Grove, IL: InterVarsity Press, 1984), 66.

[3] Ronald J. Sider, *Rich Christians in a World of Hunger* (Dallas: Word, 1990).

[4] Ellul, *Money and Power.*

[5] See R. Paul Stevens, *Disciplines of the Hungry Heart* (Wheaton, IL: Harold Shaw, 1993), 159–165.

## Further Reading

Jouette M. Bassler, *Asking for Money in the New Testament* (Nashville: Abingdon, 1991).

John Chrysostom, *On Wealth and Poverty*, trans. Catherine P. Roth (Crestwood, NY: St. Vladimir's Seminary Press, 1984).

Douglas J. Hall, *Stewardship of Life in the Kingdom of Death* (Grand Rapids: Eerdmans, 1988).

John C. Haughey, *The Holy Use of Money: Personal Finances in the Light of the Christian Faith* (New York: Doubleday, 1986).

Luke T. Johnson, *Sharing Possessions: Mandate and Symbol of Faith* (London: SCM Press, 1981).

Christopher J. H. Wright, *God's People in God's Land: Family, Land, and Property in the Old Testament* (Grand Rapids: Eerdmans, 1990).

# MARKETING THE FAITH:
# A REFLECTION ON THE IMPORTING AND
# EXPORTING OF WESTERN THEOLOGICAL
# EDUCATION

*From* Crux, *vol. 28, no. 2 (June 1992)*

In October 1989 the Carey Theological College faculty met with visitors from Baptist churches in the former USSR who were inviting us to help them establish theological seminaries throughout the Soviet Union. Leaders of churches without the benefit of seminary education were scrambling to export Western help, the faster the better. At the same time Western seminaries were scrambling to export what they had and to become one of the earliest agencies to have an extension headquarters in Moscow. A few days after this significant consultation I wrote a parable.

## The Tomato Farm

"We have come to your country to learn about hydroponic tomatoes. In our country we have state-regulated tomato culture for many years. But they were tasteless. And most people preferred their own tomatoes grown in boxes inside their windows, or in small patches of ground in some hidden place. The state tried to regulate this underground movement but finally agreed to legalize tomato-growing by the people. So now we have the opportunity of mass-producing tomatoes and educating experts in tomato culture."

The person explaining this turned to his two companions seeking their tacit approval of this presentation. They were representatives of millions of ordinary people who loved eating tomatoes and were fascinated with the abundance of tomatoes in the West. They had heard about our advanced tomato-growing techniques employing greenhouses with computerized climate control, twenty-four hour simulated sunshine and artificial ripening techniques to produce red tomatoes by passing them through special gases.

"But why do you think our tomatoes are better?" we asked.

Our visitors continued, "Tomatoes in your country are redder and bigger. They all look the same. You can grow them four times more quickly in any season of the year. Your supermarkets are well-stocked with them all the time. We need your technology. In our country we have no experts but we do have lots of people who love tomatoes. So let us send some of our best young people to your Tomato Institutes. They can learn your language and your technology and then, when they return, teach the rest of us to grow tomatoes like you, or establish Tomato Institutes such as yours. We also need your videotapes, your study guides and your programs. We have nothing like this in our country and so much to catch up in such a short time."

The Canadians were sobered by the importance of the visit. Now for the first time tomatoes could be grown by anyone, anywhere without the condemnation of the state. Here was an unprecedented opportunity and one fraught with consequences.

"But," interrupted the Canadian, "our hydroponic tomatoes do not have the flavour of tomatoes grown in real earth. In the old days before we mass-produced tomatoes we could sometimes tell where they were grown by the flavour. The plant takes on the quality of the soil. But here in the West we have largely stopped using soil and grow tomatoes in water and chemicals. If you buy into our technology your people will stop growing their own tomatoes."

"We are not sure what you mean," one said on behalf of the whole delegation.

"Growing tomatoes has become professionalized. That is what happens at our Tomato Institutes to which you want to send your best young men and women. In the Institutes they interact with books and hear lectures on the technology of tomato engineering, on the development of new strains and new techniques. They lose contact with the soil. And so your young men and women will become separated from the people who have learned to grow tomatoes in their own boxes and patches of ground. Soon they will tell people that they cannot grow tomatoes efficiently without greenhouses and chemicals. Eventually only the experts will feel competent to grow tomatoes. And ordinary people will read their books and want to be scholars like them. That is what has happened here."

The pensiveness of the visitors was evident now.

"In our country the average person does not know how to grow hydroponic tomatoes because he or she does not have access to the Institutes. Before this happened the wisdom of the art was passed from parent to child. But now the experts gather in professional societies to discuss better ways of breeding high-yield plants and more efficient ways of producing crops, but always in greenhouses."

Suddenly, the passing remark struck home. "You mean your tomato plants cannot survive outside of a greenhouse?"

"They are designed to be raised in an artificial environment and will not survive in the normal climate of our country. You cannot have everything. You can have them big, fast and red, but only if you take it away from the people and trust the professionals to manage the entire tomato production in a specially controlled environment.

"You must choose between the soil of your own country and imported hothouses. But if you choose the latter it will not be long before the former is lost...perhaps forever."[1]

In the history of theological education the ambiguity of the present moment is ironical: a Western theological degree is for most aspiring Christian leaders in the developing world a *sine qua non* at the very moment when those most responsible for that education have never been less sure of the integrity of their enterprise.[2] In this chapter I will explore the fateful fascination with Western theological education, and will ask why Western theological education is a questionable export product. We will take some biblical soundings in the course of this to consider how theological education can fit into the biblical concern for lifelong growth into maturity in Christ. Finally we will take a second look at Western theological education and some possible directions for full partnership with churches in developing countries.

## Fateful Fascination with the West

A Regent student in my class on "Theological Education Overseas" raised the naughty question: "How is it that the only form of theological education that has been given to us in Africa comes from the part of the world where the church is in decline?"

## Globalization without Contextualization

The relationship of globalization and contextualization is tricky. Globalization, as I wish to define it, is the full partnership of churches in the developed world with those in the developing world, involving mutual learning and interdependence, whereby the rich cultural and spiritual contributors of each can be appropriated by the other. Paul's vision of the interdependence of Jewish and Gentile believers is a useful paradigm (2 Cor 8:13–15; Rom 15:25–29). In theological education, globalization—according to my definition—would involve learning educationally and spiritually from younger churches as well as contributing Western resources, perspectives and the fruits of Western scholarship with cultural sensitivity. I fully understand that this loaded term is usually defined differently.[3]

Contextualization is the process by which the timeless and universal message of the Christian faith is brought "home" to multiple contexts in time and space. This term also is variously defined.[4] But the relationship between these two is awkward. The current practice of globalization tends to work against contextualization. Instead of mutual sharing and mutual learning there is usually wholesale, uncritical importing and exporting of the Western model. In other words, globalization has become the universalization of the Western model with a minimum of contextualization. This is all the more remarkable when one considers that the centre of the Christian world has moved from North America to Africa, Asia and South America.

"Need the Two-Thirds World Travel to West for Theological Circumcision?" Michael Griffiths asks in the title of his hard-hitting paper, which catalogues the incongruity: the desert experience that theological students frequently experience in the West, the boiled-down academic syllabus that fails to feed the spirit, the obsession with minutiae, the fact that the alleged neutrality of much biblical criticism is a decision against responding to the Word of God, and the suspicion that the outcome of biblical studies in the academy (as Walter Wink charges) is "trained incapacity to deal with the real problems of actual living persons in their daily lives."[5]

## The Ubiquitous Western Model

The student who wondered about the exporting to Africa of a form of theological education that appeared to be related to the decline of the Western church could be asked a naughty question: How is it that, knowing the church in the West is in decline, African denominations are so hungry to get this sort of ministerial training that the West offers? It may be instructive to consider some possible answers to that question.

First, it is not immediately apparent to the Two-Thirds World that the Western church is in decline. Judged by the wealth of resources, the proliferation of books, journals, videos and seminars, the Western church appears to be thriving. The most fascinating things about Western culture are its gadgets and technology. And they prove to be the easiest part of Western Christianity both to export and import.

Second, we now live in a global society in which the rich are getting richer and the poor poorer. Without critical reflection it appears that the only way to break the cycle of poverty and increasing national debt is to adopt the Western way totally, or nearly so. While Western political, economic and military imperialism is not acceptable in the Two-Thirds World, cultural and educational imperialism is both acceptable and, by and large, welcomed. It holds the promise of success. It takes a penetrating analysis to conclude that to get this mess of pottage one has to sell one's spiritual inheritance.

Third, Western theological education comes to the Two-Thirds World in a package that feeds the direction many people are moving towards in the increasingly urbanized developing world—secularism and rationalism. To lose heavenly-mindedness (a surpassing mark of much indigenous African Christianity) seems a small price to pay for relevance.

Fourth, pride in degrees and publishing records caters to people wanting to establish their identity in a competitive world community; the loss of humility as a Christian goal goes largely unnoticed.

Fifth, gaining cognitive information and skill development are impressive and attainable goals for theological education, even if one unconsciously relinquishes one's spiritual worldview (in which God, angels and demons are as real as one's physical environment) and abstracts education from life.

Sixth, most denominations arose from missionary activity, and the first theological educators were seminary-trained missionaries from the West.

Finally, there is the sheer energy of Western educators and missionaries (to put the matter in its best light) and their bigotry (to put it in the worst light). Theological education is one more arena for global imperialism. So we get globalization without contextualization. We ignore non-rational or supra-rational ways of learning in indigenous cultures[6] and cut all pieces of cloth to the same Western pattern. By and large, visiting Western professors talk about going overseas to learn as well as to teach, but there is little doubt about which motive is uppermost.

While it is foolish to try to replay history, it may be useful to consider what alternatives could be explored *if there were no Western-style seminaries*. Fascinating exceptions to the Western-dependent churches can be found in the indigenous denominations in Africa, which are fast-growing, eclectic and remarkably free from Western influence. With one such indigenous church, the Africa Brotherhood Church, Carey Theological College first established its partnership program. It provides a fascinating model of learning and teaching *together*.[7] But even in this experiment it became clear that part of the attraction was simply the value of an overseas certificate.

So the university-based, graduate theological program geared for producing clergy for the churches is the norm, even though it is rather a late-comer in history.[8] And the rest of the world desperately wants it now at the very moment when leaders in Western theological education are having serious misgivings about their enterprise.

### Soul-searching about the Quality of the Export

Many dedicated scholars in the Western tradition are asking themselves whether the emperor knows he has no clothes on! Successive issues of *Theological Education* and numerous books and journal articles[9] feed the misgivings expressed in the papers presented to the faculty mentioned previously (see endnote 2). What are we exporting? And is it worth exporting? Many concerns are being expressed,[10] though we will concentrate on those that most significantly affect the importing and exporting of Western theological education.[11]

### Why Go to Seminary?

Seminaries provide the professional grooming and intellectual preparation needed for people who have faith and believe they are called into "the ministry." But a shift has taken place in North America whereby students are now more often coming to a theological seminary not to prepare for a career in ministry but to find their own faith. Western seminaries are, by and large, unprepared for this shift, though Regent is probably positioned well to meet this *cri de coeur*. Would we be wise to replace "graduate theological school" on our public relations pieces with "an international centre for spiritual formation and vocational integration?"

Though many students come to find God, they experience graduate theological education as a spiritual wasteland during the time they submit to the rigours of academia, exams, research assignments and academic hierarchies. Keith Clifford, the late head of the religion department at the University of British Columbia, put the matter this way: "justification by faith or the rapture of the Holy Spirit may be helpful in heaven but they will get you nowhere in a theological college."[12] Tragically the West has sometimes infected younger churches with arid intellectualism without spiritual power.

### For What Does the Theological College Exist?

Years ago, H. Richard Niebuhr said that the ultimate purpose of the Western theological college was to be "the intellectual centre of the church's life."[13] But Niebuhr's stated purpose is being questioned from inside and outside academia: outside, by the church, which is not sure it needs and wants an intellectual centre, and inside, by the theological college, which is no longer sure that its primary purpose is to help the church think biblically and critically. The unstated purpose of many theological educators is the replication of their scholarship. Without realizing it, students submit themselves to an imitation process in which they become "like their master" as Jesus himself said (Lk 6:40). It is not surprising that students find themselves enthralled with scholarship and lose interest in pastoral or evangelistic ministry or involvement in society.

Undoubtedly part of the confusion is caused by a failure to distinguish between the goal of theological education and the purpose of a theological college. Theological education is the lifelong process of forming Christian persons into the maturity of Christ and equipping them to serve God's purposes in the church and world.[14] A theological college can only engage a part of that purpose, a truth usually not appreciated by incoming students. In the West the confusion is problematic. Overseas, it is debilitating as newer churches without an evolved history of theological education try to make their Bible schools and theological colleges perform the *whole* task of theological educaton.[15]

### The Academy-Congregation Connection

Western faculty members are frequently alienated from the contexts in which their students will eventually serve—the local church or, in the case of non-clergy laity, the world. Linda Cannell adds to a chorus of other spokespersons[16] in questioning whether Western theological education is not setting people up for failure by preparing them to serve a church that is "stuck," or dysfunctional. She argues:

> For the most part we are equipping people to preserve a church that is growing more and more distant from the culture in which it must minister. Graduates, be they lay or professional, will serve these churches for a time; but there will come a time (probably within three years) where they will find themselves butting up against a brick wall. They will make the wrong assumptions about why this is happening and will further alienate themselves from the people with whom they should be serving. They won't be able to counter the charge of the non-Christian but interested young woman, who asks, "Why is your gospel so interesting and why are you so damn dull?"[17]

Cannell cites the fact that recent graduates and long-term clergy are turning to seminars for the help they did not get and will not get from seminaries.[18] She concludes: "I tend to agree that we cannot teach ministry through courses in a formal program." A scholarly work based on an influential essay by James F. Hopewell on "The Congregational Paradigm for Theological Education" has addressed the need for the academy to relate to the congregation,[19] and some vital experiments in church-based graduate-level theological education are being explored, including the Seattle Association of Theological Education, in which Fuller Seminary and Regent College cooperate with ten Seattle churches.

Speaking to the Canadian situation, Keith Clifford has documented the drift of the theological colleges away from the church. He notes:

> Thirty years ago the theological colleges were seen as servants of the church. But today they appear as if they are much more concerned with their relationships to the university (because this relationship controls government funding which is more important for their survival than church funding), to the ATS (because this relationship controls their accreditation), and to their partners in the ecumenical clusters, than they are with their own denominations.

> During these three decades two profound shifts have taken place in the structure of theological education in Canada: first, the formation of university departments of religious studies, and second, the forming of ecumenical clusters of theological colleges in major university centres.[20]

One result of these two trends, Clifford notes, is that the seminaries are no longer the main institutional locale within higher education for the study of religion, a phenomenon Clifford does not welcome. But he ends his penetrating analysis by noting that while the theological colleges cannot afford to risk being marginalized by withdrawing from the university, the college must remain subject to the church, and its control, a principle he admits violates the ground rules of every university.[21]

Generally, there is a more interdependent relationship between churches and colleges in developing countries, and the West has much to re-learn from newer churches in this matter.

## The Quest of Pedagogy

There is no clarity in Western theological institutions on how theory and practice should relate. The linear approach (first you learn the theology and then you graduate and put it into practice) is widely understood to be deficient. But the solution is quite apparently *not* to add more "how-to" and applied theology courses to the curriculum. While Liberation Theology may fairly be critiqued for having a faulty theoretical structure,[22] it has posed an undeniable challenge: people learn in *praxis*, by doing as well as by studying. Francis of Assisi put it this way: "mankind has only as much knowledge as it executes." Scripture will not allow the separation of knowing and acting, being and doing. In *Pedagogy of the Oppressed* Paulo Friere's idea is that the teacher is no longer the one who teaches but a fellow learner-teacher.[23] This has not gained wide acceptance in the West, but many voices in the adult education field are saying something remarkably similar: adults learn best in situations where they begin with their own experience and engage that experience with materials being studied on a continuing basis.[24] What is really needed is a spiral of learning: theory followed by *praxis* followed by reflection on theory and so on. For the seminary this boils down to the question of whether theological education must be education *for* ministry or education in ministry. In place of the classes and field education we need an integrated cycle of *praxis*, instruction and reflection.

What one frequently finds overseas is an educational system in seminaries and colleges that exemplifies the worst of Western educational theories or educational styles that have long proven unsatisfactory, with one possible exception: overseas seminaries place more stress on actually doing ministry, planting churches and engaging in evangelistic crusades.

### Should Theological Education be Reserved for the Professional Minister?

George Bernard Shaw once said that every profession is a conspiracy against the laity. Regent College, in contrast, prides itself on challenging people from societal careers to return to their work in the world as a mission. But in reality, many Regent students who come from a "secular" career in vocational transition succumb to the magnetic attraction of the professional ministry.[25] The same appears to be true of the London Institute for Contemporary Christianity (now called Christian Impact), a supposedly lay institution. Remarkably, Peter Stone's analysis of the London Institute shows that about 42% of the students were clergy, and Stone argues that the Institute could only remain a lay movement, as opposed to an academic faculty for laity administered by clergy and academics, if the Council made major adjustments in its courses, policies and faculty.[26] It is simply a fact that a full-time residential program will have its greatest appeal to people who are preparing for a Christian service career. They gain a marketable skill and a valuable career credential; laypersons doing graduate theological education lose one or two years of the career advancement while they pursue what their employers regard as an unprofitable "diversion."

In spite of what I have called the magnetic attraction of the Christian service career, it is important to point out that clericalism is threatened in the West, perhaps much more than in developing countries. A multitude of books and articles emphasizing the ministry of all the people of God, along with numerous attacks on professions as a whole, have taken their toll.[27] Along with growing anti-clericalism there has been a spate of books negatively critiquing the contemporary church with the net result that by the late 1960s, few self-respecting young people wanted to pursue a career in such an irrelevant institution. There has been some numerical recovery in recent years but there can be no return to the clericalism of the '60s. Keith Clifford says that this has put most traditional seminaries between a rock and a hard place. On the one hand, it has undermined the idea of a ministerial elite for the church, an idea upon which the seminary has thrived for decades. On the other hand, turning seminaries into lay training centres, as has been proposed within at least one Canadian denomination,[28] also poses insurmountable problems along the lines of admission requirements and the availability of courses to the people unable to attend a residential college, not to mention the perceived inability of seminary professors to address the real issues of people in the marketplace. Those of us who do believe in a clerical ministry welcome this ambiguous situation as a divine opportunity to liberate and educate the laity (including the pastoral leadership).

It is almost impossible to generalize on the state of clericalism globally. But a few points can be made: the clergy-lay problem is perpetuated globally by the seminary system exported largely from the West; in countries where the church is growing quickly (for instance, in Africa, where some denominations grow at 25 percent per year), lay ministry is not an optional extra and the West has much to learn from churches where *most* church leadership and ministry is undertaken by untrained and nonprofessional ministers; the West has very few models of theological centres for the education of the non-clergy laity either for voluntary tent-making leadership in the church, as proposed by the visionary Roland Allen in *The Case for the Voluntary Clergy*, or for equipping lay Christians for their societal ministry. Tragically, the few models of theological education for the laity in the West are probably not workable elsewhere.[29]

## The Loss of Integration

Edward Farley has written extensively on the loss of unity in theological education.[30] Unity in Christ, on which the medieval university was founded, has dissolved into departmental specializations. Interdisciplinary Studies has become a discipline in its own right! With the information explosion, increasing specialization appears to be a self-defeating exercise, but we continue to pursue it with ever-increasing passion. Sadly, it is usually left for the student to make the integration. Faculty members do not read each other's books, attend each other's lectures or interact with each other on their growing edges of intellectual and spiritual growth. What a tragedy it would be to export this atomization of theological education into countries that have not gone through the Enlightenment and have no need to recycle our recent history.

## Bring the Student to the Educational Institution or Take the Education to the Student?

Eastside Foursquare Church in Seattle has over twenty people on staff. Only one has formal theological education and the senior pastor has not completed his degree. They are asking for graduate level theological education but with this crucial proviso: "Don't take us out of ministry!" Increasingly there are calls for new formats and new delivery systems.

Many are saying to us, "Come to us with theological education because we cannot come to you." The demand for part-time involvement in the context of part-time remunerated work on the staff of a church or in a societal occupation is increasing daily. The average student at Regent College is half-time, though we still plan as though we were a residential community of full-time scholars offering a unique experience to an elite group.

Preparing laypersons (non-clergy laypersons, that is) for their societal mission is the founding vision of Regent College. But in a shrinking global economy, this primary target group is less likely than ever to risk losing their jobs by taking a year off to come to Regent. Those in vocational transition may take this risk, but most will have to be reached in the context of their normal occupational experience: in the marketplace, in concentrated short courses accessible to people unable to devote full time to an educational program. For some people this will provide the best possible education in work and ministry, especially if we learn how to enhance the mentoring opportunities and engage people in guided reflection on their Christian service in the world. A balance of residential community and extension programs seems not only to be the inevitable shape of the future but the best of all possible educational worlds. Some people cannot be expected (and should not be asked) to leave their professions for one to three years to gain a degree that will not advance their careers.[31] Fortunately, sheer necessity has forced churches in developing countries to be more innovative and flexible on this matter, as evidenced in the growth of theological education by extension.[32]

### A Crisis of Escalating Costs

The cost of graduate theological education for the average full-time student in North America is $16,000 per year.[33] At Regent our cost per student is lower than that amount; however, approximately one-half of the cost is passed on to the student in the form of tuition fees. But in Third World countries, where the buying power of a person's earnings may be one-tenth of ours, the cost of providing graduate level education at North American standards is out of sight. Western theological education is an alabaster jar. Should it be broken for clergy in the church, let alone for laity in the world? Most North American theological institutions are now considering strategies for surviving the inevitable financial crunch. With theological institutions competing for relatively few students and for even fewer donors, new partnerships and institutional networks seem inevitable.

In countries where the rich are getting richer and the poor poorer, the financial issue is even more serious. The final chapter of Rene Padilla's volume summarized the findings of the Latin American Theological Fraternity. Conspicuous in these findings is the observation that for theological education to be made available for the whole people of God as that people seeks to bring in the Kingdom of God and serve God's justice (a Latin American contribution to the discussion of goals), theological education itself must cease existing for itself or "exclusively for the equipping of a (clerical) elite."[34] The cost of this slavish replication of Western curriculum and educational philosophy is quite simply economic dependence on the West because of the lack of national professors."

## The Demise of Thinking in the West

In Allan Bloom's *Closing of the American Mind* and Alastair MacIntyre's *After Virtue* the demise of straight thinking in Western culture is carefully analyzed.[35] Viewed from the point of view of the three dimensions of classical education (*theoria, poesis* and *praxis*[37]) the most significant failure in Western theological education may not be in *praxis* or *poesis* but in *theoria*. We have a decadent *theoria*. Dr. Craig Gay, responding to my paper on "Globalization and Contextualization," notes that it is precisely the contextualizing of Western scholarship that has led to its decadence. Contextuality (in this sense), he maintains, is the AIDS virus of the intellect; it does not kill you outright but leaves you defenceless against attack from such overpowering cultures as the New Age Movement, which can be viewed as another name for "postmodernism."

So there are at least nine dimensions to the crisis of Western theological education. But there is another way of looking at the present situation. It is often noted that the Chinese word for "crisis" is composed of two characters, one meaning "danger" and the other meaning "opportunity." These multiple crises give us occasion to rediscover new forms and old foundations. I believe in reinventing the wheel. Each generation should have the privilege of contributing its own unique perspective on the equipping of the saints to grow into the full measure of the stature of the headship of Christ. But now we must learn to do this globally, and the West will have much to learn from the rest of the world.

## Pathways Toward a Full Partnership

Dean Gilleland of the Fuller School of World Mission notes that "based on sheer numbers, Christianity has already been handed to the young, the poor, and the non-white peoples of the world."[38] So finding ways to achieve genuine partnership in theological education between churches globally[39] must now become a missional-level commitment of every North American seminary and college. As a basis for further discussion and research, the following strategies are offered.

### Enriching the Goal of Theological Education: the Mature Person in Christ Serving his Purposes in the World

The West should contribute its scholarship to the world by reclaiming Niebuhr's proposed goal of the college as the "intellectual centre of the church's life." But in genuine humility the Western institutions should profit from the goal of theological education in other cultures and sensitively incorporate these dimensions into their educational programs.[40] From South America the West can learn about justice and the *theoria-praxis* connection. The proposed purpose of theological education stated by Latin American scholars meeting in Quito, Ecuador is "the kingdom of God and his justice, directed towards the total renewal of the student and his or her situation."[41] And from Africa and Asia, the West can learn spirituality[42] and the formation of persons able to give spiritual discernment and to engage in spiritual direction. Prayer, exorcism and healing are as natural to African Christians as being "busy" or giving a rational explanation of a biblical truth are to Western Christians. Some time ago a student asked me a hard question about the non-verbal message given by the faculty at Regent in their manner of life: "Is the mature Christian, as modelled by our faculty, a person who accepts every speaking and writing opportunity that one can cram into one's life without jeopardizing health?"

### Learning from Alternative Models

There are, fortunately, some inspiring exceptions to this universalizing trend of the university-based graduate school of theology in the West, exceptions that prove to be prophetic challenges to the infractible institutions of the West: the base ecclesial communities of Latin America,[43] a Catholic experiment in lay education at the grassroots level, as well as Theological Education by Extension, which arose first in Guatemala in 1963 in answer to pressing problems in a growing church, including the fact that most seminary graduates did not want to return to rural areas and gifted leaders were not able to be involved in the traditional program.[44] In North America an experiment similar to the proposed

Seattle program was made in the eastern United States under the banner of "Seminary of the East," a conservative Baptist seminary without walls dedicated to working in partnership with churches, where most of the learning takes place.[45]

Perhaps in the light of these fruitful experiments the Western church should welcome greater diversity in theological education patterns and *credential them*, while maintaining a limited number of traditional theological colleges, especially those capable of developing research scholars and research practitioners for the church.

## Sharing Theological Resources

Today everyone deserves and needs an international education. Western theological institutions should carefully invite scholars from the Third World to be present on their faculty for limited periods of time, but not in a way that would rob precious resources from institutions of the developing world. Short courses, sabbaticals and part-time arrangements are to be preferred to taking full-time faculty from newer churches. In turn, when Western academic scholars go to teach extension courses in other countries they should observe the mandate given by their own anatomy: two ears and one mouth. They should do twice as much listening as they do teaching. They should normally go to the country for a period of time in which they do no teaching but rather actively listen. This militates against the parachute approach that is almost universal (and often welcomed by the host country). Further, when teaching in an international college such as Regent,[46] professors should develop sensitivity to the cross-cultural issues of teaching an international class. That means that our international students are not only a challenge but a God-given resource for the education of the faculty.

## A Network for Graduate-Level Theological Education

To the best of our knowledge there does not exist a forum for interchange and mutual encouragement for those involved in the pioneering of graduate theological education for the laity. It is urgently needed. Through a simple exchange newsletter and an international gathering of educators every three years, significant deepening of our enterprises could be accomplished. In North America a gathering of "Lay Leaders in America" took place in September 1991 under the auspices of the Vesper Society (*Laity Exchange*) and it was profoundly rewarding to discover more resources and more kindred hearts than one thought existed.

## Practice in Cross-Cultural Ministry

Three years ago Ward Gasque and I developed a course that was profoundly satisfying to the teachers: "Theological Education Overseas," now taught by Thena Ayres. Our hunch was that most overseas students at Regent were going to return to become theological educators in their home country, and that many of our North American students were considering ministries in teaching overseas. We were concerned that our overseas students should be able to handle their experience of Western education in the context of critical reflection and discernment, and that the North Americans should have an experience of contextualizing theological education before going overseas. So why not get the overseas students and the North Americans to teach each other? [47] But there is a needed next step: a practicum in theological education overseas. We should identify several centres in various developing countries where there is a national or a sensitive missionary capable of mentoring a small number of Regent students who would come for a three-month practicum. During this time they would listen, teach classes, join the classes that are being taught and do research on the culture and the learning patterns of that culture.[48]

## Contextualized Extension Centres

Regent has two opportunities to regularize its commitment to globalization: first, in selecting and nurturing a small number of extension centres overseas, probably one in each of Africa, South America, Asia and Europe. The choice should be made on the basis of several criteria: the need for Regent's lay emphasis and the availability of alumni and friends of the College who have a vision for establishing and maintaining such a centre. Most, though not all faculty members, could thus be encouraged to teach overseas at least once every two years. But replication of the Regent vision offers another opportunity, especially where there is a fledgling institution already in existence, such as the Institute for Interdisciplinary Studies started by our Regent alumni, Marcos Feitosa and Paul Freston, in Sao Carlos, Brazil. In many locations in the world, an appropriate centre already exists and would be substantially encouraged by a formal connection with Regent College and the opportunity from time to time to offer credit courses transferable to the Regent diploma.[49] Scholars from these communities could be invited to spend sabbaticals at Regent and eventually a few could be jointly appointed. It can hardly be emphasized enough that each of these centres and institutional partnerships must be contextualized. Some Regent students might choose to do part of their course work overseas in order to enrich their degree program in Vancouver.

## Creative Faculty Enrichment

Emilio Castro has wisely said that "the methods of theological education will depend exclusively on the answer we give to two basic questions: *where?* and *for what?* [50] "Where" is generally answered in the context of a university, theological college or seminary, stressing residential life, classroom instruction and the rational interpretation of historical texts, along with withdrawal from actual ministry. "For what" is generally answered in terms of preparation of men and women for professional leadership in the church. A strand of witness throughout the Old and New Testaments is education *in* the thick of life and *in* the context of ministry. In his lecture in "Theological Education Overseas," Ward Gasque noted several themes of theological education in the Bible: the family as the primary educational unit, the reinforcement of public festivals, structured patterns of instruction through creeds and stories, the schools of the prophets, congregational instruction in the synagogue, the disciple community around Jesus engaged in action and withdrawal for reflection, Paul's travelling seminary with his missionary co-workers (Timothy, Gaius, Tychicus and Trophimus), the Hall of Tyrannus as education in the marketplace (Acts 19:9–10) and local household churches as the primary place for the education of the laity. In other words, there was simply nothing like the university academy as a community of scholars learning and living in separation from the ongoing life and mission of the church. Even synagogue schools were closer to the household church environment than they are to the modern seminary. Jewish yeshivas may be considered an exception to this, although it must be added that they are not envisioned in Scripture and may be critiqued in the light of the fundamental scriptural witness for education in the context of the normal gathered and dispersed experience of the people of God.

Faculty could prepare to be better educators by considering some life-changing and challenging alternatives for a sabbatical: becoming a theologian-in-residence in a business, doing research in a Third World college, living among the poor, volunteering to be part of a pastoral team in a local church or working as a theologian-in-residence in a mission context. Melba Maggay, a believer working in the Philippines, writes: "the fact that most people are poor means that most Christians should do theology from the underside...Well-educated non-Westerners must decolonize their imaginations and learn to write from a position of powerlessness."[51] For systematic integration of academy, marketplace[52] and congregation[53] to take place in Western institutions, the faculty must lead the way by experiencing that integration within themselves individually and among themselves communally.

In the closing comments of the Quito consultation, a remarkable statement is made about the need for Western theological education and the possibilities of reforming them to be of greater use to the global church:

> It is obvious that for the future, it will not be possible to totally discard conventional structures (resident or extension programs). Nevertheless, these will need to be adapted to specific contexts and will need to maintain the tension between information and formation, reflection and action, orthodoxy and orthopraxis, Word and context...Although it is too frequently thought that theology is a luxury which the evangelical churches of Latin America cannot afford, there is an urgent need to train experts in the different theological disciplines, so that they may serve as teachers of the teachers of God's people...Theologians are needed, but theologians who work in close contact with the marginalized sectors of the population, who themselves know their needs, and who can articulate the Gospel in the socio- cultural contexts in which the majority live...This willingness to be identified with the poor and humble will save theologians from the pride that so often traps scholars and leaves them feeling as if God were absent. Furthermore it will produce a theology forged by dialogue with the people and their struggles and sufferings, their aspirations and longings.[54]

Each generation needs to rediscover the forms of theological education that best fulfils the biblical and the cultural mandate of the day. But today we fulfil the educational mission of the church in the context of one earth, one world and one church, with a meaning impossible to any previous generation. To experience this continiung refomation, Western theological educators must now sit at the feet of people who have but recently been brought to the Lord, or who represent traditions that have emerged in other cultural contexts, some with other ways of reasoning, thus embracing true partnership globally. To accomplish this educators must sit lightly to the academic traditions and credentials that once guaranteed their tenure or secured their superiority. But the result of this will not be the elimination of Western theological education but its much-needed reformation and deepening. We may also anticipate the exquisite experience of Christ that Paul anticipated at the conclusion of his own Jew-Gentile partnership, when he told the Romans that he would come, after visiting Jerusalem with the Gentile love-gift, "in the full measure of the blessing of Christ" (Rom 15:29).

## Endnotes

[1] Just three years before this event, in the period before the opening of the Soviet door, my wife and I spent a half-day eluding the KGB in order to spend five precious hours with an underground pastor in a swampy park in the suburbs of Moscow. As we repelled the attacks of militant Soviet mosquitoes, I asked, "What is your biggest challenge in church leadership?" I could hardly believe his response: "Women's ministry!" "Tell me more," I said. The young pastor explained, "In my church they say I am not fit to be a pastor because I treat my wife as an equal." "But where did they get the idea that she was not equal?" The pastor explained that the only book on marriage and family life translated into Russian (from the West) was Larry Christianson's *The Christian Family*, which teaches a chain-of-command: God over the husband, over the wife, over the children. "There is another way of understanding the Bible," I offered, and for four hours we walked from Genesis to Revelation and tried to unlearn the imported viewpoint.

[2] The context of this paper is a series of faculty discussions and papers that are part of Regent's continuing pursuit of a new form of theological education:

(1) In 1987 John Zimmerman offered a paper on an apprenticeship model of pastoral education used extensively in the New England states prior to the formation of seminaries.

(2) In January 1989 Michael Griffiths gave a public lecture prior to his appointment on the subject, "Need the Two-Thirds World Travel West for Theological Circumcision?"

(3) In February 1990 I presented to a faculty retreat and later to a Strategic Planning Committee of the Board a working paper titled, "On Lifting the Green Roof: Globalization and Contextualization."

(4) In February 1990 Walter Wright (then President) presented a paper to the Strategic Planning Committee on the Seattle experiment (later called SATE), a church-based, mentoring, lay-oriented, urban, Pacific Rim and inter-disciplinary model.

(5) On March 5, 1990, Al Bussard, our missionary-in-residence, challenged the faculty with a paper entitled, "Tension in Mission: The Dilemma of Western Energy."

(6) In March 1991 Linda Cannell raised the question of whether we were equipping people to serve in a dysfunctional church with her paper, "Regent College: Theological Education and the Church, the Church and Theological Education."

(7) In June 1991 I summarized my reflection on Carey Theological College's four-year experience of institutional partnership with an African indigenous denomination (The Africa Brotherhood Church) in a paper submitted for publication to *Missiology*. It is entitled: "Equipping Equippers Cross-Culturally: An Experiment in the Globalization of Theological Education."

[3] The term "globalization" has at least four distinct meanings in theological literature: (1) the church's universal mission to evangelize the world, (2) ecumenical cooperation between the various parts of the church, including the challenge of growing equality and mutuality of churches in the first and third worlds, (3) the dialogue between Christianity and other religions, and (4) the mission of the church not only to convert and to evangelize but to improve the lives of millions of poor and disadvantaged people. "Globalization and the Task of Theological Education in North America," *Theological Education* 23, no. 1 (Autumn 1986): 43–44.

[4] Max L. Stackhouse, "Contextualization and Theological Education," *Theological Education* 23, no. 1(Autumn 1986): 67–84.

[5] Michael Griffiths, "Need the Two-Thirds World Travel West for Theological Circumcision?" (unpublished lecture delivered at a Regent College Forum, January 1989).

[6] A fascinating study was made by Herbert V. Kine on oral art in Nigeria: "*Oral Communication of the Scripture: Insights from African Oral Art* (Pasadena: William Carey Library, 1982).

[7] See the article mentioned above, "Equipping Equippers Cross-Culturally: An Experiment in the Globalization of Theological Education."

[8] Other historical models in Christian history have been *the catechetical model* (for the transmission of the apostolic tradition by pastors and bishops), *the monastic model* (such as the "school for service to the Lord" established by Benedict as a prototype of the monks and bishops who would provide a mystical ascetic education), *the scholastic model* (with the birth of the university at the end of the medieval period, in which university professors sought to synthesize reason and faith and systematize theological formulations with the love of knowledge for its own sake often being uppermost) and *the seminary model* (originally started by Ignatius Loyola in 1550 for the provision of highly trained future priests). The early reformers believed in an educated clergy and established many schools, the Geneva Academy of Calvin being one of the most

famous. The period following the Reformation was characterized by (1) the continuation of the university and formation of colleges (in North America), where general instruction would be combined with theological study and (2) the founding of separate seminaries, especially in North America. As Sidney Rooy notes, the ubiquitous seminary model is dedicated to producing a professional pastor instead of presenting the whole person mature, attaining to the measure of the fullness of Christ. Sidney Rooy, "Historical Models of Theological Education," in *New Alternatives in Theological Education,* ed. Rene Padilla (Oxford: Regnum Books, 1988), 51–72.

[9] Edward Farley, *Theologia: The Fragmentation and Unity of Theological Education* (Philadelphia: Fortress Press, 1983); Max Stackhouse, *Apologia: Contextualization, Globalization, and Mission in Theological Education* (Grand Rapids: Eerdmans, 1988); Joseph C. Hough, Jr., Barbara G. Wheeler, eds., *Beyond Clericalism: The Congregation as a Focus for Theological Education* (Atlanta: Scholars Press, 1988). See also, "Readings for Theological Education Overseas" (unpublished lecture, Regent College, Vancouver, BC 1989) and Paul Wikes, "The Hands that would Shape our Souls," *The Atlantic* (Dec 1990): 59–88.

[10] Ten concerns can be noted in North American theological education: (1) the changed motive for seeking theological education—not so much to prepare for ministry as to find one's faith; (2) the crisis of relevance as educators consider whether they are preparing people to serve in a dysfunctional church; (3) pedagogical misgivings, particularly the questioning of the linear (theory to practice, classes followed by field ed) approach to learning; (4) misgivings about clericalism and the professionalism of ministry; (5) the disintegration of the unity of the disciplines and the effect of hyperspecializations; (6) the demand for new delivery systems since many people can no longer afford to come to a residential-based, full-time academic community; (7) the crisis of escalating costs; (8) confusion about the purpose of theological education (is it to critique the faith, to prepare mature Christians or to train ministers?); (9) philosophical concerns about the erosion of Western thought and the loss of a sound *theoria*; (10) the location of theological learning and the increasing alienation of the academy from the congregation and the marketplace.

[11] I will pass over an obvious one only because this paper is written in an evangelical context. Old-style liberal theology has been widely exported to developing countries with, in some cases, disastrous effects, as observed by Michael Griffiths, in his case study of the slow church growth in Japan as compared to Korea. The West has often dumped its unsold books and unsold scholarship on a hungry world. For example, in the small library of 100 (total!) volumes in the theological college of the African Christian Churches and Schools, with which

Carey Theological College will be in partnership from 1991–1995, there is only one complete commentary: *The Interpreter's Bible*, obviously a cast-off from a North American pastor's library.

[12] N. Keith Clifford, "Universities, Churches and Theological Colleges in English-Speaking Canada: Some Current Sources of Tension," *Studies in Religion/Sciences Réligieuses* 19, no. 1 (1990): 10.

[13] H. Richard Niebuhr, *The Purpose of the Church and its Ministry: Reflections on the Aims of Theological Education* (New York: Harper and Bros., 1956), 107.

[14] Biblical theological education is a complex reality involving many strands of learning, faith development and active ministry evoked by authentic relationship with the living God and described in Scripture. Texts such as Colossians 1:28 and Ephesians 4:11–16 are especially seminal in discerning the biblical shape of Christian theological education: it is community-oriented (rather than individualistic), cooperative (rather than competitive), life-centred (rather than merely school-based), oriented towards obedience (rather than the mere accumulation of cognitive information), life-long (rather than concentrated in a degree program) and available for the whole people of God, the *laos* (rather than a clerical elite).

[15] Another way of looking at this is to say that newer churches may, in their theological education programs, be more in harmony with the ultimate purpose of theological education since they usually stress the devotional life and practical service more than in the West and do so in a residential community of learning and serving. However, the vision of giving theological education to the whole people of God, the *laos*, has hardly caught on anywhere in the globe!

[16] See Farley, *Theologia*.

[17] Linda Cannell, "Regent College: Theological Education and the Church, the Church and Theological Education" (unpublished paper presented to the Regent College faculty, March 1991), 9.

[18] Ibid.

[19] Hough and Wheeler, *Beyond Clericalism*. See also John M. Freme "Proposal for a New Seminary," *Journal of Pastoral Practice* 11, no. 1 (Winter 1978): 10–17.

[20] Clifford, "Universities, Churches and Theological Colleges," 3.

[21] Ibid., 16.

[22] See Stackhouse's critique of faulty *theoria* in Liberation Theology in *Apologia*, 84–105.

[23] Paulo Friere, *Pedagogy of the Oppressed*, trans. Myra Bergman Ramos (New York: Continuum, 1987), 67.

[24] Robert J. Schreiter, "Teaching Theology from an Intercultural Perspec-

tive." *Theological Education* 26, no. 1 (Autumn 1989): 13–14.

[25] See the results of the questionnaire in the ATS 1990 Self-Study of Regent College (Appendices H and I).

[26] Peter Stone, "Theological Education for the Laity: Part 1: Policies and Practices at the London Institute for Contemporary Christianity," *Journal of Christian Education*, papers 94 (April 1989): 21.

[27] N. Keith Clifford, "The Paradoxes of Professionalism: A Brief Look at the Context of Theological Education in British Columbia," in *The Journey Continues: The VST Diamond Jubilee Lectures,* ed. R. Gerald Hobbs (Vancouver: Vancouver School of Theology, 1987).

[28] Learning on the Way, a United Church document, cited by Clifford, "Universities, Churches and Theological Colleges," 9.

[29] While Regent College has nurtured the vision of replication globally, it has become apparent to many of the friends of the College that while the idea of Regent can be replicated, the *structure* as a graduate theological college with full ATS-type accreditation and a library of 100,000 volumes is a form that cannot be replicated in most developing countries. However, a number of significant centres for lay theological education have emerged internationally, including some of the following: The Center for Interdisciplinary Theological Studies (CITI) in Buenos Aires, Argentina; Centre Interdisciplinar de Estudos Cristaos in Sao Carlos, Brazil; Zadok Centre in Australia; Christian Impact (London Institute for Contemporary Christianity) in U.K.; New College Berkeley in U.S.; Institute for Christian Studies in Toronto, Canada; Daystar University in Nairobi, Kenya; Biblical Graduate School of Theology in Singapore, and many centres that combine undergraduate with graduate study, or who have special programs relating to laity: Schloss Mittersill, Austria; God on Monday Project in Cambridge, U.K.; Crossroads in U.S.

[30] Farley, *Theologia.*

[31] This appears to be experienced by New College Berkeley and is evidenced in the real statistics of Regent students intending to return to a societal career. See ATS Self-Study (Appendix).

[32] F. Ross Kinsley, ed., *Ministry by the People: Theological Education by Extension* (Maryknoll, NY: Orbis Books, 1983).

[33] See ATS Theological Education Facts, 1991.

[34] Rene Padilla, "Summary of Findings," in *New Alternatives in Theological Education,* ed. Rene Padilla (Oxford: Regnum Books, 1988), 174.

[35] Ibid., 168.

[36] A stunning example of poor thinking or weak *theoria* is cited by a Catholic author, William Rademacher, who shows that the contemporary Roman Catho-

lic justifications of celibacy on the basis of being "eunuchs for the sake of the Kingdom" (Mt 19:12) are merely recent attempts to use Scripture to enforce ecclesiastical law, whereas the real source of celibacy, he argues, is the Neo-Platonism embraced by the church centuries before. See *Lay Ministry: A Theological, Spiritual and Pastoral Handbook* (New York: Crossroad, 1991), 67.

[37] Stackhouse, *Apologia.*

[38] Quoted by Miriam Adeney in an unpublished paper, "What the Church Nationally and Globally Needs from the Fuller School of World Mission in the 1990s," delivered to the faculty of Fuller School of World Mission, 1991.

[39] It is noteworthy that the Association of Theological Schools (U.S. and Canada) have made globalization a priority for the decade of the '90s. Some of the study articles are: Don S. Browning, "Globalization and the Task of Theological Education in North America," *Theological Education* 23, no. 1 (Autumn 1986); David S. Schuller. "Globalization in Theological Education: Summary and Analysis of Survey Data," *Theological Education* 22, no. 2 (Spring 1986); and Robert Schreiter, "Teaching Theology from an Intercultural Perspective," *Theological Education* 26, no. 1 (Autumn 1989).

[40] I am not satisfied that a theological college should relegate the non-academic dimensions of theological education to the local church on the assumption that the theological college is *only* the intellectual centre of the church's life and does not need to embrace the wider mission of theological education: spiritual formation, praxis, etc. Indeed, the college has a responsibility for modelling the integration of mind, heart, spirit and action that ought to be obtained in a lifelong experience of learning and growing in Christian discipleship and service.

[41] Padilla, "Summary of Findings," 174.

[42] See Tukunbob Adeyerno, *Salvation in African Tradition* (Nairobi: Evangel, 1979); Richard J. Gehman, *African Traditional Religion in Biblical Perspective* (Kijabe, Kenya: Kesho Publications, 1989); Byang Kato, (Bristol: Arrowsmith, 1985).

[43] Guillermo Cook, *The Expectation of the Poor: Latin America Base Ecclesial Communities in Protestant Perspective* (Maryknoll, NY: Orbis Books, 1985).

[44] J. Norberto Saracco, "Search for New Models of Theological Education," in *New Alternatives in Theological Education*, ed. C. Rene Padilla (Oxford: Regnum Books, 1988), 28.

[45] "Seminary of the East," P.O. Box 611, Drescher, PA 19025. This is a refreshing experiment in which field education is not the added extra for "practical application" but the centre-piece of the learning, matched with one day a week in classroom learning. The program is spread over longer than the conven-

tional three-year program and involves extensive self-directed learning.

[46] Regent has the sixth largest number (not percentage) of non-North American students in a North American theological college. See Schuller, "Globalization in Theological Education."

[47] The course does have, in addition to its seminar component, a major didactic section that encompasses the history of theological education, educational theory, new and old patterns of theological education and an examination of biblical dimensions of lifelong education for maturity and service in Christ. Some of this material is included in the "Readings for Theological Education" prepared for the course.

[48] It is a matter of interest that one of the students in our first offering of TEO, Gerry Schoberg, did just this. He went to Zambia for eight months to supply teach for a Regent alumnus on sabbatical.

[49] See the places named above.

[50] J. Andrew Kirk, *Theology and the Third World Church* (Downers Grove, IL: InterVarsity Press, 1983), 48–49.

[51] Quoted by Miriam Adeney, "What the Church Nationally and Globally Needs," 3.

[52] I make some concrete suggestions for equipping worker-priests in the marketplace in my book *The Equipper's Guide to Every-Member Ministry* (Downers Grove, IL: InterVarsity Press, 1992).

[53] In "Liberating the Laity," chapter 3, I explore the idea that the local church is the best arena for equipping the saints for the work of the ministry (Eph 4:11–12).

[54] Padilla, "Summary of Findings," 176–178.

# STRUGGLING WITH GOD:

# A SERMON ON GENESIS 32

*From* Crux, *vol. 37, no. 1 (March 2001)*

Then the man said, "Let me go, for it is daybreak." But Jacob replied, "I will not let you go unless you bless me." The man asked him, "What is your name?" "Jacob," he answered. Then the man said, "Your name will no longer be Jacob, but Israel, because you have struggled with God and men and have overcome." (Gn 32:26–28)

Regent is a dangerous place. It is highly likely that we will meet God and ourselves at the same time, as was wonderfully true for Jacob.

One of the Grimm fairy tales is a story called "Iron John" or "Iron Hans." As the story starts, we find out that something strange has been happening in a remote area of the forest near the king's castle. When hunters go into this area, they disappear and never come back. Twenty others go after the first group and do not come back. In time, people begin to get the feeling that there's something weird in that part of the forest, and "they don't go there anymore."

One day an unknown hunter shows up at the castle and says, "What can I do? Anything dangerous to do around here?" The king says, "Well, I could mention the forest, but there's a problem. The people who go out there don't come back. The return rate is not good."

"That's just the sort of thing I like," the young man says. So he goes into the forest and, interestingly, he goes there alone, taking only his dog. The young man and his dog wander about in the forest and they go past a pond. Suddenly a hand reaches up from the water, grabs the dog and pulls it down. The young man doesn't respond by becoming hysterical.

He merely says, "This must be the place."

## This Must Be the Place

Recently some of us received an e-mail from a Regent graduate studying in Scotland who shared a quote that sums up in a way the message I wish to bring from Genesis 32. "Struggle with me; I want to name you" (God is speaking).

I wonder if you are willing to consider a motif of the spiritual life as not only a journey as not only as a desert experience, but a passionate struggle.

Jacob is a struggler. Jacob, struggling in the womb, the second-born of twins, came out grabbing his brother's heel. So they named him, "Heelgrabber," the one who grabs from behind, the one who takes hold of his brother's heel. Denied being first, condemned to being second, Jacob chose to fulfill the sinister side of his name and to do everything he could to grab his brother's heel, to gain the rights of the firstborn, the leadership of the family and, above all else, the blessing—that treasured inheritance passed on from Abraham to Isaac that God would make a great family, would give them the land and would bless all the nations through his own people.

The name derives from the root *akov*, which means "crooked, indirect." It will be his characteristic always to have a plan, to lead from behind, to get in by the back door, to choose the way of the snake. Jacob defines himself as Esau's shadow, the one who comes behind, the one with a blurred identity.

This is a narrative that gives shape to and evokes our own story. In the narrative Jacob does not use his own name for twenty years—this seems deliberate, ominous, lucid, provocative—and it is a powerful hint that Jacob is not willing to admit who he is, that he has an incomplete fragmented identity, that he is inauthentic, not real. God wants to bless Jacob but cannot bless him until he will admit his own name.

When Jacob brings in the roasted goat, he is wrapped in goatskins to simulate his brother's hairy arms and neck, and blind Isaac asks, "Who is it?" (27:18). God is confronting Jacob with the question of his own identity. Jacob answers, in effect, that he is an impersonator, that he is taking on the role of the first-born, that he wishes he were someone else: "I am Esau," he says (27:19).

So Jacob gained his brother's blessing but lost himself. He now becomes a fugitive, like Cain, running for protection. But he is also running from himself. God is determined to bless him, just as he is determined to bless us.

The Christian faith is a love affair of the heart, but it begins with God's pursuit of us. God meets Jacob at Bethel. Then Jacob finds his way to Paddan Aram, where he meets the woman of his dreams at the well and, technically, the one for whom his father and mother have sent him abroad. But he does not use his own name. "He told Rachel that he was a relative of her father and a son of Rebekah" (29:12).

God's plot is to bring this man to himself in order to bring him to God and life itself. There can be no blessing ultimately for a trickster, since there is no authenticity, no real person to bless. One who enters the world of seeming, performance or assumed identities cannot know God because he does not know himself—the double knowing about which Calvin spoke. With deep insight the Talmud links idolatry with this fundamental inauthenticity since idolatry is simply worshipping a semblance of God, an appearance.[1]

So God brings into Jacob's life an untarnished mirror in his father-in-law, Laban, who also has a plan, who also leads from behind, who also grabs by the heel. Laban slips Leah into the marriage tent after seven years of love-work for Rachel. And, according to a Jewish commentary, when Jacob protests to Leah in the morning, "'Deceiver, daughter of a deceiver! Did I not call you Rachel last night and you answered me?!' She replied, 'Is there a master without students? Did your father not call you Esau and you answered him?!'"[2] The morning after, Jacob protests to Laban in words that are reminiscent of his own name. "Why have you deceived me?" (29:25) is roughly equivalent to "Why have you *jacobed* me?" We get as we give. Laban changes his wages ten times and finally, in desperation and in answer to a divine call, Jacob decides to leave Haran and make for home.

Home is a complex thought, as many Regent students have found when they returned "home" only to find it was no longer home. It is much more than a physical environment, just as Jacob's journey home is more than a mere physical journey. He is coming to the place. Jacob is not at home with himself, not at peace. He has no rest, has not yet entered sabbath/salvation (Heb 4:1–13). So on the way home he meets not only his brother but himself! And God!

Now, with his family having forded the Jabbok brook, Jacob is "left alone" (32:24). Until now he has avoided naming himself and defined himself by his brother. He has also defined himself by sheep and goats and camels and wives—by his accomplishments. Just as many who have come to Regent were somebody before they came to this place—somebody in ministry in the church, on the mission field, in business or professional life—and in this place they are left alone. They are nobodies. Just as faculty can define themselves by books published, conferences addressed, places travelled, but when stripped of that, when alone with God, they simply are. But in this dangerous place of solitude with God, struggling, we are left alone, as Jacob was.

### This is the Place

What happened that dark night by the Jabbok brook is emphasized by a play on three words that have a similar sound: "He struggled/wrestled" is closely related to the word "Jabbok" and probably even the name Jacob. At Jabbok, Jacob *jacobed*. It was a fight, a wrestling match with intimate embrace as each tried to gain the advantage. But with whom did Jacob wrestle? The narrative is deliberately opaque and mysterious, as Jacob himself apparently did not know who had confronted him in the dark by the struggling brook. As Annie Dillard said, "We awake, if we awake at all, to mystery."[3]

Who grabbed the heel-grabber? Some Jewish commentators suggest it might be the angel of Esau, since his struggle with himself and God was played out in relation to his brother (as is darkly suggested in Hosea 12:4–5). Did Jacob that night review his whole life, especially his relationship with Esau, and his own dissembling, role-playing, inauthentic performance? Did that physical struggle externalize a personal and spiritual battle within, one in which Jacob had to come to terms with himself—struggling with God in the context of life, in relationships with his brother, his father, his mother, his father-in-law, his wives? And with himself?

In *The Sacred Romance,* Curtis and Eldredge note that we have two deep desires: "the longing for adventure that requires something of us, and the desire for intimacy...These two desires come together in us all as a longing to be in a relationship of heroic proportions."[4] Nothing will satisfy that longing but relationship with the living God.

In the process of theological studies we do most of the things that Jacob had been doing for twenty years: we eat, we relate to family, we sleep and often dream, we mate, we marry, we work, we worship, we journey. In addition, we study. Instead of seeing these as diversions from our real life in God, why not see them as the very context in which we can be found by the seeking Father, as Jacob was? God is inescapable, wonderfully inescapable!

Your theological studies and the high-pressure role of faculty are a furnace of transformation, inviting us to know ourselves and God at the same time. Why am I driven? Why lazy? Why do I fill in the blanks in my date book? Whom am I pleasing? (When I became Dean at Regent, the President, Walter Wright said, "It will be a place, a context in which you will have to deal with yourself, especially your desire to please others.") Why am I afraid to tell people who I am? And God...why are you so distant? Why have you denied me meaningful employment, a spouse, a perfect body? All this is coming to a head by the brook.

The most astonishing words to the reader, who knows that God was struggling with Jacob, is verse 25: "When the man saw that he could not overpower him, he touched the socket of Jacob's hip so that his hip was wrenched as he wrestled with the man." If this is God after all, cannot he prevail over his own creature? Or does God deliberately make himself vulnerable to his own creature? This seems to be a moment of profound discovery for Jacob, for at the moment of his seeming triumph, he is wounded. Must he, through this wounding, know that it is in weakness rather than autonomous strength that he will truly be the leader of the people of God? He is not totally self-sufficient. In that wounding Jacob realizes he is encountering an opponent with supernatural power. But the man wants to be released as day is breaking. Jacob is determined—now that he knows God is in this—to wrest a blessing.

He has a passion for the blessing of God and will lie and cheat and fight to get it, which is better than being apathetic. Esau was the epitome of spiritual *ennui*. He sold his blessing for a bowl of porridge.

I fear apathy more than anything—called by the ancients *acedia*—spiritual boredom. Especially perhaps in a theological college, we are in danger of *acedia*, where we are tempted constantly to be handling the outside of holy things. Richard Neuhaus says, *"Acedia* is apathy, the refusal to engage the pathos of other lives and [the passion] of God's life with them."[5]

"I will not let you go unless you bless me" (Gn 32:26). Jacob now wants God with his whole heart and will not release God until God has blessed him. The kingdom of God, Jacob now knows, is not for the mildly interested but for the desperate.

And how about you? Will you say to God—not only in the sanctuary but in everyday life—in eating, working, relating, studying? "I will not let you go unless you bless me."

We are now at the climax of the struggle. The man asked Jacob, "What is your name?" This is the question that Jacob has been avoiding for twenty years. For the first time in the narrative, Jacob confesses, "Jacob." This is not merely an identification. It is an admission of guilt, a disclosure of his character, the taking off of the mask, becoming real. He is not now Esau in disguise, not merely his mother's son. He is himself. It is his moment of authenticity, of integration, of coming home.

The man—representing God's presence—did more than bless him. He gave him a new name indicating his identity and his vocation: "Your name will no longer be called Jacob, but Israel, because you have struggled with God and with men and have overcome" (Gn 32:28). Jacob wants the messenger's name, but this is denied, lest it be abused (Jgs 13:17–18; Ex 20:7). This is Jacob's rebaptism into Israel, the leader of the nation. The precise etymology of Israel means "El (God) fights," but popular etymologies generally take the form of a play on the name rather than an exact translation. So Jacob became the one who triumphed in his struggle against men (Esau and Laban being conspicuous examples) and, most surprising of all, God! Jacob knows he has met God and calls the place "Peniel" because he has seen God "face to face and yet my life was spared" (Gn 32:30).

With considerable insight Wenham notes the paradox implicit in Jacob's new name: "while Jacob struggled with God, it was God who allowed Jacob to triumph in the fight."[6] Simply put, both prevailed—both God and Jacob. It was win-win.

Perhaps there is nothing so damnable as apathy. God is not looking for compliance. What God most wants from us is not compliance but love, passion.

So Jesus in the garden of Gethsemane takes the disciple's prayer on his own lips—"Thy will be done"—showing that submission is not the same thing as compliance to impersonal fate or karma, that praying for God's will is not passive but active. P. T. Forsyth once said that "we say too often, 'Thy will be done'; and too ready acceptance of a situation as his will often means feebleness or sloth. It may be his will that we surmount his will." Forsyth continues, "does not Christ set more value upon importunity than on submission?" Refering, as Forsyth refers, not only to Jacob wrestling, but to the parable of the unjust judge, the incident of the Syrophenician woman, Paul beseeching the Lord thrice, Abraham pleading—yes haggling—with God for Sodom, Moses interceding for Israel. "We have Job facing God, withstanding him, almost berating him and extracting revelation…So the prayer that resists his dealing may be part of his will and its fulfilment…It is a resistance that God loves."[7]

This must be the place.

What is your name?

Struggle with me. I want to name you.

I will not let you go unless you bless me.

## Endnotes

[1] Avivah Gottlieb Zornberg, *The Beginning of Desire: Reflections on Genesis* (New York: Doubleday, 1995), 154.

[2] Ibid., 185–6.

[3] Quoted in Brent Curtis and John Eldredge, *The Sacred Romance: Drawing Closer to the Heart of God* (Nashville: Thomas Nelson,1997), 13.

[4] Ibid., 19.

[5] Richard Neuhaus, *Freedom for Ministry: A Critical Affirmation of the Church and its Mission* (San Francisco: Harper & Row, 1956), 202.

[6] Gordon Wenham, *Genesis 16–50* (Word Biblical Commentary), vol. 2 (Dallas: Word, 1994), 303.

[7] P.T. Forsyth, *The Soul of Prayer* (London: Independent Press, 1954), 86–88.